Meeting the
Employment Challenge

MEETING THE
EMPLOYMENT
CHALLENGE

Argentina, Brazil, and Mexico in the Global Economy

Janine Berg, Christoph Ernst,
and Peter Auer

LYNNE RIENNER PUBLISHERS

HD
8266.5
.B47
2006

μι

Published in the United States of America in 2006 by
Lynne Rienner Publishers, Inc.
1800 30th Street, Boulder, Colorado 80301
www.rienner.com
ISBN-13: 978-1-58826-443-5 (hardcover : alk. paper)
ISBN-10: 1-58826-443-2 (hardcover : alk. paper)

and in the United Kingdom by
Lynne Rienner Publishers, Inc.
3 Henrietta Street, Covent Garden, London WC2E 8LU

Published in Switzerland in 2006 by the
International Labour Office
CH-1211 Geneva-22, Switzerland
www.ilo.org/publns
ISBN-13: 978-92-2-117947-4 (ILO hardcover : alk. paper)
ISBN-10: 92-2-117947-8 (ILO hardcover : alk. paper)

Library of Congress Cataloging-in-Publication Data
Berg, Janine.
    Meeting the employment challenge : Argentina, Brazil, and Mexico in the global economy /
Janine Berg, Christoph Ernst and Peter Auer.
        p. cm.
    Includes bibliographical references and index.
    1. Labor policy—Argentina.   2. Labor policy—Mexico.   3. Labor policy—Brazil.
I. Ernst, Christoph.   II. Auer, Peter.   III. Title. HD8266.5.B47 2006
331.1098—dc22

                                                                2006002390

British Cataloguing in Publication Data
A Cataloguing in Publication record for this book
is available from the British Library.

Printed and bound in the United States of America

∞   The paper used in this publication meets the requirements
     of the American National Standard for Permanence of
     Paper for Printed Library Materials Z39.48-1992.

5   4   3   2   1

Contents

Tables and Figures

Tables

Figures

Foreword

W hat policies would be appropriate if the goal of creating employment were truly at the center of economic and social policies? Would the focus of policies have to be changed, or do present policies accommodate the employment goal sufficiently? This is the basic question addressed by this book with regard to selected micro, meso, and macro policies of Argentina, Brazil, and Mexico. The broad answer is that a new set of policies that promote employment needs to be designed and implemented. These policies should not be limited to microeconomic variables that affect the supply of labor, but must also include different macroeconomic and mesoeconomic aspects that affect employment demand. Monetary and fiscal policy, but also trade, industrial, and service policy, all have important implications for employment and should thus be designed to achieve a high rate of employment growth. Nevertheless, the employment objective must also include qualitative aspects of employment, considering underemployment and informal employment and, related to this, the improvement of productivity and incomes as well. Thus the final and long-term objective is greater and better-quality employment—in other words, the attainment of decent work.

These policies should include a more proactive stance by government and social partners (including civil society). Together, these actors could develop policies that not only increase their countries' integration in the global economy, and thus increase the value-added of exports, but also consider the domestic market and internal sources of financing. A coherent set of labor market regulations and policies that provide security at work and security in change are also needed. These are the topics that this book addresses in detail and also reflect policy areas that have become prominent topics of discussion in the three countries concerned.

Meeting the Employment Challenge analyzes economic and labor market developments in Argentina, Brazil, and Mexico during the 1990–2004 period. It draws lessons from the different macroeconomic and mesoeconomic policies implemented as a result of liberalization, as well as from the changes in the microeconomic areas of labor market regulations and the conduct of labor relations, with the aim of providing policy advice for promoting the growth of decent work.

The 1990s saw sweeping reforms as the countries abandoned import-substitution industrialization, liberalized their current and capital accounts, privatized public enterprises, imposed fiscal and monetary austerity, and reformed their labor markets. These far-reaching structural changes—not carried out to the same extent by all three—were expected to boost economic growth, especially through increased exports, with positive effects on the nontradable sector. Higher growth rates and labor market deregulation resulting in better adjustment capacities would in turn lead to additional employment growth and reduce unemployment, underemployment, and poverty.

Yet the expectations for economic and employment growth and poverty reduction did not materialize. While economic growth and per capita growth improved in relation to the "lost decade" of the 1980s, it remained weak and volatile compared to the 1960s and 1970s. Imports grew more than exports, and the massive inflows of foreign investment not only failed to create much employment but also had some perverse macroeconomic effects, such as an exchange rate and interest rate appreciation, that hurt domestic investment. Indeed, over the whole period there were few employment successes, limited mainly to the Mexican maquiladora sector between 1995 and 2000 and, more recently, to the employment recovery in Argentina following the deep crisis of 2001–2002. Furthermore, during the 1990s a disbelief in the role of institutions and governments as well as social partners prevailed. The institutional vacuum left by the retreat of the state was not filled by the traditional social partners or by emerging social actors, which impeded the formulation or implementation of policies to create quality employment.

The new millennium is a better era for employment growth: the international financial institutions have changed their view somewhat regarding the supremacy of market forces after reckoning some failures in their former policy advice and acknowledging the positive effects that government policy can have on development, as well as the contributions that institutions and social policy can make. Policymakers in Argentina, Brazil, and Mexico have also come to understand that too much dependence on external financing restricts their flexibility on national policy and that they need more autonomy in developing their own economic and social policies.

But many employment challenges in Argentina, Brazil, and Mexico remain. There is insufficient new job growth to cope with the increases in labor supply. Compared with 1990, employment rates in 2004 were lower in Argentina and Brazil; the share of workers employed in the informal economy was higher in Brazil and Mexico; and average real manufacturing wages increased only marginally in Brazil and Mexico, and declined in Argentina. Social security covered less than half of the working population in Argentina, 63 percent in Mexico, and 69 percent in Brazil. The traditional skewed distribution of income and wages, evident in high Gini coefficients, is partly the result of these labor market patterns and continues to be a major source of concern.

What Janine Berg, Christoph Ernst, and Peter Auer propose in this book is a change in policy, so that the creation of good-quality employment once again becomes a goal for policymakers. For this to occur, there needs to be a more proactive stance by government and social partners, as opposed to just relying on market forces and free trade. Indeed, employment is not just a derivative of economic policies that can be relegated to active policies under the responsibility of a labor ministry. Employment must be a priority of the political, economic, and social agenda of government. All ministries need to design policies that can contribute, coherently and consistently, to this overarching strategy of government.

—Daniel Martínez
ILO Regional Director for the Americas

Acknowledgments

We would like to thank Adalberto Cardoso Moreira and Adriana Marshall for providing background studies that formed the basis for Chapters 6 and 7. We also appreciate the collaboration of Maria Cristina Cacciamali and Enrique Dussel Peters.

This book has benefited from feedback at ILO departmental seminars, as well as from comments from Ajit Ghose, David Kucera, and Muhammed Muqtada. We have also received helpful comments from experts outside the ILO, in particular Alfredo Calcagno of UNCTAD, and from academics, government officials, and social actors in Argentina, Brazil, and Mexico during country visits in 2003 and 2004, and during seminars in May 2005. The book was also reviewed by one ILO and two external experts, whose valuable suggestions are gratefully acknowledged.

The authors are especially thankful for ILO support from Rizwanul Islam, director of the Employment Strategy Department; Daniel Martínez, regional director for the Americas; and the ILO offices in Brasilia, Buenos Aires, and Mexico City.

The authors express their special thanks to Christine Alfthan, Geneviève Domon von Richthofen, and Anne Drougard for secretarial support. Research assistance was provided by Miriam Bird, Alfons Hernández Ferrer, Francesco Paolini, and Matthew Schneid, to whom we wish to express our gratitude. The provision of various regional employment data by Bolivar Pino from ILO-SIAL in Panama is gratefully acknowledged. Parts of the book were edited by Praveen Bhalla. Rosemary Beattie, May Hofman Öjermark, and Alison Irvine at the ILO were responsible for guiding the manuscript through to publication.

—*Janine Berg,*
Christoph Ernst,
and Peter Auer

1

Introduction

The economies of Argentina, Brazil, and Mexico are vastly different entering the twenty-first century than they were in 1990. Yet many of the same employment challenges remain today and new challenges, arising from integration in the global economy, have been added. The reforms of the late 1980s and 1990s, which centered on the liberalization of financial and goods markets, the privatization of public enterprises, and in some cases labor market "flexibilization," were undertaken with the belief that a more open and competitive economy would produce higher growth rates, with benefits for workers and society at large.

Yet, unfortunately, unemployment, underemployment, poverty, and informality remain pressing concerns, and in many cases have been exacerbated by the economic reforms. This negative labor market outcome is perhaps the greatest disappointment of the new development strategy. That growth and employment suffered as a result of the policies advocated by the "Washington Consensus" has been observed both in critical appraisals of the strategies of the 1990s (for example, Stiglitz, 2003) and in empirical work on the region (for example, Stallings and Peres, 2000). But since the new development strategy had no explicit employment goal—and, as a consequence, no mechanisms were in place to achieve such a goal—the poor employment performance is not surprising. Instead, it was assumed that employment would automatically derive from the reorientation of the economy.

Thus the challenge of creating employment, and especially decent employment, remains for Argentina, Brazil, and Mexico. Though each now places a higher priority on employment because of its positive effect on growth and poverty reduction, and on the socioeconomic fabric of society in general, the question remains: What economic policies are needed to put employment at the center of economic and social policies? That employment takes the central role of economic and social policies is advocated by the ILO's *Decent Work Agenda* and *Global Employment Agenda* as well as by the Employment Policy

1

Convention, 1964 (No. 122), and its more up-to-date Employment Policy (Supplementary Provisions) Recommendation, 1984 (No. 169), requiring that governments advance "policies to promote full, productive and freely chosen employment."

What this volume proposes is that governments make employment a central goal of economic and social policy to spur the creation of quality employment. Attaining higher employment levels and better-quality jobs requires not only strong economic growth, but also explicit employment goals and policies. The government, along with social partners, should work more closely together to develop these policies, as market forces alone are not sufficient.

Based on a comparative analysis of Argentina, Brazil, and Mexico, this study draws lessons from the different macroeconomic and mesoeconomic policies implemented as a result of liberalization, as well as from changes in labor market regulations and the conduct of labor relations. It ultimately aims to provide policy advice for promoting the growth of productive employment.

Policies for Employment and Decent Work

Based on the findings of the study, a set of policies over three dimensions—macro, meso, and micro—is proposed. The policies demand a more proactive stance from the governments of Argentina, Brazil, and Mexico, which should intervene more forcefully in economic affairs than they did in the 1990s, as well as a proactive and constructive role for social partners. The broad lines for a more balanced policy agenda to create decent work are the following:

1. Employment needs to be regarded as an essential goal for economic and social policies. "Employment targeting" subject to an inflation and debt constraint should be a central macroeconomic goal. Employment targeting, as opposed to inflation targeting, makes employment a direct policy goal. Often, exaggerated price stabilization hampers economic growth and employment, rather than achieving it, as the policy intended. Targeting employment, which may imply the loosening of price stabilization, might at times imply tough choices between short-term stability and expansion, but because of the beneficial effect that more employment creation will likely have on the economies, it can be expected that these policies will become complementary over the longer term and lead to sustainable economic growth.

2. Both export industries as well as industries serving the domestic markets should be promoted. Or as D. Rodrik (2001a, 2001b) states, an outward-oriented strategy should be combined with a "homegrown strategy." Though primary exports remain important for these countries, it is also important that they promote an export specialization in higher value-added goods to improve their competitiveness in the world market, help stabilize and increase export earn-

ings, and have a multiplier effect on growth and employment. Specific attention should be given to small and medium-sized firms, to increase their participation in both the world market and the hitherto neglected domestic market.

3. Regional integration creates bigger domestic markets, which through
supranational cooperation and increased economies of scale can bolster the development of higher value-added industries. Regional integration also gives
the countries a stronger position in international trade negotiations, potentially
improving the prospects for economic development of member countries. But
since trade liberalization can result in more volatility in labor markets, even
among members of a regional agreement, such agreements must be flanked by
adequate social protection and labor market policies. It is therefore necessary
that labor and social issues gain a more prominent role in regional agreements.

4. In order for employment to be sustainable, a basic set of labor market
regulations must exist. The exact level and form of protective mechanisms,
such as employment protection legislation, notice periods, severance pay, regulation of part-time and temporary contracts, and minimum wages, should be
set by the social partners in a national context that accounts for regional variation and takes into account possible disincentives for hiring and investment.
ILO conventions and recommendations on various aspects of labor relations
can provide useful guidance for the balanced design of such regulations.

5. The labor markets of the countries under review are already quite
volatile and tend to become more volatile and more informal because of increasing competitive pressure facing firms. Active labor market adjustment
and safety nets are a good example of the functional integration of social and
economic policies, as they alleviate firms from some of their social responsi-
bilities, while providing security in change to workers, through income replacement and enhanced employability. Thus safety nets should be expanded,
but as permanent features of economic and social policies to improve worker
security in a time of globalization, rather than as quick-fix crisis solutions.
Making labor market policies a permanent feature of government policy also
has positive macroeconomic benefits, as they can mitigate recessions and the
negative effects of structural change.

6. Social dialogue is necessary to respond to the challenges of globalization. Economic openness and restructuring as a result of the policies of the
1990s has led to increased firm and labor market churning. Because appropriate policies need to be developed to help firms and workers adjust, it is important that the views of employers and workers be represented. Previously, the
governments formed corporatist alliances with the social partners, but now
worker and employer organizations are more autonomous. This independence
requires coordination among government and the social partners through continuous dialogue (beyond wage bargaining rounds), as well as greater responsibility from all parties to shape economic and social issues. Policy formulation would also benefit from including new social actors representing informal

workers and the unemployed. But for social dialogue to be sustained and effective, it must be institutionalized through, for example, social and economic councils that entail obligatory consultation with the social partners. The active adjustment and security safety net and its possible trade-off with employment protection could be one of the issues discussed.

In sum, coping with trade-offs in all these areas can render policies more complementary: it is not inflation control or employment creation but employment creation *and* inflation control. Nor is it outward orientation or inward orientation but outward *and* inward orientation. Complementarities should also govern the search for flexibility and security in labor markets. A last area concerns overcoming opposing policy stances: a true social dialogue that allows the voicing of these oppositions to enable compromise, so that employment creation can be achieved.

All of this calls for concrete policies and for a more proactive role of the main stakeholders in society: government at all levels, employer and worker organizations, and civil society. If employment is a major target of economic policy, it is clear that the government must be the main actor, as the central objective of individual firms cannot be the maximization of jobs. The recommendations do not imply a return to state planning of economic activity, but rather the creation of institutions to frame market forces and repair market failures, while trying to prevent policy failures. ILO conventions—many of which have been ratified by Argentina, Brazil, and Mexico—can be a guideline for policy action. Yet making employment central to economic and social policies implies a direct route to more jobs instead of detours via an exclusive focus on macroeconomic stabilization and economic opening with uncertain employment effects.

Overview of Chapters

The study is structured around five policy areas: macroeconomic policy and employment (Chapter 3), trade policy and employment (Chapter 4), policies to boost employment through foreign direct investment (FDI) (Chapter 5), labor market regulations and labor market policies (Chapter 6), and social dialogue and employment (Chapter 7). In addition, Chapter 2 gives an overview of the principal employment challenges facing Argentina, Brazil, and Mexico through an analysis of employment trends during 1990–2004. The main findings and policy conclusions are summarized in Chapter 8. A brief overview of the main findings follows.

Chapter 2 highlights the employment challenges facing Argentina, Brazil, and Mexico. Though the growth rate of labor supply has been decreasing in the three countries, and younger generations are more educated and thus seem better prepared for the labor market, formal labor demand in all three countries is insufficient in terms of both quantity and quality. Associated challenges are the increased informalization of jobs, unemployment and underemployment, as well as "working poverty." All have negative consequences for working conditions, but also for the tax base and social security financing. High income concentration is also of concern. Compared internationally, job tenure is low and was further reduced in Argentina. Real wage growth has been volatile in the countries as a result of the economic shocks, though wages have begun to recover in Argentina, and in Brazil and Mexico have recovered to precrisis levels. Minimum wages, on the other hand, have increased in Brazil and most recently in Argentina, but have lost ground in Mexico. Brazil, and more significantly Argentina, have experienced a deterioration in social security coverage levels, another indication that decent jobs are losing ground. Coverage has increased in Mexico, but still remains at a level lower than in Brazil.

Chapter 3 discusses the shift in macroeconomic policy in the three countries since the late 1980s and early 1990s, and its effect on economic performance. On the whole, economic growth in Argentina, Brazil, and Mexico has been highly volatile and at the same time low, with growth during 1990–2003 averaging just 2.2 percent in Argentina, 2.4 percent in Brazil, and 3 percent in Mexico, higher than in the 1980s but remarkably lower than in former decades. The difference in growth rates is reflected in the performance of employment, with Mexico faring better than Argentina and Brazil, yet still at a level lower than in the 1960s and 1970s. The overall poor macroeconomic performance stemmed from a combination of domestic and external factors, most importantly the decision to open the economies to financial and trade liberalization under a fixed exchange rate regime, which led to a series of undesirable effects. Argentina, Brazil, and Mexico now have floating exchange rates, yet macroeconomic policy, both fiscal and monetary, remains restrictive because of the policy of inflation targeting pursued by the central banks as well as the need to control and reduce the large debt burden. Thus, monetary policy has centered on using the interest rate to rein in economic growth and keep inflation low. Fiscal policy has centered on controlling government spending and using the primary surplus to service the debt. The countries have experienced success in maintaining low inflation, and all have been managing to control their debt burden. Nevertheless, these policy objectives have come at the cost of job creation, as the excessive reliance on high real interest rates has aggravated the availability of credit, particularly in Brazil. As a result, domestic investment has been tempered, resulting in a weak economic recovery and few new jobs.

Chapter 4 discusses the new export-oriented development strategy adopted by the countries in the late 1980s and early 1990s, which involved trade liberalization, regional trade agreements, and the curtailment of government industrial policy. In particular, the chapter assesses the outcome of this policy shift on trade specialization as well as the labor market, in particular on employment and wages. The chapter finds that, in general, trade liberalization and regional integration did not have the expected strong positive impact on production or employment during the period of analysis. Instead, there was a steep rise in imports and little export dynamism. Exchange rate appreciation contributed to the rise in imports while hurting exports, which, coupled with a lack of public support to firms during the adjustment process, meant that export growth, measured in quantity or by type of export, was not as dynamic as had been foreseen. Only Mexico experienced an export boom in manufacturing production and employment due to growth in the maquiladora sector. Argentina and Brazil, on the other hand, decreased their specialization in dynamic products vis-à-vis the world market, specializing instead in primary and semiprocessed primary products. Moreover, the exports of more sophisticated products, in particular from the maquiladora industry, did not lead to value chain upgrading, since the import content of exports also rose significantly. With the exception of the maquiladora industry, restructuring in manufacturing was not particularly beneficial to job growth, as there were few new production plants and the job-creating sectors were of low labor intensity.

Chapter 5 analyzes the evolution and nature of FDI inflows in Argentina, Brazil, and Mexico and their impact on the labor market. Attracting FDI has been a key aspect of the countries' outward-oriented development strategy, as FDI is seen as compensating scarce domestic financial resources that are needed to help modernize production and to facilitate integration into the world market. As such it is considered crucial for output growth and employment generation. The new outward-oriented development strategy of the 1990s and the increased globalization of production worldwide led to a boom in FDI. The impact of large FDI inflows on employment, however, was to a large extent disappointing. This unfavorable outcome is explained by the type of investment, which mostly came in the form of mergers and acquisitions, often as a consequence of the privatization of public utility companies or bank restructuring. As a result, few productive assets with additional employment potential were created. Overall, foreign direct investment was often associated with restructuring, implying rationalization measures and labor shedding. Only Mexico escaped the trend as a result of investment in the maquiladora sector, mainly of greenfield plants using labor-intensive production methods, leading to substantial job growth during 1995–2000, though since 2000 the sector has lost jobs. In Argentina and Brazil, FDI helped to modernize the economies, but without creating jobs.

Chapter 6 discusses the prevailing labor market regulations and the reforms undertaken during the 1990s, as well as the labor market policies used to promote labor market integration and greater worker security. Regarding labor market flexibility, Argentina was the most ambitious reformer. Reforms in Brazil were also geared toward making employment more flexible. Though the reforms undertaken by Argentina and Brazil were designed to stimulate employment creation, the policies were largely unsuccessful. Mexico has had several labor market reform proposals under discussion since the late 1980s, yet no legal reforms have been approved. Nevertheless, many changes have been achieved through collective bargaining, particularly relating to functional and numerical flexibility at the workplace. During the 1990s and early 2000s, labor market policies, comprising active and passive measures, were increasingly used to confront labor market problems and alleviate poverty. Both Argentina and Brazil expanded their unemployment insurance systems, but coverage is only significant in Brazil. Compared with Brazil, Argentina and Mexico have relied more on active measures such as direct employment creation and training programs. Additionally, the countries have a number of programs to foster self-employment and microenterprise creation. Yet despite recognition of the importance of labor market policies, expenditure and coverage in the countries remain low and program design and implementation can be improved. Moreover, no attempt has been made to make labor market policies a permanent tool for providing security to workers during the continuous and accelerating structural change that characterizes present times.

Chapter 7 presents the argument that social dialogue has been used insufficiently to address the employment challenges that the three countries face. During the period of import-substitution industrialization, the lack of social dialogue was not a major concern, as state, labor, and capital relations were regulated via the legal system. The structural and economic reforms of the 1990s, however, demanded more extensive social dialogue to compensate for the retreated position of the state and the challenges brought by liberalization. Yet unions did not effectively represent workers' interests in negotiations on economic and labor reforms. The absence of much voice in an environment of increased labor market insecurity further weakened social dialogue, which, coupled with job losses in traditional manufacturing, has led to a decline in union membership, particularly in Argentina and Mexico. Similarly, employer organizations lost influence as the state sharply curtailed industrial policies and foreign investors increased their influence in the economies. As a result of the shortfall of the traditional actors to fully address the concerns of broader society, new social movements have emerged. Nevertheless, there still remain some concerns as to how these groups should be represented in social dialogue. Where social dialogue has been successful in maintaining employment and improving the local economy, it involved negotiations that were broad-based and confronted issues of adaptation and security for firms and workers.

2

The Evolution
of the Labor Market in
Argentina, Brazil, and Mexico

What are the employment challenges that Argentina, Brazil, and Mexico face? To a large extent, this question can be answered by determining the quantitative and qualitative gap between the supply of labor (the number of individuals seeking work) and the demand for labor (the amount of work available to individuals). However, it is not simply how many new jobs have been created, but whether these jobs are of sufficient quality to ensure decent work.

The economic reforms that Argentina, Brazil, and Mexico undertook during the 1990s had profound effects on the labor markets of these countries. The rapid opening of the economy, the subsequent macroeconomic crises, privatization, and labor market deregulation entailed major shocks to the labor market that affected employment rates, the distribution of employment, and job quality. This chapter gives an overview of the principal employment trends in Argentina, Brazil, and Mexico between 1990 and 2004. The supply of labor, its demand, as well as the characteristics and quality of employment, for women, men, and youths, are discussed with a view to assessing the employment challenges that the countries face.

Labor Supply

Labor supply, the amount of labor available for work, indicates the number and types of jobs that an economy needs to create. The size of the labor force is determined by demographic factors, fertility rates, and life span, by migration, both inward and outward, as well as by cultural and social norms. Individual and household decisions are influenced by family structure (e.g., single- or double-income-earning households), educational choices that affect entry into the labor market, childcare facilities, transport, housing, and, of course, the prevailing labor market situation. An important indicator of the

9

quality of labor supply is the amount, as well as the quality, of schooling and training received by labor market participants.

The working-age population comprises the number of potential labor force participants. In Argentina, Brazil, and Mexico, the fall in fertility rates has contributed to a decline in the growth rate of the working-age population. In Brazil, the decline has been quite sharp, from an average annual growth rate of 2.7 percent between 1980 and 1985, to an annual average rate of 1.9 percent between 2000 and 2005, according to the Economic Commission for Latin America and the Caribbean (ECLAC) (2004e). Similarly, Mexico's growth rate in working-age population has declined from 3.2 to 2.5 percent, and Argentina's from 2.3 to 1.8 percent (see Figure 2.1). Because of the slow-down in population growth rates, some of the pressures of finding productive employment for youths will be alleviated, as in the future they will constitute a smaller portion of the working-age population.

If more potential participants choose to enter the labor force, then labor supply will increase at a rate faster than the growth rate of the working-age population. Indeed, in all three countries, the growth in the labor force (employed and unemployed), also called the economically active population, is greater than the growth in the working-age population. Based on ECLAC estimates, the economies needed to produce a 1.9–2.6 percent increase in jobs annually during 2000–2005 to accommodate the increase in supply (see Figure 2.2). Although the pressure is strongest in Mexico, it is mitigated by emigration. Mexican emigration to the United States is an important source of work and income for Mexicans, with roughly 9 percent of the Mexican-born population residing in the United States (see Box 2.1).

Figure 2.1   Growth of Working-Age Population, Five-Year Periods, 1980–2005

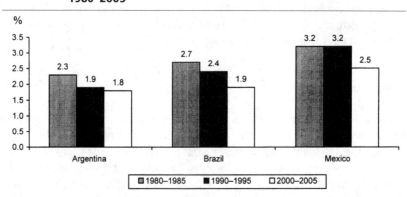

Source: ECLAC, 2004e.

Notes: Working-age population defined as persons over ten years of age in Brazil and Mexico, over fifteen years of age in Argentina. Forecasts for 2000–2005.

Figure 2.2   Growth of Economically Active Population, Five-Year Periods, 1980–2005

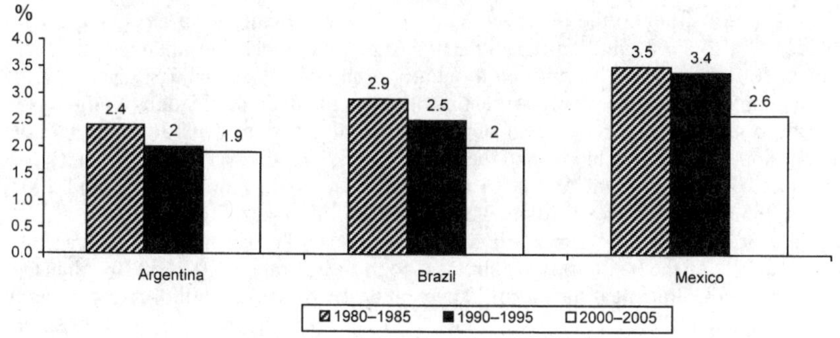

Source: Author calculations based on ECLAC, 2004a.

Box 2.1
Migration and the Supply of Labor

In 2000, 8.7 percent of the Mexican-born population resided in the United States, compared with 5.9 percent in 1990 and 1.6 percent in 1970. The United States is a natural destination for Mexicans because of geographic, historical, and cultural proximity as well as strong economic ties. Although it was believed that the North American Free Trade Agreement (NAFTA) would curb the flow of migrants, it was not very successful in this regard. The economic crisis in 1994 and 1995, but also the strong decline in agricultural employment in Mexico, led to a continued and steady migration flow that reached almost 4 million during 1990–2000. The income earned abroad was beneficial to the families of the migrants, who received on average US$3,000 in 2000, up from US$2,100 in 1992 (Moreno-Fontes, 2004). Mexico also has substantial within-country migration, especially toward Mexico City and the northern border states. Indeed, in 2000, 17.7 percent of the population lived in a state that was not their place of birth.

By contrast, Argentina and Brazil, both belonging to the Mercado Común del Sur (Mercosur; Southern Cone Common Market), have not had the same opportunities for migration as has Mexico. Yet the two Mercosur countries, unlike the United States and Mexico, have agreed to open their borders to Mercosur-member countries and extend the same rights and protections to migrants as their citizens have. Currently, there are an estimated 2.5 million people living illegally or undocumented in Argentina and Brazil who would be granted full status under these regulations (Rohter, 2002). While relations between the Mercosur countries are meant to improve intraregional labor mobility, one of NAFTA's primary purposes was to deter migration.

continues

Box 2.1   Continued

Argentina, unlike the other two nations, has historically been an immigrant receiver. Out of the 36 million inhabitants of Argentina reported in the population census in 2001, there were 1.5 million foreign-born inhabitants, equal to 4 percent of the total population. Until recently, Argentina has been the main destination of migrants in South America, drawing workers from the surrounding nations. Only recently, with the expansion of Chile's economy and the shrinking of Argentina's, has there been a small outflow of workers from Argentina to Chile. In addition, between 2001 and 2003, about 255,000 Argentines emigrated to Europe (Jachimowicz, 2003).

In Brazil, migration is primarily internal and toward urban areas. In 1999, according to data from the Instituto Brasileiro de Geografia e Estatística (IBGE; Brazilian Geographical and Statistical Institute), 39 percent of Brazilians, 63 million, were living in a municipality other than the one of their birth, and 16 percent were living in an entirely different federal unit. Half of the 27 million Brazilians who migrate between regions move to the southeast. There is significant mobility in Brazil, which serves to allocate labor at the national level. Unlike in Mexico, where much migration is cyclical, most Brazilians move permanently. The 2000 census revealed that over 18 million people had lived in another district without interruption for over ten years.

The growing labor forces of Argentina, Brazil, and Mexico have the advantage of being more educated than earlier generations, even if increased education remains an important challenge for the future. Adult illiteracy is low in Argentina (3 percent in 2001), close to standards in countries of the Organisation for Economic Co-operation and Development (OECD), though 12 percent of Brazil's urban population is illiterate, as is 7 percent of the Mexican population.[1] Youth illiteracy (fifteen to twenty-four years old) is significantly lower, with 1 percent for Argentina, 4 percent for Brazil, and 3 percent for Mexico, indicating a higher educational level of the younger generation. Of the three countries, Argentina has the highest educational level, based on an analysis of the educational profile of the population aged twenty-five to twenty-nine. It has by far the highest percentages of population with more than six years of education (92 percent) and more than ten years of education (53 percent), followed by Mexico with 76 and 35 percent and by Brazil with 48 and 29 percent. In Argentina, but even more so in Mexico, male students have a higher share in the six-year and ten-year educational level than female students, while in Brazil, female students are better represented. In all three countries, the younger age bracket (fifteen to twenty-four years) has received more formal education than the twenty-five to twenty-nine age cohort, which means that once these youths enter the labor market, the formal skill profile will be enhanced (see Table 2.1).

Nevertheless, a formal education and skill profile does not always correspond to real qualifications. This is true not only for the countries analyzed, but also for OECD countries. A recent OECD study, the Programme for Inter-

Table 2.1   Educational Profile of Population, National Level (25–29 years old), 1999 and 2000 (percentages)

Country	Year	6+ Years of Education			10+ Years of Education		
		Total	Male	Female	Total	Male	Female
Argentina	2000	91.7	92.6	90.8	53.1	52.5	53.6
Brazil	1999	48.2	47.7	48.6	28.6	27.3	29.8
Mexico	2000	75.8	78.3	73.5	34.6	37.0	32.4

Source: UNESCO, 2004.

national Student Assessment (PISA), evaluated the performance of fifteen-year-old students in the original OECD countries, as well as in Argentina, Brazil, and Mexico. The results are worrisome for the three countries in absolute terms, but also in comparison with the OECD countries: for students fifteen years of age, 86 percent of Brazilians, 74 percent of Mexicans, and 70 percent of Argentines had low reading performance in 2000, compared with an OECD country average of 40 percent (United Nations Educational, Scientific, and Cultural Organization [UNESCO], 2004).

Another important characteristic of the labor market is the integration of women. In May 2003, Argentina's female labor force participation (LFP) rate was 48.3 percent, just above Brazil's rate of 47.8 percent, but considerably higher than Mexico's rate of 38.9 percent. Argentina's female LFP rate has jumped tremendously since 1990, when it stood at 38 percent; in contrast, the male LFP rate fell slightly during this period, from 76 to 74 percent. The increased participation of women in Argentina is the result of their increased educational attainment, which, coupled with declining family incomes as a result of the economic crises of the 1990s and early 2000s, forced many women to enter the labor market. However, gender gaps remain large: a 26 percentage-point differential in Argentina, a 20 percentage-point differential in Brazil, and a 33 percentage-point difference in Mexico, despite a narrowing of rates during the 1990s.[2] Overall LFP rates were highest in Argentina at 60 percent of the urban labor force, followed by Brazil at 57 percent and Mexico at 54 percent (see Table 2.2). LFP rates in the Europe Union (EU) and the United States are much higher, averaging 70 percent in the former and 76 percent in the latter; gender gaps are also lower, at 17 percentage points in the EU and 12.5 percentage points in the United States.

Labor Demand

In general, the evolution of labor force participation responds to economic conditions, with potential workers entering the labor market when more job

Table 2.2   Urban Labor Force Participation by Sex, May 2003 (percentages)

Country	Total	Men	Women
Argentina	60.2	73.9	48.3
Brazil	57.1	67.7	47.8
Mexico	54.2	72.3	38.9

Sources: Data for Argentina for urban population 15+ years from EPHP, available at LA-CLIS/ILO database. Data for Brazil for population 10+ years in six metropolitan areas from PEM survey, available at IGBE website (http://www.ibge.gov.br). Data on Mexico for population 12+ years in thirty-two urban areas from ENEU, available at INEGI website (http://www.inegi.gob.mx).

opportunities are available, and leaving, discouraged, when opportunities are lacking. During the 1990s and early 2000s, however, Argentina had an almost steady increase in its urban LFP rates, despite declining job opportunities. Argentina's LFP rate increased from 54 percent in 1990 to 56 percent in 2002, whereas its urban employment rate fell from 50 to 46 percent (but since then increased again). In Brazil and Mexico, on the other hand, participation rates followed employment rates more closely (see Figure 2.3). In Brazil, both rates fell substantially, with participation dropping from 64 percent in 1990 to 56 percent in 2001, and employment rates falling from 61 to 49 percent. A deteriorating labor market led to a rise in discouraged workers who dropped out of the labor market, lowering the overall rate of participation. In Mexico, both rates moved upward despite a slight fall during the 1994–1995 economic cri-

Figure 2.3a   Urban Labor Force Participation and Employment Rates, Argentina, 1990–2002

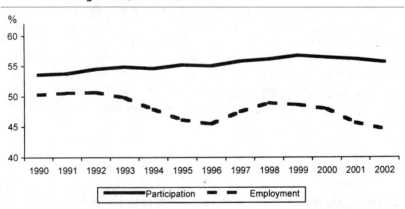

Source: ILO, 2004b.

Figure 2.3b Labor Force Participation and Employment Rates, Brazil, 1990–2001

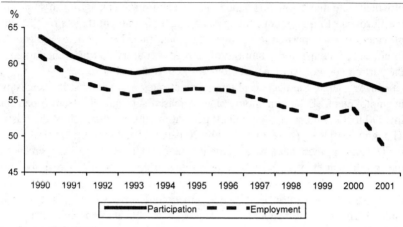

Source: ILO, 2004b.

Figure 2.3c Labor Force Participation and Employment Rates, Mexico, 1990–2003

Source: ILO, 2004b.
Note: Data for Argentina are not available for 2003, and for Brazil for 2002 and 2003, because of a methodological change.

sis; LFP increased from 52 percent in 1990 to 56 percent in 2003, whereas employment rates increased from 50 to 54 percent.

The employment rate is a particularly useful indicator of labor market performance. Because it is measured as the percentage of working-age population who are employed, it reveals not only trends in job growth, but also trends in the participation of workers in the labor market. Thus, if labor force participation declines, the employment rate will decline as well, whereas the unemployment rate may show no change, or even an improvement. For this reason, the European Employment Strategy bases its employment targets on the employment rate as opposed to the unemployment rate. Thus policies are geared to not only increasing the number of jobs in a country, but also encouraging the participation of women and older workers in the labor force.

In Argentina, the decline in employment rates was manifest in increasing unemployment.[3] Urban unemployment increased substantially, from 6 percent in 1990 to 17 percent in 2001 and 20 percent in 2002, at the peak of the crisis. Though unemployment remained at the 20 percent level until the first trimester in 2003, it has since fallen by a dramatic 8 percentage points, to 12.1 percent in the fourth quarter of 2004, according to data from the Ministry of Labor. In Brazil, though participation fell, unemployment also rose steadily over the decade, from 4 percent in 1990 to 8.9 percent in 2002.[4] In Mexico, the official unemployment rate remains low. Since a peak in 1995 at 6.2 percent as a result of the Tequila crisis, the unemployment rate has declined to around 3–4 percent (see Figure 2.4). Low unemployment remains one of the salient features of the Mexican labor market. In 2000, for example, the urban unemployment rate was 2.2, substantially less than the population-weighted Latin American average of 8.5 percent (10.4 percent unweighted), and below the US rate of 4 percent (International Labour Organization [ILO], 2002b).[5] Historically, unemployment has not been a problem in Mexico, and it is largely considered to be frictional (Salas and Zepeda, 2003). In 1950 the unemployment rate was 1.3 percent, in

Figure 2.4   Urban Unemployment, 1991–2004

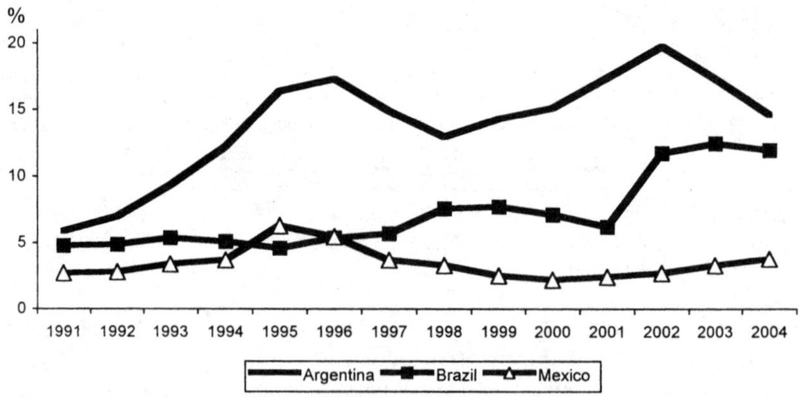

Source: ILO, 2004b.
Note: Figures for 2004 are only for the first three quarters of the year.

1969 it was 3.8 percent, and in 1990 it was 2.7 percent. Even during the severe economic crisis of 1982, unemployment only reached 8 percent (Gregory, 1986). Low unemployment in Mexico is a welcome structural feature of its labor market, though it only presents a partial picture of work in the country.

As in most countries, unemployment is greater for women than men in Argentina, Brazil, and Mexico. Over the period 1990–2003, women had continually higher unemployment rates than men, and the gap grew wider when unemployment reached double digits in Argentina and Brazil. For example, in Argentina in 2003, female unemployment was 19.5 percent, compared with a male unemployment rate of 15.5 percent. Similarly, Brazilian women had an unemployment rate of 15.2 percent in 2003, compared with the male rate of 10.1 percent. In Mexico, which has much lower unemployment, the gap in 2003 was smaller but still telling, with female unemployment of 3.5 percent compared with male unemployment of 3.1 percent. Another important dimension of unemployment is how different age groups are affected. In general, youth unemployment is around double the overall unemployment rate in the three countries (see Box 2.2). Youth face a difficult time entering the labor market because of a lack of work experience, and once employed are more likely to receive precarious contracts.

Box 2.2
The Difficult Integration of
Youth into the Labor Market

Unemployment of youth has become a major concern for Latin American governments, as their potential is underused and they can become a source of social unrest and violence. Data in the table below show youth unemployment rates to be about double total unemployment rates. Even though there has not been much change in the differences among youth and total unemployment rates in Argentina and Brazil, the levels are unbearably high in Argentina and Brazil, at almost 34 percent and 21 percent. Youth unemployment also has a strong gender dimension. Young women's unemployment has increased and is about 5 percentage points higher than that for young men in Argentina, and 7 percentage points higher in Brazil. Mexico is experiencing a different situation; even though the unemployment rate for young people is double the rate of total unemployment, it is still relatively low, at 7.2 percent overall and 5.4 percent for females. Youth in the three countries are also overrepresented in precarious forms of employment, such as underemployment, jobs without contracts, or informal employment, especially among fifteen- to nineteen-year-olds. In Brazil and Argentina, 66 percent and 42 percent of this age cohort do not have an employment contract, compared to shares among adults of 32 percent and 15 percent (Tokman, 2003).

continues

18

Box 2.2   Continued

Insufficient labor demand, coupled with inefficiencies in the education and training systems, are the main reasons for high youth unemployment. In particular, youth face a vicious cycle: with no former job experience they cannot get a job, but without a job they cannot acquire experience. Changes in labor regulations (e.g., allowing a probationary period in Argentina), and new programs such as "first employment" in Brazil, seem to have had only a marginal impact on youth employment.

Youth Unemployment Rates (15–24 years old), 1990–2002 (percentages)

Country	Year	Both Sexes		Men		Women	
		Ratio to Total	15–24 Years	Ratio to Total	15–24 Years	Ratio to Total	15–24 Years
Argentina	1990	2.2	13.0	2.0	11.5	2.4	15.6
	1997	1.7	24.2	1.7	21.1	1.7	28.9
	2002	1.8	33.8	1.7	31.7	1.9	36.3
Brazil	1990	1.8	8.3	1.8	8.7	2.0	7.7
	1996	1.9	15.1	1.9	12.8	1.8	18.2
	2001	1.9	20.5	2.0	17.4	1.8	24.6
Mexico	1990	2.5	8.1	2.5	8.4	2.5	7.6
	1997	2.5	12.5	2.4	13.8	2.6	10.3
	2002	2.1	7.2	2.1	8.2	2.1	5.4

Source: Author calculations based on data collected in ECLAC, 2003d.
Note: "Ratio to total" is the youth unemployment rate divided by the total unemployment rate of the country.

Youth unemployment is particularly high among the poor. While in Argentina the richest 20 percent of the country (fifth quintile) had a youth unemployment rate of 17 percent in 1998, the youth from the poorest 20 percent of the country (first quintile) had a rate of 48 percent. The situation in Mexico is similar and the differences are even stronger, but at a lower level (4 percent compared to 23 percent). Only Brazil is an exception, where the difference between the first quintile (18 percent) and the fifth quintile is rather low (15 percent in 1997). Poor youth are also overrepresented in precarious forms of employment. In Brazil, for example, 73 percent of the fifteen- to nineteen-year-olds in the first quintile are engaged in informal employment. In Argentina, 95 percent of this first-quintile age cohort in the Buenos Aires area do not benefit from social coverage (Tokman, 2003).

Despite an increase of unemployment among higher-educated youth, especially in Brazil and Mexico, the majority of unemployed youth have little education. Less-educated youth have the greatest difficulty in finding a job. According to R. Diez de Medina (2001), in the 1990s the share of unemployed youth with low qualification reached 50 percent for twenty- to twenty-four-year-olds in Argentina and 87 percent for fifteen- to nineteen-year-olds in Brazil. The underinvestment in education and training represents a barrier to social and economic development, as poor youths remain stuck with low skills, high unemployment, or employment of low quality (Cacciamali, 2005).

Employment by Sector, Firm Size, and Education

Employment by sector. The job gains and losses since 1990 in Argentina, Brazil, and Mexico have not been spread evenly across economic sectors. In Brazil and Mexico, agriculture declined in importance as an employer, falling from 28.3 percent of employment in 1992 to 20.6 percent in 2001 in Brazil, and from 25.7 to 17.6 percent in Mexico (see Table 2.3). The decline in agricultural employment stems from the fall of the importance of agricultural output in total output, but also from the modernization of agricultural production requiring less labor. In Argentina's agricultural sector, where 10 percent of the economically active population can be found,[6] the sector's contribution to gross domestic product (GDP) fell from 11.5 percent in the 1980s to 7.4 percent in the 1990s. The decline in agricultural output has a strong effect on employment because of the sector's potentially high employment multiplier (Kostzer and Mazorra, 2004). In Mexico, the decline of agricultural employment was due to the termination of government support to agricultural production in the late 1980s as well as the related trade liberalization process of NAFTA. These measures negatively affected agricultural employment, as the lower costs of US agricultural imports, stemming in part from high US farm subsidies, made Mexican farmers unable to compete (Polaski, 2003). The loss of agricultural jobs caused a strong exodus from rural to urban areas of about 600,000 people each year from 1992 to 2000 (Moreno-Fontes, 2004).

Changes in the share of manufacturing employment were mixed in the three countries, with Argentina seeing a dramatic decline from 32 percent in 1992 to 23 percent in 2001. Brazil, on the other hand, maintained manufacturing employment at the 20 percent level, whereas Mexico increased its share of

Table 2.3   Sectoral Evolution of Employment, 1992–2001 (percentage shares)

Sector	Argentina[a]			Brazil			Mexico		
	1992	1996	2001	1992	1996	2001	1992	1996	2001
Agriculture	0.4	0.8	0.4	28.3	24.4	20.6	25.7	21.6	17.6
Men	0.4	1.1	0.6	30.6	27.4	23.6	32.6	27.3	23.6
Women	0.3	0.2	0.2	24.7	19.7	16.1	10.1	9.7	6.1
Industry	32.1	24.9	22.9	20.4	19.9	20.0	22.9	22.8	26.0
Men	40.2	32.6	30.4	26.9	26.6	26.9	24.9	25.1	28.0
Women	18.2	12.1	12.1	10.1	9.6	9.9	18.4	17.9	22.0
Services	66.7	73.9	76.3	51.4	55.7	59.2	51.4	55.2	56.0
Men	58.6	65.9	68.8	42.6	46.1	49.1	42.5	47.0	47.9
Women	80.7	87.2	87.2	65.2	70.7	73.8	71.5	72.1	71.7

Source: ILO, 2003b.
Note: a. Only urban data for Argentina (which explains the low agricultural employment).

formal manufacturing employment from 23 percent in 1992 to 26 percent in 2001, benefiting both women and men. The gap in male-female participation in manufacturing remained low in Mexico, but was high in Argentina and Brazil. In all countries, the employment share of manufacturing is strongly correlated with the sector's contribution to economic output. For instance, the fall in manufacturing employment in Argentina stems from the fall of industrial GDP by 5.8 percent between 1993 and 2001, which led to its decline in share of output in the economy from 26.8 in the 1980s to 17.5 percent in the 1990s. Employment was also hurt by strong productivity increases as a result of rationalization.[7] On the other hand, Mexico's positive employment performance goes hand in hand with the rising importance of industrial production (from 17 percent in the 1980s to 18.6 percent in the 1990s) accompanied by slow growth in productivity.

Within the broader category of manufacturing is the construction sector, an important sector for employment because of its high labor intensity. According to ILO data at the one-digit sector level,[8] the share of construction in overall employment slightly increased to 6.2 percent in Mexico, 6.5 percent in Brazil, and 7.9 percent in Argentina in 2000–2001, with a dominant male participation of over 90 percent. Construction is a sector with a high number of low-skilled workers, but who are generally employed in low-quality jobs.[9] The output-employment elasticity in the 1990s was 0.7 in Argentina and Mexico and 0.8 in Brazil,[10] and it made a significant contribution to total employment growth in the three countries, from 3 percent in Mexico to 6 percent in Argentina to 12 percent in Brazil (see Table 2.4).

But the most important sector for employment has undoubtedly been the service sector, which continued its dominance as principal employer in Argentina, Brazil, and Mexico during the 1990s. By 2001, 76.3 percent of urban Argentine workers, 59.2 percent of Brazilian workers, and 56 percent of Mexican workers were employed in this sector. The service sector has by far the highest share of female employment, with 72 percent in Mexico, 74 percent in Brazil, and 87 percent in Argentina. Both high- and low-quality jobs have been created.

Table 2.4 gives annual employment growth rates and the contribution of different services to employment creation. As a result of financial liberalization and strong FDI inflows, the finance, insurance, real estate, and business services sector has been the source of many new jobs. The sector had an annual employment growth rate of between 5 percent (Argentina) and 6 percent (Brazil and Mexico) between 1991 and 1999. The sector created many good-quality and well-paying jobs. For example, in Argentina and Brazil, 84 percent of the workers in this sector are employed in formal jobs (Weller, 2001). Many highly educated professionals are employed in this category, and women are also well represented. Part of this sector includes support services to firms in dynamic areas such as information technology and advertising. ·

Table 2.4   Contribution to Employment Creation of Selected Sectors, 1991–1999 (percentages)

	Annual Employment Growth			Contribution to Employment Creation		
Sector	Argentina	Brazil[a]	Mexico	Argentina	Brazil[a]	Mexico
Agriculture, hunting, forestry, and fishing	n/a	–1	0	n/a	–18	0
Manufacturing	–3	0	5	–47	–2	29
Construction	1	2	2	6	12	3
Utilities, transport, storage, and communications	4	3	5	37	8	8
Wholesale and retail trade, restaurants, and hotels	0	3	4	5	27	26
Finance, insurance, real estate, and business services	5	6	6	37	14	6
Community, social, and personal services	3	3	4	63	62	28
Other	n/a	–1	0	n/a	–4	0
Total	1	1	3	100	100	100

Source: Weller, 2001.
Notes: a. Data for Brazil are from 1992 to 1999.
n/a = data not available.

Also, the utilities, transport, storage, and communications sector saw strong job growth, with an annual rate of between 3 and 5 percent between 1991 and 1999. Following privatization and modernization of utilities in the 1990s, there has been an increase in demand for highly skilled workers in this subsector, though it is also an important employer of semiskilled workers. The boom of external and internal trade, related to regional integration as well as infrastructure modernization, has had a positive impact on employment in transport and communication, though privatizations were often associated with layoffs. Transport and communication has a medium to high employment elasticity (0.5 in Argentina and 0.9 in Brazil and Mexico) and is an important employer of low- to medium-level educated workers. The female share of employment in this subsector is rather low; for example, only 15 percent of Brazilian transport and communication workers are female.

The community, social, and personal services sector, which accounted for a major share of job growth in the 1990s, is quite heterogeneous. There are many informal activities, such as domestic work, but also formal activities with an increasing share of highly qualified, often female workers, mainly in health and education. This subcategory represents the bulk of service sector job creation, accounting for over 60 percent of employment creation in Argentina and Brazil during the decade. Part of the reason for the growth has been the increased importance that governments have given to spending on social services, some of which has benefited private providers. Social services have a high employment intensity, as D. Kostzer and X. Mazorra (2004) show in the case of Argentina, though the sector has few links to the rest of the economy. In Mexico, it was the most important employment contributor during the 1990s, employing 2.2 million workers (Moreno-Fontes, 2004). Many of the providers are nongovernmental organizations (NGOs), and their increased importance as social actors in the countries is reflected in employment. In Brazil, for example, NGOs employ three times more employees than does the government—1.5 million workers, according to the Cadastro Central de Empresas (CEMPRE; Central Company Register).[11] The majority of NGOs are active in education and health, but also in human rights and the environment. In general, their workers earn wages that are slightly above the average formal wage, and female workers are well represented.

Trade, restaurants, and hotels is also a sector of high labor intensity—having an employment elasticity of 0.7 in Brazil and Mexico—that has contributed strongly to employment creation, especially among the self-employed and nonremunerated family workers. Sixty percent of new jobs in the service sector in both Brazil and Mexico have been in trade, restaurants, and hotels (Weller, 2001). Working conditions, however, are often bad, and wages are relatively low compared to other service categories,[12] but conditions are usually better than in agriculture and construction. A relatively large share of women are active in this sector (51 percent in Brazil, for example), and it is dominated by micro- and small and medium-sized enterprises. The majority of the workers have a low to medium level of education. The sector, however, has a high and rising informality level.

Employment by firm size. Disaggregating employment data by firm size reveals that, despite a policy shift toward "less state," the public sector is still an important employer. It has even slightly increased its relative importance since 1990–1991 in Argentina (21 percent in 2003) and Brazil (14 percent in 2003) (see Table 2.5). Only Mexico managed to significantly reduce public employment, from 19 percent in 1990 to 14 percent in 2003. Micro firms, defined as having fewer than five employees, have increased their employment share in the region, particularly in Mexico, with a growth from 15 percent in 1990 to 18 percent in 2003. The large category of formal sector firms of small to large size (firms with five or more employees) has the highest employment share, with over 40 percent in Brazil and Mexico, but only 33 percent in Argentina, due to the continued strong presence of the public sector. While the importance of small to large firm employment rose in Argentina and Mexico during the 1990s, Brazil saw a decline in favor of informal and public employment.

Table 2.5   Distribution of Urban Employment by Firm Size, 1990–2003
            (percentage shares)

Country	Year	Micro Firms	Total Informal Sector	Public Sector	Small to Large Firms[a]
Argentina	1991	18.8	52.0	19.3	28.7
	2003	19.7	46.5	20.9	32.6
Brazil	1990	13.5	40.6	11.0	48.4
	2003	14.3	44.6	13.8	41.7
Mexico	1990	14.8	38.4	19.4	42.3
	2003	17.9	41.8	14.2	44.0

Source: ILO, 2004b.
Note: a. Firms with five or more employees.

An alternative breakdown for employment by firm size is employment in micro- and small and medium-sized enterprises (SMEs), or firms with fewer than 200 employees in the case of Argentina, and fewer than 250 employees in Brazil and Mexico. Based on this definition, 71 percent of Argentines worked in micro enterprises or SMEs, compared with 60 percent in Brazil and 49 percent in Mexico (Ayyagari et al., 2003). Although the employment share in micro enterprises and SMEs is much smaller in Mexico than in Argentina or Brazil, small-firm employment grew by 11.4 percent between 2003 and 2004, compared with a decline in large-firm employment of 2 percent (Galhardi, 2005).

Employment by educational level. A breakdown of employment rates by educational level shows rather mixed results among the countries (see Table 2.6). While workers with no schooling improved their employment rate in Argentina and Mexico, they lost ground in Brazil. The employment rate of workers with completed primary education improved in Mexico, but worsened in Argentina and Brazil. Workers with completed secondary education lost ground in Argentina and Brazil, but their employment remained stable in Mexico. Workers with tertiary education also saw a decline in employment rates in Argentina and Brazil, but remained stable in Mexico. In terms of wages, however, workers with completed university education gained the most during the 1990s in all three countries. Compared with secondary-educated workers, the returns to schooling for university-educated workers increased from 13 to 18 percent in Argentina, from 23 to 26 percent in Brazil, and from 14 to 17 percent in Mexico. Secondary-educated workers saw a decline in their returns compared with primary-educated workers, from 10 to 9 percent in Argentina, 19 to 14 percent in Brazil, and 8 to 7 percent in Mexico (Inter-American Development Bank [IADB], 2004).

Table 2.6 Employment Rates by Educational Level, 1992–2001 (percentages)

Country	Year	No Schooling			Primary Complete			Secondary Complete			Any Tertiary		
		Total	Male	Female	Total	Male	Female	Total	Male	Female	Total	Male	Female
Argentina	1992	35.7	44.4	31.0	59.2	83.1	37.1	67.5	89.1	51.1	72.5	81.6	64.3
	2001	38.8	51.1	28.0	52.8	69.9	35.8	60.7	75.5	47.3	67.1	74.1	61.7
Brazil	1992	54.7	77.9	35.6	61.3	81.6	42.4	72.7	86.5	61.2	81.7	88.1	75.9
	1999	51.6	72.1	33.7	59.2	76.5	43.0	70.2	82.3	60.8	79.2	85.5	73.9
Mexico	1992	42.6	73.0	25.7	54.5	84.3	30.0	59.0	78.2	49.2	68.2	78.7	51.3
	2001	47.8	74.1	33.5	56.9	85.5	35.0	59.8	79.4	48.0	68.1	78.5	55.8

Source: IADB, 2004.

In all three countries the lowest male-female gap in employment rates is among those with tertiary education. With some exceptions (e.g., a low gender gap for those with no schooling in Argentina, and a high gap for those with primary education in Mexico and Argentina), this holds true for all education levels: the greater the education, the higher the employment rate and the lower the gender gap. It should be stressed that Mexico has a significantly higher employment gap between male and female workers than do Argentina and Brazil, among those with both low and high education.

Informal Sector, Informal Economy, and Informal Employment

The informal sector is an important characteristic of the economy and employment in Argentina, Brazil, and Mexico, as it is in many other economies of the world. Employment in the informal sector represents a considerable part of total employment in Argentina, Brazil, and Mexico, accounting for 42 to 47 percent of employment. Informal sector employment is characterized by low levels of organization of work, labor relations that are based more on social relations between the parties rather than contractual agreements, low income and low productivity, instability, lack of social protection, and limited prospects for labor upgrading. In sum, it can be summarized as activities carried out at the margin of governmental regulation (see Box 2.3).

Based on the *Labour Overview* definition of employment in the informal sector, measured informality between 1990 and 2003 grew to around 45 percent in Brazil and 42 percent in Mexico, whereas employment in the informal sector in Argentina shrank from 52 to 47 percent (see Table 2.7). Thus, in Argentina, as

---

Box 2.3
How to Define Informality?

Defining informality has many difficulties. This is due to the existence of different, and somewhat intertwined, definitions, such as "employment in the informal sector" and "informal employment," both of which refer to different sources of the informalization of work as a global phenomenon.

The fifteenth International Conference of Labour Statisticians (ICLS) (1993) defined the informal sector in terms of the characteristics of the enterprises in which the activities take place, rather than in terms of the characteristics of the persons involved or the characteristics of their jobs. With the passage of time, it became apparent that the term "informal sector" hid much of the diversity and complexity of informality. Thus the ninetieth International Labour Conference (2002) used the term "informal economy" to refer to "all economic activities by workers and economic units that are—in law or in practice—not covered or insufficiently covered by formal arrangements" (ILO, 2002a).

continues

Box 2.3   Continued

Later on, it was decided that it would be more appropriate to complement the definition of informal sector and informal economy with a definition and measurement of informal employment, given the amount of informal employment found in the informal sector. For this reason, the seventeenth ICLS (2003) defined informal employment as "the total number of informal jobs, whether carried out in formal sector enterprises, informal sector enterprises, or households, during a given reference period." It includes (1) own-account workers and employers employed in their own informal sector enterprises, (2) family workers, (3) employees in informal jobs, whether employed in formal sector enterprises, informal sector enterprises, or households, (4) members of informal producers' cooperatives, and (5) own-account workers engaged in production of goods exclusively for own final use (ICLS, 2003).

This book, however, has mostly followed the definition of informal sector employment used by the *Labour Overview,* an annual publication of the ILO in Latin America, whereby employment in the informal sector comprises the following categories: (1) independent workers (including family workers and own-account workers, except administrators, professionals, and technicians), (2) domestic servants, and (3) persons employed in micro enterprises, defined as firms having up to five employees.

It is worth noting the many similarities between the definition of informal sector employment used by the *Labour Overview* and that of informal employment of the ICLS. To begin, the category of independent workers includes family workers and own-account workers, with the exception of certain more skilled occupations. The second category, of domestic servants, does not have a direct correspondence with the definition of the ICLS, but it reflects the importance of this occupation in the region. The final category makes reference to the place of work, defined by the number of employees, and does not correspond directly with the ICLS definition. Thus the definition used by the *Labour Overview* leaves out many important features that define informal employment, especially those related to the specific characteristics of the job, given in the third category of the ICLS definition (employees in informal jobs). The ICLS definition is based more on the job's characteristics and secondly on whether the job is carried out in a formal sector firm, an informal sector firm, or a household. Finally, it should be noted that an important difference between both definitions centers on the question of legality: the definition used by the *Labour Overview* does not consider the legal standing of the firms of the employees, whereas the ICLS definition considers the legality of the productive units.

opposed to Brazil and Mexico, the decrease of formal sector job opportunities was reflected in increasing unemployment rate rather than in the rise of informal sector jobs. Indeed, the share of informal sector jobs in total employment fell by 5.5 percent between 1991 and 2003. The decline in the informal sector in Argentina is due to a strong decrease in the share of self-employed (from 27.5 to 19.5 percent), while the increase of employment in the formal sector is linked to the strong rise of employment in firms with more than five workers (from 28.7 to 32.6 percent). The statistical decline can also be explained partly by the Programa de Jefes y Jefas de Hogar Desocupados (Program for the Unemployed

Table 2.7 Structure of Nonagricultural Employment, 1990–2003
(percentages)

Sector	Argentina		Brazil		Mexico	
	1991	2003	1990	2003	1990	2003
Informal sector						
Total	52.0	46.5	40.6	44.6	38.4	41.8
Self-employed						
Total	27.5	19.5	20.3	21.0	19.0	19.5
Men	28.2	22.4	19.6	22.7	19.1	18.9
Women	26.5	15.6	21.3	18.8	18.7	20.6
Domestic service						
Total	5.7	7.3	6.9	9.3	4.6	4.4
Men	0.5	0.2	0.5	0.9	0.7	0.9
Women	14.3	16.7	16.7	20.1	12.0	10.5
Micro enterprise						
Total	18.8	19.7	13.5	14.3	14.8	17.9
Men	21.2	24.5	16.0	16.9	17.8	21.6
Women	14.7	13.3	9.6	10.9	9.2	11.4
Formal sector						
Total	48.3	53.5	59.4	55.4	61.6	58.2
Public sector	19.3	20.9	11.0	13.8	19.4	14.2
Firms with more						
than five workers	28.7	32.6	48.4	41.7	42.3	44.0

Source: ILO, 2004b.

Heads of Households), which included informal sector workers among its beneficiaries, who were then counted as being in the public, formal sector. Yet measured as the percentage of nonregistered employment, informality has increased
sharply in Argentina since 1990. At the beginning of the decade, nonregistered
employment affected about 25 percent of workers, rising to 39 percent in 2001,
only to hit a maximum of 50 percent in the aftermath of the crisis, in the second
half of 2003.[13] There was slight improvement during the recovery of 2004; yet
nearly half of Argentine workers remain without a formal work contract and its
related benefits.

The rise of employment in the informal sector in Brazil is likely due to the
low rate of economic growth and the lack of new and sufficient employment
opportunities in the formal sector, in particular in the first half of the 1990s,
which resulted in a growing gap between labor supply and demand in the formal sector. This can be seen clearly in the decline of the formal sector's share
of employment, which fell from 48.4 percent in 1990 to 41.7 percent in 2003;
the nearly three-percentage-point gain in public employment—from 11 to 13.8
percent—could not make up for the shortfall. As a result, excess labor was absorbed by the informal sector, for example by domestic work, which engaged

mainly women with little education. Alternatively, informality in Brazil can be measured by the share of workers without a signed formal work contract *(carteira de trabalho assinada)*. In 2003, as in 1999, 35 percent of waged workers did not have a signed contract, according to the Pesquisa Nacional de Amostra de Domicílio (PNAD; National Household Sample Survey).

In Mexico, the increase in employment in the informal sector, from 38.4 percent in 1990 to 41.8 percent in 2003, shows that even a rise in formal manufacturing employment and continued migration flows to the United States were not enough to cope effectively with the number of new entrants into the labor force. The increase in informal sector employment can be attributed to the rise in employment in micro enterprises, despite a slight decrease observed both in the self-employed and domestic service component. The slight decrease of formal sector employment is due to a reduction of employment in the public sector, which could not be compensated by the surge of employment in large firms. Informal employment, measured as the percentage of workers who are not protected by formal labor regulations and thus do not receive any social benefits, constituted 48.7 percent of the working population during the 1991–1999 period, according to data from the National Employment Survey (Llamas Huitrón and Garro Bordonaro, 2003).

The characteristics of informal sector workers differ across the three countries. In Argentina, informal workers are generally older and better educated (32 percent had completed more than thirteen years of schooling in 2002) (Orsatti and Calle, 2004). In Brazil, on the other hand, a large proportion of informal workers are children or youths (59 percent among those twelve to thirty-four years old in 2002) and half of them have less than five years of schooling. As for the educational distribution, Mexico is closer to Brazil, with a high share of low-skilled informal workers (26 percent had only three years of schooling and 23 percent had just six years of schooling in 2002).[14]

Table 2.8 demonstrates that the gap between men and women with regard to informal sector employment has been narrowing. In the case of Argentina, it has even been reversed: only 45.6 percent of women work in the informal

Table 2.8   Participation in Total Informal Employment by Gender, 1990–2003 (percentages)

Country	Year	Men	Women
Argentina	1991	49.8	55.5
	2003	47.2	45.6
Brazil	1990	36.1	47.6
	2003	40.5	49.8
Mexico	1996	37.6	39.9
	2000	41.4	42.5

Source: ILO, 2004b.

sector, compared to 47.2 percent of men. This trend has been partly driven by creation of emergency employment programs (which are counted as formal employment). In Brazil, the informal sector gender gap is shrinking, but in 2003 almost 50 percent of female workers were employed in the informal sector. This is mainly attributed to the importance of females in domestic work (20.1 percent compared to 0.9 percent for men). Informality also involves blacks more than whites; black women in particular have a high rate of informality (66 percent as opposed to 56 percent for black men) (ILO, 2003c).

Job Rotation and Transitions Between Formality and Informality

The labor markets of Argentina, Brazil, and Mexico appear to be quite mobile, with job turnover rates higher or equal to those in developed countries. In a study comparing job reallocation in the manufacturing sector in Latin America and the OECD during the 1990s, Brazil had the highest job reallocation rate, with 32 percent of workers switching jobs each year, followed by New Zealand, with 30 percent. In Mexico, 28 percent of manufacturing workers switched jobs; in Argentina, 15 percent switched (Micco and Pagés, 2004). Part of labor market mobility concerns movements between formality and informality, which appear to be quite commonplace, particularly in Brazil and Mexico.

Indeed, in Mexico and Brazil, movements between the formal and informal sector have been helpful in mitigating employment pressures during economic crises (Maloney, 1999; Camargo, 1997). One of the reasons for the fluidity between the formal and informal sectors in Brazil and Mexico is low formal sector wages. Studies of Brazil (Carneiro, 2003) and Mexico (Maloney, 1999; Calderon-Madrid, 2000) revealed that low formal sector wages and inefficient social protection encouraged movements from formality into informality. Formal jobs on the informality frontier often have equally low labor productivity and wages. This suggests that if joining the formal sector is not concomitant with social or economic improvement, then workers might rationally choose to work in the informal sector.

As discussed, Argentina in the 1990s had rising unemployment with a declining share of workers in the informal sector, suggesting that the informal sector was not considered as a realistic alternative to workers who lost formal jobs. Moreover, government income support and labor market programs, mainly the Jefes y Jefas de Hogar Desocupados program during the crisis of 2001–2002, meant that workers who lost formal employment and participated in these programs were considered formal workers. These programs also attracted informal workers.[15] It should be noted, however, that when economic growth picks up, it creates not only wage employment but also self-employment opportunities; thus faster growth in wage employment is not necessarily accompanied by decreases in self-employment, which is an important component of informality. The present upswing in Argentina, for example, includes a rise in self-employment.

Quality of Jobs

A well-functioning labor market should create not just employment, but quality employment. Quality employment consists of jobs that provide decent wages, reasonable and desired working hours, job security and stability, but also sufficient social security for times when workers are out of jobs because of disability, unemployment, training, or retirement.

Wages

Wages are an important element of the decency of jobs, as they determine standards of living. They also have an important macroeconomic function affecting both consumption and savings in an economy. Figure 2.5 shows the evolution of real manufacturing wages in Argentina, Brazil, and Mexico since 1990. Argentina experienced a slight decline between 1990 and 2001, due to the provision in the Convertibility Plan, which prohibited wage increases unless it could be demonstrated that they were tied to improvements in productivity. The crisis in 2001 and the devaluation caused a sharp fall in wages, so that by 2003 real wages were at 76 percent of their value in 1990. The downward movement has been halted and most recently the trend is again upward. In Mexico, after a strong fall during the 1980s, real manufacturing wages rose significantly at the beginning of the 1990s, but then fell sharply with the devaluation in December 1994 and the economic crisis of 1995. It then took

Figure 2.5　Real Urban Manufacturing Wages, 1990–2003

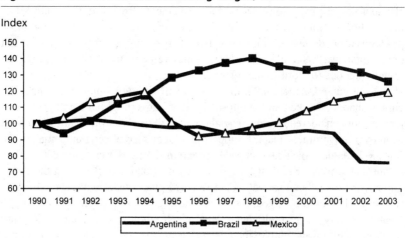

Source: ILO, 2004b.
Note: Index 100 = 1990.

Mexico's wages almost ten years to reach their 1994 level. In Brazil, average real manufacturing wages started to increase beginning in 1991, at an annual rate of 4 percent, until 1998, when they peaked at a level 40 percent higher than in 1990. The economic crisis and the strong devaluation, followed by a period of weak economic performance, led to a steady decline of the real average wage, and in 2003 it was only 26 percent higher than in 1990. In Brazil and Mexico, real average wages have mimicked the evolution of manufacturing wages (see ECLAC, 2004d).

Another characteristic of salaries in Argentina, Brazil, and Mexico is the pervasive gender wage gap, which is still significant, though it has declined slightly since 1990, mainly in Brazil but also in Mexico. In Greater Buenos Aires, the gender wage gap was 24 percent in 1990, meaning that female workers earned on average 24 percent less than male workers in comparable jobs; it then narrowed to 21 percent in 1999, but increased again to 29 percent with the crisis in 2002. Brazil experienced the strongest reduction in the gender wage gap, from 35 percent in 1990 to 14 percent in 2001, while Mexico saw a slight decrease from 14 percent in 1990 to 13 percent in 2002. Taking into account the educational level of female workers, recent data show that the gender wage gap increased with years of schooling in Argentina and Brazil, but not in Mexico, where the results were mixed (ECLAC, 2004d). In Brazil, race also played an important role in determining gender wage gaps. While women in 2001 received 79 percent of men's salaries, black women only received 39 percent (Abramo, 2003).

In Mexico the real minimum wage declined from the beginning of the 1990s due to deliberate government policies to increase the global competitiveness of labor (Polaski, 2003). The fall was aggravated by the crisis in 1994–1995 due to the abandonment of real minimum wage indexation. The minimum wage then stabilized after 1996 at a level of about 71 percent of its 1990 level. Contrary to Mexico, in Brazil, after a bumpy start, the real minimum wage increased in 1994 by 10 percent following the introduction of the Real Plan, which stabilized prices. After 1994 the minimum wage increased steadily, reaching a level in 2003 that was 60 percent higher than in 1990 (see Figure 2.6). Argentina also saw a strong surge in its real minimum wage in the first years of the Convertibility Plan, when it almost doubled. After 1994 it stabilized. In 2002, however, the devaluation and economic crisis caused a fall in its value, even though it recovered again due to a special government effort that increased the minimum wage by almost 60 percent in 2004. Purchasing power parity (PPP) figures in US dollars allow a comparison of the minimum wages in Argentina, Brazil, and Mexico in 2004. Mexico had the lowest minimum wage, with US$177 in PPP, followed by Brazil with US$235 PPP and Argentina with US$532 PPP.[16]

The level of the minimum wage relative to the average manufacturing wage is useful for determining whether the minimum wage may be set too high,

Figure 2.6   Real Urban Minimum Wages, 1990–2003

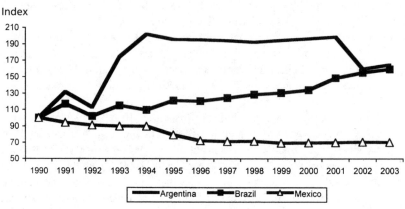

Source: ILO, 2004b.
Note: Index 100 = 1990.

or too low, and whether it might represent an impediment to formal employment creation for low-skilled workers. According to a recent study by W. Maloney and J. Mendez (2004), Mexico had a low relative value of its minimum wage to average wage (0.34), which was far below the average for Europe (0.45), Colombia (0.40), or Honduras (0.62), but higher than Argentina (0.26)[17] and Brazil (0.24).[18] D. Bienen (2002), analyzing trends in this ratio over the 1980s and 1990s, shows the strong decline in this relative value, particularly in Argentina, where it had a value of over 40 percent in 1980, but also in Brazil. In both countries, as well as in Mexico, where the minimum wage is at a very low level, the minimum wage does not represent a major barrier to job creation.[19] The minimum wage in Mexico is below the poverty line, in Brazil it is slightly above, whereas in Argentina, following the recent and substantial increase in the minimum wage since 2003, it is now well above the poverty line.[20]

Nevertheless, there are still substantial portions of the working populations in Argentina, Brazil, and Mexico who earn poverty wages, defined as earning less than US$1 per hour adjusted for purchasing power parity. According to IADB data, in 1999, 19 percent of Argentine workers, 55 percent of Brazilian workers, and 41 percent of Mexican workers earned poverty wages (see Table 2.9). However, there were substantial fluctuations in these levels throughout the 1990s, mainly due to fluctuations in the real exchange rate. In Brazil, for example, there was a strong decline in poverty wages in the middle of the decade as a result of the macroeconomic stabilization program, while the economic devaluation following the Tequila crisis caused a sharp increase in poverty wages among Mexican workers.

Another important question concerns whether the evolution of wages has reduced the disparity in income distribution in these countries, which has tra-

Table 2.9   Percentage of Workers with Poverty Wages, Urban Areas, 1992–1999

	1992[a]	1996	1999[b]
Argentina	17.8	15.2	19.0
Brazil	72.8	54.6	55.4
Mexico	29.0	44.3	40.8

Source: IADB, 2004.
Notes: Poverty wage defined as earnings of less than US$1 per hour in the worker's primary job, adjusted for purchasing power parity.
a. For Argentina and Brazil, 1993.
b. For Mexico, 1998.

ditionally been among the most unequal in the world. Table 2.10 shows the Gini coefficient of wages and income (including wage and nonwage income) for the three countries during the 1990s. In Argentina and Brazil both Gini coefficients increased during the 1990s, though they fell in Mexico.[21] In Brazil, the Gini income index showed a stronger increase than did the Gini hourly wages coefficient, mainly due to the declining wage share in GDP.[22] Mexico was thus the only country that managed to significantly reduce income and wage inequality. The Tequila crisis of 1994–1995 caused wage equality to deteriorate, but growth in GDP and employment during 1997 and 2000 led to an improvement in the Gini, as can be seen in Figure 2.7.

Table 2.11 gives information on the evolution of wages by occupation and in rural and urban areas, in multiples of each country's poverty line, allowing us to assess how different workers have fared during the 1990s and whether this has contributed to inequality. In Brazil and Mexico, rural workers continue to earn significantly lower wages than urban workers, though the wage decline in rural areas in Brazil was less than that of urban areas. In Mexico, rural wages fell to 2.3 times the poverty line in 1996, but then recovered so that by 2002 they were at the same level as in 1989. Employers have by far the highest

Table 2.10   Income and Wage Distribution, 1990–2001 (Gini coefficients)

	Argentina		Brazil		Mexico	
	1992	2001	1992	1999	1990	2001
Gini hourly wages	0.343	0.385	0.366	0.369	0.372	0.350
	1990	1999	1990	1999	1989	2000
Gini income	0.501	0.542	0.606	0.625	0.53	0.493

Sources: For Gini hourly wages, IADB, 2004. For Gini income, ECLAC, 2004a.

Figure 2.7   Income Distribution, GDP, and Employment, Mexico, 1990–2003

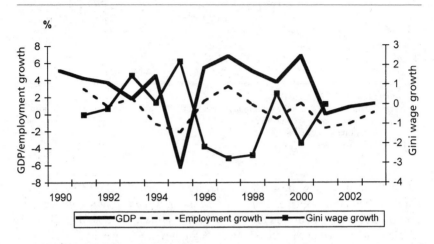

Sources: IADB, 2004; ECLAC, 2004e.

wages in Argentina, Brazil, and Mexico, followed by professionals and public sector workers, but also self-employed workers, particularly in Argentina. Domestic workers and microenterprise workers have the lowest incomes.

An analysis of the evolution of wages by occupation gives some explanation for the rising income inequality in Argentina. The only group that increased their income with respect to the poverty line was employers (+1.4 percentage points), while professionals witnessed a fall of 3.2 points in their average incomes respective of the poverty line, followed by a fall of 3.1 points for self-employed workers and of 1.5 points for microenterprise workers. The declining Gini coefficient in Mexico can be partially explained by the strong fall in average income of employers (–6.9) and the improvement in incomes of those employed in firms with more than five workers (+0.3). In Brazil, while most occupations witnessed a relatively similar deterioration in incomes with respect to the poverty line, the income rise of domestic workers (+0.7) is striking.

Thus, in Argentina, greater inequality was driven by increased wage disparity, whereas in Brazil it was driven by increased disparity in nonwage income. As a result, the labor market can only explain part of the high disparity of income distribution in the region. Inequality of land distribution is very high and historically has contributed to the high income Ginis of the countries. The Gini for land distribution was close to 0.9 in Argentina, over 0.8 in Brazil, and over 0.6 in Mexico between 1960 and 2000, compared to Thailand with a value of less than 0.5 and China and the Republic of Korea with less than 0.4 (World Bank, 2003). With regard to another asset, education, Argentina, Brazil, and

Table 2.11 Average Incomes of Labor Force by Rural/Urban Location and Occupation, 1990–2002 (in multiples of country per capita poverty line)

Country	Year	Rural Total	Urban Total	Employers	Wage or Salary Earners Total	Public Sector	Private Sector Total	Private Sector Professional	Nonprofessional, Nontechnical Firms with More Than Five Persons	Firms with Less Than Five Persons	Domestic Workers	Self-Employed
Argentina	1990	n/a	7.3	22.2	5.1	n/a	5.1	11.4	4.7	3.7	4.4	9.4
	2002	n/a	5.7	23.8	4.0	3.9	4.0	8.2	3.3	2.2	3.6	6.3
Brazil	1990	2.0	5.7	17.2	4.8	n/a	4.8	11.3	4.2	2.8	1.3	4.9
	2001	1.7	5.1	15.8	4.7	8.0	4.1	8.8	3.4	2.2	2.0	4.0
Mexico	1989	3.0	5.1	23.4	3.8	n/a	3.8	7.8	3.3	n/a	2.1	6.1
	2002	3.0	4.9	16.5	4.0	5.8	3.6	8.3	3.6	2.3	2.0	4.9

Source: ECLAC, 2004d.
Note: n/a = data not available.

Mexico are catching up in literacy and primary enrollment, but the gap is still big in other areas such as secondary enrollment (see also Islam, 2006).

Working Hours

Working hours are also an important element of job quality, affecting workers' individual preferences for balancing work and family, as well as determining overall pay. In terms of hours worked, Argentina, Brazil, and Mexico rank among those countries with long annual working hours, like Japan, Australia, and the United States, and have significantly longer working hours than most European countries (see Table 2.12). Nevertheless, ILO data show a strong decline of working hours in Argentina in the 1990s, a slight decline in Brazil, but a rise in Mexico. The declining hours in Argentina and Brazil do not reflect better working conditions, but rather declining employment and thus underemployment. Indeed, monthly average working hours by the unskilled declined in all three countries during the 1990s.

The reduction of working hours is explained to a large extent by the rise in involuntary part-time work, which is one of the forms of undesired work. The number of workers who work fewer than thirty hours per week, but who would like to work more, increased from 7.4 percent in 1992 to 19.5 percent in 2001 in Argentina. The level in 2001 was much higher for female workers (26 percent) and unskilled workers (31.6 percent) (IADB, 2004). Recently in Mexico, the share of involuntary part-time workers also increased slightly, from 7.9 percent in 2002 to 9.5 percent in 2004,[23] at the same time that unemployment rose. Female workers still work fewer hours than their male col-

Table 2.12   **Average Annual Hours Worked per Person, Argentina, Brazil, and Mexico Compared to Selected Industrialized Countries, Various Years**

Country	Year	Annual Hours
Argentina	1990	2,013
	1999	1,820
Brazil	1990	1,796
	1999	1,689
Mexico	1990	1,767
	2000	1,888
Australia	2002	1,824
France	2002	1,545
Germany	2002	1,444
Japan	2002	1,821
United States	2002	1,815

Source: ILO, 2003b.

leagues. This gap increased slightly in Brazil, from 4.2 average monthly hours in 1990 to 5.4 in 2001, and more strongly in Argentina, from 16.7 hours in 1992 to 22.2 hours in 2001 (IADB, 2004).

The distribution of working hours shows a strong concentration of workers in the range of forty to forty-eight hours per week in Mexico (47 percent) and Brazil (49 percent). For men, this trend is even greater, with 51 percent in Mexico and 55 percent in Brazil working in this range per week, compared with 41 percent of female workers in Mexico and 43 percent in Brazil. More detailed figures on Brazil show forty to forty-four hours per week to be the dominant range (32.4 percent), in comparison with forty-five to forty-nine hours (17.1 percent) (see Figure 2.8). In Argentina and Brazil, the difference

Figure 2.8   Distribution of Working Hours, Brazil, 2003, and Mexico, 2002

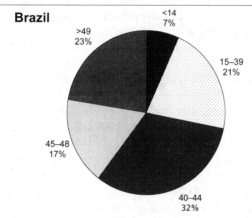

Source: IBGE, PNAD, 2003.

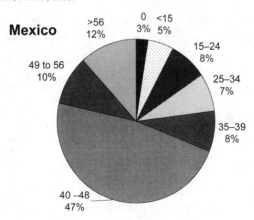

Source: INEGI, 2002.

in working hours between formal and informal sector workers has decreased. While in Argentina the self-employed worked in 1992 on average 3.4 percent more hours than formal workers, by 2001 they worked on average 6 percent fewer hours. In Mexico, working hours have remained about the same, with informal employees averaging 5 percent more hours per week and the self-employed averaging 13 percent fewer hours (see Table 2.13).

Employment Tenure

Stability in employment is an important source of economic security for workers and is thus an important indicator of job quality and job satisfaction. Stability is measured by employment tenure, the amount of time a worker has spent with the same employer. Average tenure in Argentina was 6.7 years in 2001, a drop from 7.1 years in 1992. In Brazil, average tenure in the 1990s fluctuated at just over 5 years.[24] In comparison, average employment tenure was 6.6 years in the United States in 1998, 12.2 years in Japan in 2001, and 10.7 years in Germany in 2002. Disaggregating the tenure data by the distribution of workers with short and long tenure, we see that the short tenure range (less than 1 year) and the long tenure range (over 10 years) lost importance in favor of the medium tenure ranges (1–5 and 5–10 years) (see Table 2.14). The situation in Brazil is slightly different, with short tenure losing ground in favor of medium (1–5) and long tenure. Analyzing the breakdown by skill level, in Argentina the gap between skilled workers (25.8 percent) and unskilled workers (31.8 percent) among the short tenure range (less than 1 year) increased, and fewer unskilled workers benefited from long tenure (26.1 percent in 1992, declining to 19.9 percent in 2001). In Brazil, there were no significant changes. The IADB data also show that the share of female workers was higher in the shorter tenure range (0–5) than in the longer tenure range (over 5 years) in Argentina and Brazil during the 1990s. In sum, Argentina did see a decline in overall job stability, possibly as a combined result of the crisis and economic and labor market reforms of the 1990s, but there was no such effect in Brazil.

Table 2.13   Relative Working Hours, 1992–2001

	Argentina		Brazil		Mexico	
	1992	2001	1995	2001	1996	2000
Informal	94.9	92.8	110.2	107.6	105.2	105.1
Self-employed	103.4	94.0	93.3	93.0	86.2	87.4
Formal	100.4	104.9	103.7	103.4	105.8	104.3

Source: Gasparini, 2004.
Note: 100 = national average working hours.

Table 2.14   Distribution of Job Tenure of Employees Measured as Years on the Job for Total, Skilled, and Unskilled Workers, Argentina and Brazil, 1992–2001 (percentage shares)

Country	Year	Ability	Years on Job 0–1	1–5	5–10	10+
Argentina	1992	Total	30.4	29.3	16.4	23.8
		Skilled	30.3	31.1	16.1	22.5
		Unskilled	30.4	26.4	17.0	26.1
	2001	Total	27.5	34.0	17.3	21.2
		Skilled	25.8	35.3	17.1	21.8
		Unskilled	31.8	30.5	17.9	19.9
Brazil	1992	Total	39.1	30.9	14.7	15.3
		Skilled	36.8	32.0	15.3	16.0
		Unskilled	42.1	29.8	13.8	14.4
	1999	Total	37.3	31.6	14.7	16.4
		Skilled	37.2	32.2	14.4	16.1
		Unskilled	36.9	30.7	15.2	17.1

Source: IADB, 2004.

Social Security Coverage

Another important indicator of employment quality and economic and labor market security is social security coverage. Social security coverage—measured as the amount of workers who pay into and are thus part of the system—declined sharply in Argentina between 1990 and 2003, from 62 to 48 percent of total workers, with both formal and informal sector workers suffering. Formal sector coverage fell by over 20 percentage points, from 86 to 64 percent, and coverage of microenterprise employees also declined sharply, from 38 to 23 percent. Coverage also fell in Brazil, though not as dramatically, from 74 percent of workers in 1990 to 69 percent in 2003 (see Table 2.15). Domestic workers were the exception, however, increasing their coverage by 5 percentage points. Mexico had been the country with the lowest levels of social security coverage, but with the decline in Argentina and an increase in Mexico, it now ranks second. Coverage in the formal sector increased by over 8 percentage points, possibly stemming from the reforms to the social security system, including the issuing of personal tax identification numbers as well as privatization of the system for non–public sector workers. In the informal sector, there was a strong increase in coverage of domestic workers, from 4 to 9 percent, though coverage of microenterprise workers declined. The falling coverage of microenterprise workers is likely related to the strong growth in employment in these firms, which typically have lower coverage rates than do larger firms. With regard to gender, it should be stressed that in Mexico, women and men

Table 2.15   **Percentage of Salaried Workers Who Pay into the Social Security System, 1990–2003**

| Country | Year | Total | Informal Sector | | Formal Sector |
			Domestic Service	Micro Enterprise	
Argentina	1990	61.9	7.8	38.1	86.2
	2003	48.2	4.0	23.0	64.0
Brazil	1990	74.0	24.9	45.8	86.1
	2003	69.2	29.7	37.9	83.8
Mexico	1990	58.5	4.2	15.3	72.9
	2003	63.4	9.2	11.9	81.2

Source: ILO, 2004b.

had the same level of social coverage in 2003, while in Argentina and Brazil, even though it declined during the 1990s, there was still a gap of 3.4 percent and 6.2 percent in favor of male workers in 2003.

Narrowing the analysis to pension fund rights, the percentage of workers who declared having the right to a pension in household surveys in Argentina declined sharply, from 87 percent of formal sector workers in 1992 to 79 percent in 2001. Similarly, in the informal sector, there was a decline from 35 to 25 percent. In Brazil, pension fund entitlements in the informal sector increased, from 49 to 52 percent, whereas formal sector coverage was stable, at 84 percent (Gasparini, 2004).

Efficient unemployment insurance and its ample coverage are a sign of a well-functioning labor market, as they can facilitate the matching process between demand and supply, and provide security in times of job loss or job change. Unemployment insurance does not exist in Mexico, and in Argentina its coverage is still quite limited, with approximately 17 percent of the unemployed in Buenos Aires entitled to benefits (Marshall, 2004). The Brazilian unemployment insurance program, the Fundo de Amparo ao Trabalhador (FAT; Workers Protection Fund), is substantially more developed, with 60 percent of unemployed salaried workers having coverage (Gasparini, 2004).

Conclusion

The effect of the economic reforms of the 1990s on the labor markets of Argentina, Brazil, and Mexico is clearly evident. Economic opening affected the distribution of employment across economic sectors. In Brazil and Mexico there was a notable decline in the population employed in agriculture; manufacturing's share of employment fell in Argentina, remained stable in Brazil, and increased in Mexico in response to the insertion of these sectors in global trade; and in all three countries the service sector increased its importance as an employer. In Brazil and Mexico, there was also a shift in employment to the informal sector, and rising informality (unprotected employment) became a dominant feature of employment in Argentina. Different occupations and skill levels were also affected by the reforms. Though employment rates for skilled workers did not increase much, the skilled did see a greater increase in their returns to schooling than less-educated workers. This was particularly true in Argentina, where employers were the only occupational category to increase their average incomes with respect to the poverty line during the 1990s. In Mexico, low-educated workers with completed primary education improved their employment rate, and microenterprise workers were the sole occupational category to increase their average incomes with respect to the poverty line. In Brazil, the employment rates of both skilled and low-skilled workers fell, and incomes with respect to the poverty line did not improve either, with the exception of domestic servants.

Overall, between 1990 and 2004, Mexico had the most favorable labor market evolution of the three countries, reflecting some of the positive aspects of its international insertion, including the strong economic and job recovery in the second half of the 1990s. New jobs were created following the 1995 crisis, formal unemployment remained low, youth unemployment was not a major problem and social security coverage improved. Nevertheless, Mexico still faces some important employment challenges. There has been a lack of job creation since 2000, and real minimum wages lost significant ground during the 1990s. Though manufacturing wages recovered following the crisis of 1995, real incomes in Mexico are still far below the level they were in 1980. Social security coverage is also low and needs expanding, particularly to microenterprise workers and domestic servants (see Table 2.16).

Argentina's labor market has had the worst evolution of the three countries since 1990, clearly reflecting the negative effect of the economic reforms on the country's work force. The most notable change in its labor market is the high rate of unemployment, which remains in double digits despite substantial improvement since the economic crisis. There has also been a worsening of job quality measured by the sharp increase in the number of workers who do not hold a formal work contract, by increasing underemployment (measured in hours worked), and by greater instability in jobs. Though the minimum wage has recovered its losses since the crisis, wages, proxied by the manufacturing sector, declined sharply over the period.

Brazil's labor market evolution has been more mixed, though negative on the whole. In particular, there has been a deterioration in the country's employment rates, reflected in both higher unemployment, particularly of women and youths, and lower participation rates. The fall in employment in firms with more than five workers was partly compensated with an increase in employment in

Table 2.16   Summary of Employment Trends of Selected Indicators

Indicator	Argentina	Brazil	Mexico
Economically active population	Declining	Declining	Declining
Participation	Rising	Declining	Rising
Employment			
Overall	Stable	Declining	Rising
In agriculture	Stable	Declining	Declining
In manufacturing	Declining	Stable	Rising
In services	Rising	Rising	Rising
Informal	Declining	Rising	Rising
Unemployment			
Overall	Rising	Rising	Stable
Youth	Rising	Rising	Declining
Working hours	Declining	Declining	Rising
Social security coverage	Declining	Declining	Rising
Wages			
Real wages	Declining	Rising	Stable
Real minimum wages	Rising	Rising	Declining
Wage Gini	Rising	Rising	Declining

micro enterprises and domestic service, but this has not helped to increase the number of workers with a formal work contract. Indeed, the percentage of salaried workers who pay into the social security system has fallen. On the positive side, real minimum wages and manufacturing wages increased during the period, causing a fall in the percentage of workers with poverty wages.

Appendix Table 2.A   Summary Trends from a Gender Perspective

	Argentina		Brazil		Mexico	
Indicator	Gap Trend	Difference	Gap Trend	Difference	Gap Trend	Difference
Labor market participation	Declining	<	Declining	<	Declining	<
Unemployment	Rising	>	Rising	>	Stable	>
Youth unemployment	Rising	>	Rising	>	Declining	<
Informal employment	Declining	<	Declining	<	Declining	>
Real wages	Rising	<	Declining	<	Stable	<
Social security coverage	Declining	<	Declining	<	Rising	=
Working hours	Declining	<	Declining	<	n/a	n/a

Notes: "Difference" refers to the difference between male and female worker, with "<" indicating, for example, that the female participation rate is lower than, ">" greater than, and "=" equivalent to, the male participation rate. "Gap trend" refers to the gap between the female and the male participation rate.

n/a = data not available.

Notes

1. Data from UNESCO Institute for Statistics, Country Profile (http://www.uis
.unesco.org/countryprofiles).
2. ECLAC data on labor force participation indicate increasing female participation in Mexico (by 9.5 percent between 1992 and 2002) and Brazil (by 4.3 percent during the same period) and thus a shrinking gap between male and female participation rates (http://www.eclac.cl/badeinso/badeinso.asp).
3. The rate of unemployment in a labor market corresponds to the gap between participation rates and employment rates and is measured as the percentage of labor market participants who are out of a job.
4. The 8.9 percent unemployment rate figure for 2002 is calculated using the old methodology. Changes in the methodology of the Monthly Employment Survey in Brazil in 2001 led to an increase of the urban unemployment rate of almost 2 percentage points, making the 2002 unemployment rate 10.8 percent. For more details on the change in methodology, see ILO, 2003c.
5. There are some differences regarding how unemployment data are collected in Mexico compared with the United States. G. Martin (2000) adjusts Mexican unemployment data to US definitions and finds that this raises the Mexican figures by approximately 1.5 percentage points, an insufficient difference to explain variations in country unemployment rates.
6. Data from the Food and Agriculture Organization (2004).
7. For more details, see Chapter 4.
8. International Standard Industrial Classification (ISIC) Revision 3 for Argentina and Mexico and Revision 2 for Brazil.
9. ECLAC data reveal both low schooling levels and high informality levels in the construction sector. For example, Brazilian construction workers have fewer than five years of schooling on average, and 46 percent of Mexican construction workers are informal.
10. Based on author calculations. Argentina: 1993–2000; Brazil: 1996–2000; Mexico: 1994–2000.
11. *Journal do Brasil,* December 11, 2004.
12. According to ECLAC data, relative wages in this sector were 91.3 percent compared to the average wage in Brazil in 1996 and 85.1 percent in Mexico in 1997, while finance, business, and insurance services had relative wages of 257.3 percent in Brazil and 170.2 percent in Mexico.
13. Data from the Instituto Nacional de Estadística y Censos (INDEC; National Institute for Statistics and Census) and reported in "El trabajo en negro volvió a crecer," *El Clarín,* March 2005.
14. Data from the Instituto Nacional de Estadística, Geografía e Informática (INEGI; National Institute for Statistics, Geography and Informatics), 2002.
15. See Chapter 6 for more information on labor market policies.
16. Purchasing power parity in US$ from 2003. Data from International Labour Organization (ILO), Conditions of Work and Employment Programme, *Minimum Wage* database.
17. Following the latest minimum wage increases in 2004, this value reaches about 36 percent, which is about Mexico's level (Ministerio de Trabajo, Empleo y Seguridad Social [MTSS], 2004).
18. These results were confirmed by a similar analysis undertaken by the ILO (2004b) (period of 1997–2002), as well as by S. Waisgrais (2003) for Argentina and D. Bienen (2002) for Argentina and Brazil.

19. A Kernel-density analysis by W. Maloney and J. Mendez (2004) showing the distortionary effect of a minimum wage on income distribution demonstrates similar results for our three countries, with a slightly distortionary effect for Brazil, but not for Argentina and Mexico. S. Suarez Dillon Soares (2002) comes to similar results for Brazil using the same Kernel-density methodology as well as labor income elasticities with relation to minimum wage (1995–1999).

20. According to ECLAC's *Social Panorama of Latin America 2002–2003* (2004d), the monthly minimum wage (in 2002 US$) in Mexico was US$123 compared with the urban poverty line of US$154; in Brazil the minimum wage was US$69 compared with an urban poverty line of US$54; and in Argentina the minimum wage was US$153 compared with a poverty line of US$55.

21. It also fell in Brazil in the mid-1990s, but then increased again to reach a higher level at the end of the 1990s than at the beginning. The Gini income coefficient reached 0.628 in 2001 according to ECLAC, 2003d.

22. This share went down from 45.4 percent in 1990 to 37.9 percent in Brazil, while it went up from 29.5 percent to 31.3 percent in Mexico, according to ECLAC (http://www.eclac.cl/badeinso/badeinso.asp).

23. Involuntary part-time work is defined as the percentage of urban workers who involuntarily (i.e., for market reasons) work less than thirty-five hours per week. Data from INEGI, Encuesta Nacional de Empleo Urbano.

24. Tenure data for Argentina and Brazil from Inter-American Development Bank (IADB), 2004. Data for Mexico were not available.

3

Macroeconomic Policy and Employment

Macroeconomic policy is a fundamental determinant of economic growth and employment. Higher economic growth rates, particularly when concentrated in employment-generating activities, increases labor demand in an economy, leading to faster job growth. Economic growth also spurs investment, which improves productivity and ultimately the level of income in an economy. But how best to achieve higher economic growth is a matter of economic debate. Beginning two decades ago, Argentina, Brazil, and Mexico radically changed their macroeconomic policy in an effort to control inflation as well as realize the benefits of increased integration with the world economy. Since then, economic growth has been volatile and, on average, relatively low, affecting the ability of the economies to create employment, particularly in the formal sector.

The external opening of Argentina, Brazil, and Mexico to international competition in goods and financial markets provides a number of important lessons on how to integrate employment objectives within macroeconomic policy. Macroeconomic policy in the 1990s was dominated by the belief, which remains today, that countries must first "get prices right" in order to stimulate economic activity. This was first pursued via the fixed exchange rate policy adopted by the countries during the 1990s and has currently been replaced by inflation targeting. Employment, on the other hand, has taken a back seat. This chapter analyzes why monetary, exchange rate, and fiscal policy have not supported employment growth and, based on this assessment, makes recommendations on how macroeconomic policy can be more effectively directed toward job creation.

Macroeconomic Performance and Employment

During 1990–2003, growth averaged 2.2 percent in Argentina, 2.4 percent in Brazil, and 3 percent in Mexico. By historical standards, economic growth during this period compares unfavorably with earlier decades, particularly in Brazil and Mexico. Mexico averaged 9 percent real growth during the 1960s and 1970s, followed by 2 percent average growth in the 1980s and 4 percent in the 1990s (see Table 3.1). Brazil's average growth in the 1990s fell to 3 percent, compared with 8 and 13 percent in the 1960s and 1970s. In Argentina, growth was slow overall, with the performance in the 1990s matching the 1960s.

The performance of the macroeconomy affects employment creation in three ways: by the amount of growth in the economy, the stability or volatility of that growth, as well as its structure. During the 1990s, economic growth was not only relatively low, but also quite volatile. In Argentina, between 1990 and 2003 the standard deviation of economic growth was 6.4 percent, nearly three times the average growth rate. In Brazil and Mexico, economic growth has also been volatile, though much less than Argentina, with the standard deviation matching the growth rates (see Figure 3.1).

A stable macroeconomic growth rate is preferable to volatile growth marked by booms and crashes. Even though recessions lead to job loss, if a recession is mild, dismissed workers will be rehired when economic growth resumes. In contrast, in a severe recession, firms are more likely to go bust and exit the market, making it more difficult for these workers to be rehired in a recovery. Stable growth also ensures a better environment for investment, since stability lessens uncertainty, which is a deterrent to business investment.

The nature of economic growth is another important determinant of employment. If an economic boom period is due to a boom in financial markets, employment may not increase much, as investment may be destined toward speculation in the real estate or stock markets, as opposed to productive investment in new firms or firm expansion that can create jobs. In contrast, if eco-

Table 3.1   Average Real GDP Growth Rates, 1960–2003 (percentages)

Period	Argentina	Brazil	Mexico
1960–1970	4.9	7.5	9.2
1970–1980	3.2	12.9	8.7
1980–1990	−1.0	1.7	1.9
1990–2000	5.0	2.9	4.1
1990–2003	2.2	2.7	3.6
2000–2003	−4.4	1.6	1.3

Source: ECLAC, various years.

Figure 3.1   Real Economic Growth, 1990–2003

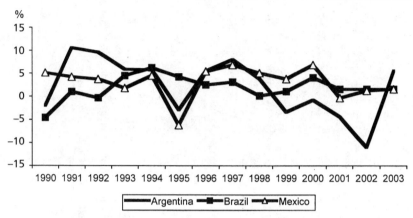

Source: ECLAC, various years.

nomic growth is driven by increased demand for labor-intensive goods or services, then employment growth is likely to be strong, particularly if this sector
has strong multiplier effects on other areas of the economy. For example,
heavy public investment in infrastructure and housing is also generally associated with strong employment growth, as the construction sector is highly
labor-intensive.

The employment intensity of economic growth can be determined roughly
through elasticities, which measure how much employment increases for every
1 percent increase in economic growth. Table 3.2 compares employment-
output elasticities during different expansions and recessions in Argentina,
Brazil, and Mexico. In Argentina, employment-output elasticities averaged
0.29 during the expansion of 1991–1994, substantially lower than the employment impact of the expansions in the 1980s, when the elasticity was 0.67 during 1983–1984 and 0.84 during 1986–1987. In the 1995 recession, the very
high, negative employment-output elasticity shows a reversal in relation to the
1980s, when economic crises had not been accompanied by declining employment (Marshall, 1998). The economic crisis of 1999–2002 resulted once again
in a negative employment-output elasticity (employment did not fall with output), most likely due to the significant job-shedding that took place before the
crisis as well as the implementation of the emergency employment program.
As a result, the recovery has had a strong labor intensity.

In Brazil, employment-output elasticities were at a low of 0.43 during the
1993–1997 expansion, and even lower throughout the stagnation of 1998–
1999. The elasticity, however, increased noticeably in 2000–2002, a period of
very modest expansion. In Mexico, employment-output elasticities during the
expansions of the 1990s fell slightly as compared with their historical trends:

Table 3.2   Employment-Output Elasticities, 1981–2002

Expansions			
Argentina I	Argentina II	Brazil	Mexico
[0.67 (1983–1984)]	–0.09 (1994)	0.43 (1993–1997) [0.45]	0.67 (1988–1994)[a]
[0.84 (1986–1987)]	0.64 (1996–1998) [0.66]	0.02 (1998–1999) stagnation [–1.14]	0.51 (1996–2000) [0.48]
[0.29 (1991–1994)]		1.08 (2000–2002) moderate expansion [1.08]	
[0.64 (1996–1997)]			

Recessions			
Argentina I	Argentina II	Brazil	Mexico
[–0.24 (1981–1982)]	1.04 (1995)	1.56 (1992) [1.56]	0.75 (2001)
[–0.18 (1985)]	0.03 (1999–2002) [–0.15]		
[–0.63 (1988–1990)]			
[0.58 (1995)]			

Source: Marshall, 2004.

Notes: The table measures elasticities corresponding to annual average rates of variation of employment and output in each economic phase. Periods start with year of first rate of change.

[ ] = average of annual elasticities in each economic phase. Argentina I and Argentina II based on different GDP series (at constant market prices of 1986 and 1995, respectively).

a. Estimates from López, 1999.

0.59 in 1970–1981, 0.67 in the moderate expansion of 1988–1994, and 0.51 in the expansion of 1996–2000 (Marshall, 2004).

Thus, overall economic performance in the 1990s in Argentina, Brazil, and Mexico was unfavorable to employment creation. Growth was slow, volatile, and not employment-intensive. The relatively poor performance is associated with a sharp shift in macroeconomic policy.

The Adoption of a New Model and the Preeminence of the Washington Consensus

After a half century of import-substitution industrialization, the Argentine, Brazilian, and Mexican economies undertook ambitious economic reform in the mid 1980s and 1990s, including trade and financial liberalization, privatization of state enterprises, and market deregulation. Inflation control became the centerpiece of macroeconomic policy, based on the idea that a stable economic environment would provide the best possible scenario for the resumption of economic growth. Nevertheless, all three countries struggled to achieve stability, with each country attempting to combat inflation by anchoring the exchange rate, at varying degrees, to international currencies. Unfortunately, this policy stance would have strong negative effects on economic competitiveness, yet it was only after the economies experienced financial crises that the fixed exchange rate regimes were abandoned. The end result: highly volatile and overall low economic growth rates in the 1990s.

The timeline of the economic reforms differs slightly. Argentina made a first attempt at trade liberalization during 1976–1981, which would foreshadow many of the problems of the liberalization of the 1990s, since this first liberalization was also undertaken during a period of real exchange rate appreciation. The manufacturing sector was negatively affected under liberalization, losing 3 to 4 percent of its share in gross domestic product (GDP) by the time the program was abandoned in 1982 (Gerchunoff and Llach, 2003). Nevertheless, toward the end of the 1980s the country would once again liberalize, reducing average tariffs from 43 to 30 percent between 1987 and 1988 and removing quantitative restrictions. The process accelerated in the 1990s, with average import tariffs further reduced to 10 percent in April 1991.

The opening of Argentina's current account went hand-in-hand with the opening of its capital account. In March 1991 the government passed the Convertibility Law, which set a fixed parity between pesos and dollars that transformed the newly independent central bank into a currency board, automatically linking the money supply to the amount of foreign currency reserves held by the bank (Calcagno, Manuelito, and Titelman, 2003). Liberalization was further promoted by the passing of laws to promote foreign investment, principally the 1989 Laws of State Reform and Economic Emergency, which established the legal basis for the privatization of state-owned enterprises, granted equal treatment for foreign and domestic capital, and eliminated the requirement of prior approval for direct foreign investment. The legal reforms gave way to a surge in privatizations, and by 1994 most state-owned firms producing goods and services had been sold (Frenkel and González Rozada, 1999).

Mexico was also an early reformer, taking its first steps in the late 1980s, motivated by negotiations for a North American Free Trade Agreement (NAFTA). In 1985, Mexico eliminated import licenses on capital and intermediate goods and reduced tariffs, so that by 1993 the weighted average tariff level was 8 percent (Lustig, 2001). Beginning in 1998, the process of financial liberalization began, first with the elimination of credit quotas as well as the liberalization of reserve requirements, followed by the privatization of the banks. The government also issued a decree removing previous legislation that had limited foreign ownership to 49 percent; the decree opened the domestic stock market to foreign investment as well (Ros and Bouillon, 2000). By 1990, when Mexico initiated discussions on NAFTA, it was one of the most open developing countries in the world (Organisation for Economic Co-operation and Development [OECD], 2002).

Brazil opted to open its economy, with the 1990 announcement by the Fernando Collor administration of a trade-opening program. The program called for the immediate removal of import prohibitions and nontariff barriers, followed by a gradual reduction of tariff rates, from an average of 32 percent in 1990 to 14 percent in 1993. Following the establishment of the Mercosur Customs Union in January 1995, the average import tariff was further reduced to 13 percent (World Trade Organization [WTO], 1996). Brazilian financial liberalization entailed the removal of prohibitions on foreign investment in the stock exchange as well as the liberalization of legislation regarding foreign financing of domestic firms. Investors were given access to the options and future markets in 1992. However, Brazil did take some steps to limit short-term capital flows after the Tequila crisis, though in 1997, following massive capital flight as a result of the Asian crisis, the government eliminated this restriction in an attempt to attract external resources.

In Argentina, Brazil, and Mexico, trade and financial liberalization were thought to open new investment opportunities that would increase the efficiency of the economies and restore them onto a growth path that had been lacking during the 1980s. These opportunities were believed to be conditional on the maintenance of a stable macroeconomic environment with low fiscal deficits and low inflation. Once this could be achieved, then liberalization would lead presumably to a resumption of growth, as financial opening would jump-start investment by making domestic credit available and by lowering the rate of interest; trade opening would result in a better alignment of resources, efficiency gains, and greater growth. But in order to guarantee price stability, Argentina, Brazil, and Mexico had to take drastic measures, using their currency as an "anchor" against inflation.

Mexico's decision to use its exchange rate as a nominal anchor stemmed from its frustration in restoring stability during the 1980s. In December 1987 a tripartite board agreed to a stabilization program known as the Pact of Economic Solidarity, which included fixing the exchange rate to control inflation. The exchange rate was fixed in 1988, though by 1989 it was replaced by a crawling peg and later by an exchange rate band (Lustig, 1998). Following several bouts of hyperinflation in the 1980s, Argentina, in 1991, established parity between the US dollar and the peso, and enshrined this parity in law. In 1994, after a series of frustrated attempts to curtail hyperinflation, the Brazilians adopted the Real Plan, consisting of miniband margins that facilitated minor adjustments to the exchange rate. In all countries, the policies achieved their target of controlling inflation below one digit.

Implications of the New Policy Stance in a Volatile External Environment

In a span of just six years, the three largest economies of Latin America opened their current and capital accounts to the external market. This external liberalization had a number of simultaneous effects on the economies, effects that had—and continue to have—important repercussions for the labor market. The decision to liberalize the capital account, undertaken with complementary legislation removing restrictions on foreign ownership and massive privatization programs, led to a surge in capital inflows in all three countries. In Mexico, for example, between 1988 and 1994, GDP grew at an annual average rate of 4 percent, whereas there was 375 percent annual growth of capital inflows (Lustig and Ros, 2000). Similarly in Brazil, after capital account liberalization, portfolio investment jumped from US$3.8 billion in 1992 to US$38.8 billion in 1997, a 180 percent annual increase (Baumann, 1998). In Argentina, portfolio investment was US$12 billion in 1992, jumped to US$50 billion in 1993, and then peaked at US$92 billion in 1999.[1]

The inflow of capital heated the economies, resulting in domestic inflation that was higher than inflation in the countries to which the currencies were pegged. As a result, the real exchange rates appreciated.[2] Under an appreciation, the price of goods produced abroad cheapens relative to goods produced in the home country. Unfortunately, this shift in relative prices happened at the same time that domestic companies were being exposed to foreign competition, after previously being protected under import-substitution industrialization.

Consequently, the changes in the financial side of the economy had spillover effects on the real side. The expansion of domestic credit can be a boom for investment and economic growth, but its effects will only be lasting if the credit is used to finance productive investment as opposed to consumption. In Argentina, Brazil, and Mexico, the credit boom occurred before many of the newly exposed industries had had time to adjust to foreign competition, and at a time when adjustment was further complicated by exchange rate appreciation. The exchange rate overvaluation was a disincentive toward business development, and as a result the increase in credit was directed toward investments in the housing and stock markets, leading to a boom in asset prices. The credit boom also had adverse effects on the rates of domestic savings, as households went on a consumption spree, unfortunately directed toward the purchase of imported, as opposed to domestic, goods.

With foreign investment flows and the domestic credit expansion directed toward consumption and nonproductive investments, imports boomed, outweighing the export push intended under the export-led growth model and causing negative trade balances. Figure 3.2 shows the evolution of exports and imports in Argentina, Brazil, and Mexico between 1985 and 2001, measured in constant 1995 US dollars. In Argentina by 1991, tariff reduction had been completed and the convertibility system was instituted. From then until January 2002, when the country devalued its currency, imports grew at an average annual rate of 16 percent, compared with 11 percent growth in exports. In Brazil, from 1993, when tariffs were reduced, until currency devaluation in January 1999, imports grew at an average annual rate of 18 percent, compared with 3 percent annual export growth. Similarly in Mexico, between the time it instituted a currency peg, when the process of tariff reduction was almost complete, and 1994, when the currency devalued, imports grew at an average annual rate of 28 percent, compared with a 13 percent export growth rate.

One of the selling points for trade liberalization was the belief that labor would benefit, since production for export was believed to be more labor-intensive than production for the internal market. By opening the economy and thus removing price distortions, it was argued that the combination of a more efficient resource distribution based on the country's comparative advantage of abundant labor, coupled with more dynamic growth, would stimulate job growth.[3] Moreover, because demand for low-skilled labor would increase relative to demand for skilled labor, it was also argued that low-skilled workers would receive greater pay increases relative to skilled workers, thus compressing the unequal income distribution that has plagued the countries, especially Brazil and Mexico, for decades.

Exports did increase in all three countries under liberalization, yet the performance was much less than expected, and insufficient to compensate for the increase in imports. The appreciation of the exchange rate was partly responsible for this disappointing performance, since appreciation increased the price of the exported goods calculated in dollars. This meant, as well, that workers' wages calculated in dollars increased, even when the workers' wages in local

Figure 3.2   Exports and Imports, 1990–2001

Argentina

1995, US$millions

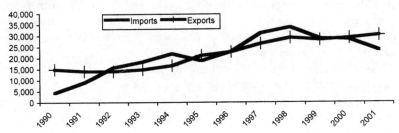

Brazil

1995, US$millions

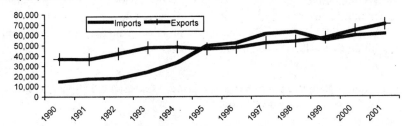

Mexico

1995, US$millions

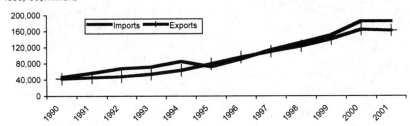

Source: ECLAC, various years.

purchasing power did not. As a result, competitiveness, gauged in terms of labor costs, deteriorated (Frenkel and Ros, 2003). For example, in Mexico, between 1988 and 1997, real manufacturing wages increased slightly, only to then fall, so that by 1997 they were lower than their 1988 value. Yet calculating the same wages in dollars shows a large and continual increase in dollar wages that hurt the competitiveness of Mexican labor until 1995, when the exchange rate was devalued (see Figure 3.3). Thus the Mexican economy was hurt externally by the rising dollar cost of its exports, and internally because lower wages resulted in weak internal demand.

A similar scenario of deteriorating competitiveness and stagnant internal demand occurred in Argentina and Brazil as a result of currency appreciation. In Argentina, the appreciation was particularly severe, hurting competitiveness throughout the decade-long appreciation. In 1994, for example, real manufacturing wages stood at 101 (based on an index where manufacturing wages in 1990 equaled 100), whereas measured in dollars, manufacturing wages had increased from 100 to 198.[4] Since devaluation in late 2001, real wages in pesos and dollars had both fallen sharply, reversing the competitive situation, so that by 2002, dollar wages were half of their real value in pesos. Similarly in Brazil, competitiveness was jeopardized until devaluation in 1999. Since then the competitive exchange rate has helped the trade balance (see Figure 3.3).

As a result of opening the previously protected manufactured goods sector with an overvalued exchange rate, demand was weakened and companies

Figure 3.3a   Real Wages in Manufacturing, Mexico, 1988–1997 (in local currency and dollars, 1990 = 100)

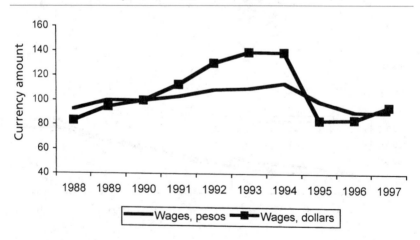

Source: Frenkel and Ros, 2003.

Notes: Dollar manufacturing wages are calculated by dividing real wages in pesos by the real exchange rate. Index 100 = 1990.

Figure 3.3b   Real Wages in Manufacturing, Argentina, 1988–1997

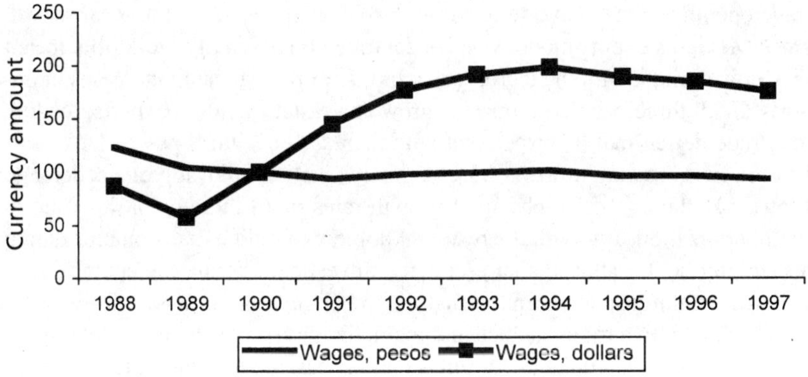

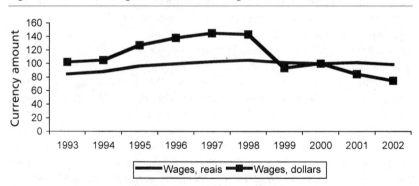

Source: Frenkel and Ros, 2003.
Notes: Dollar manufacturing wages are calculated by dividing real wages in pesos by the real exchange rate. Index 100 = 1990.

Figure 3.3c   Real Wages in Manufacturing, Brazil, 1993–2002

Source: Author calculations based on ILO and ECLAC 2004e.
Notes: Dollar manufacturing wages are calculated by dividing real wages in pesos by the real exchange rate. Index 100 = 1990.

in the tradable goods sector either curtailed production or went out of business, or adjusted by increasing labor productivity. Productivity increases stemmed from labor reorganization and shedding, as well as from the importation of machinery, which was made more affordable by the overvaluation of the local currency. Another reason for the disappointing employment performance is that only in Mexico did export orientation shift toward labor-intensive manufacturing, as was argued by the Washington Consensus. In Argentina, export industries were, and continue to be, concentrated in the processing of natural resources, which is capital- as opposed to labor-intensive. In Brazil, although its export structure has a better mix of labor- and capital-intensive production, trade opening did not favor any particular labor-intensive sectors.[5] Moreover, since Mexico's export model was concentrated on assembly work, this meant that, concomitant with the increase in exports, were associated increases in imports. In all three countries, imports grew at a faster rate than exports, leading to a trade deficit that had to be met with increased capital flows.

At first, capital inflows were a great injection into aggregate demand growth, explaining the high initial growth rates in all three countries following liberalization. But with the resultant domestic credit expansion unleashing a spending boom rather than a productive investment boom, the countries developed the unfortunate scenario that they were relying on these inflows to finance the negative trade balance and maintain the fixed exchange rate system. By opening their capital and current accounts, passing legislation to ensure independence of the central bank, and fixing their currencies to establish price stability, Argentina, Brazil, and Mexico lost monetary policy independence. This is because open capital markets force a country to choose between controlling its exchange rate and controlling its interest rate. Thus, under a fixed exchange rate regime, countries must set interest rates at levels consistent with the exchange rate target. Typically, this means that the central bank must keep interest rates high enough to prevent capital from fleeing the country, thus alleviating the pressure on the currency to depreciate.

So long as capital continued flowing into the countries, the system was sustainable. But this meant that sovereign nations were reliant on the whims of international investors to ensure continued flows. When capital stopped flowing in or left, the other policy option available besides changing the interest rate was to have the central bank sell currency reserves. Doing so bolsters the value of the home currency, since more foreign exchange will be available for purchase at the prevailing exchange rate. All three countries attempted this strategy at one point, in Argentina and Brazil during the Tequila crisis of 1995 and the Asian crisis of 1997. In 1999, Argentina once again defended convertibility through the selling of reserves, following the Brazilian devaluation. The prolonged selling of reserves is risky, however, since it weakens the central bank's ability to defend the exchange rate if there is a speculative attack. Without any reserves left, a central bank will be forced to abandon its intervention, forcing a devaluation of the currency (Blecker, 1999).

Unfortunately, all three countries faced a speculative attack, which forced devaluation and caused an immediate crisis. Mexico's crisis came in December 1994, and although with hindsight the causes of the buildup may be clear, the crash of a "model reformer" less than one year after NAFTA took effect was a large and surprising letdown to its policy-backers. But what explains the turn of events?

Between 1987 and 1993, Mexico's current account fell from a surplus of US$4.2 billion to a deficit of US$28.8 billion, equivalent to almost 8 percent of its GDP at that time (Blecker, 1999). Capital inflows buoyed by the NAFTA negotiations and signing, and from privatization, actually exceeded the current-account deficit, leading to an overall balance-of-payments surplus and the buildup of reserves. Yet much of this investment was speculative, as can be seen by the dramatic increase of the Mexican stock exchange whereby the share price index rose from 250 in 1988–1989 to over 2,500 in early 1994 (Pieper and Taylor, 1998). In 1994 the trade and current-account deficits continued to increase, but capital flows started to leave the country, as the rise in US interest rates decreased the Mexican-US interest rate spread that had existed previously, and the stock exchange stopped rising. Political events also damaged investment prospects, beginning with the January 1994 Chiapas uprising, followed by two high-profile political assassinations in March and September of 1994. With money leaving the country, the central bank chose to sterilize the outflows rather than raise interest rates, which might have encouraged some investment to stay (Lustig, 1998). However, the government did try to encourage investors to keep their money in the country and even went so far as offering investors wary of devaluation the opportunity to switch from peso-denominated short-term government debt, to debt indexed to the dollar, called Tesobonos.[6] Yet money continued to leave the country, and with reserves dwindled by the end of 1994, the central bank could no longer defend its currency and was forced to devalue. The devaluation caused a major financial crisis in Mexico, with spillover effects into other Latin American countries.

Brazil was a relative latecomer and a less ambitious reformer than Mexico or Argentina, but nevertheless suffered a similar fate of stability-cum-crisis. Although liberalization took place in the early 1990s, Brazil maintained a positive trade balance until 1994, when the newly implemented Real Plan initiated a currency appreciation. As a result, the trade balance shifted from positive to negative and the current account increased in deficit from US$1.1 billion (0.2 percent of GDP) in 1994 to a deficit of US$30.5 billion (4.2 percent of GDP) by 1997. The negative current account was being financed by a boost of portfolio investment—in 1994 it accounted for 60 percent of all foreign investment in Brazil—leading to a dependence on continued external financing. Unfortunately for Brazil, this dependence occurred at a time of international financial market shocks that took the allure out of "emerging market" investment, beginning with the raising of US interest rates in 1994 and followed by the Tequila crisis, the Asian crisis, and the Russian crisis. All of the crises had a strong negative effect on foreign investment in Brazil. For example, as a result of the Asian crisis, the Bovespa stock exchange fell 27 percent between July and November 1997 (Guillén, 2000). By the end of 1997, foreign investors began to demand a substantial risk premium for keeping their funds in the country, leading to further real interest rate hikes in order to maintain the exchange rate. Yet the increase in the real interest rate, which rose to more than 20 percent in 1998, worsened the fiscal situation of the government, as it caused a sharp increase in debt payments. To attract investment the government removed the short-term capital controls that had been put in place after the Tequila crisis; it also negotiated a US$40 billion International Monetrary Fund (IMF) loan in the fall of 1998. In early 1999, however, the government of the state of Minas Gerais announced a moratorium on its debt, which aggravated speculation against the real and culminated in the depletion of reserves and the abandonment of the adjustable peg exchange rate system. The currency lost 80 percent of its nominal value compared to the US dollar in the first three months after devaluation, then recovered slightly to finish the year with a devaluation of 49 percent.

Argentina was the most ardent of the reformers. Throughout the 1990s it maintained exchange rate convertibility with the dollar, despite being severely bruised by numerous international financial crises. At the beginning of the decade, the convertibility-liberalization program was quite successful, with the surge in capital inflows leading to an expansion of economic activity and average annual growth rates of 7.6 percent between 1991 and 1994. This initial success partly explains the zealousness with which the Argentine government maintained convertibility throughout a series of adverse shocks. The first important shock—and a turning point in the economic performance of the country—was the Tequila crisis, which resulted in a restriction of credit and an increase in interest rates (Calcagno, 1997). As a result, GDP contracted, falling to –3 percent in 1995. The crisis also halted private capital inflows, forcing the government to assure sufficient external financing from 1995 onward. Yet the cost of capital increased as the country's risk premium rose with each international financial crisis. To maintain the trust of investors, the government was forced to abide by a highly restrictive, procyclical fiscal policy, but these cutbacks in government spending together with the loss in Argentine competitiveness—particularly against its major trading partner, Brazil, following the devaluation of the real in 1999—pushed the country deeper into recession. Finances worsened and, as a result, the fiscal deficit increased. An increasing exodus of capital forced the government to abandon convertibility in January 2002, and switch instead to a floating exchange rate combined with exchange and capital controls; the country was also forced to declare a moratorium on its debt.[7]

The economic crashes of Argentina, Brazil, and Mexico had different effects on the labor market depending on the severity of the crash, its run-up, and its aftermath. In Mexico, GDP fell 6.2 percent and urban unemployment nearly doubled, from 3.7 percent in 1994 to 6.2 percent in 1995. Yet by 1997, urban unemployment had returned to its original level of 3.7 percent. The relatively quick turnaround was aided by the strong boost in output in the maquiladora sector, whose competitive position had been restored by the devaluation. As a result, maquila jobs expanded by over 20 percent annually in 1996 and 1997 and continued double-digit growth until 2000, when the sector reached a peak of 1.3 million jobs.

In Argentina, the economic crash of 2002 was severe, causing GDP to fall 11 percent and making 2002 the fourth consecutive year of negative economic growth. Economic growth had been volatile throughout the 1990s, causing a steady deterioration in the labor market. Thus, although urban unemployment only increased by a little over 2 percent the year of the crash, it had steadily worsened since 1992, culminating in the alarming rate of 20 percent in 2002. The job losses of the 1990s mainly affected male, head-of-household workers, particularly in manufacturing, where employment fell dramatically over the decade. Indeed, manufacturing's share of total employment fell from 24 percent in 1990 to 15 percent in October 2002. Since the economic crisis, Argentina's tradable sector (agriculture, fishing, mining, and manufactured goods) has been revitalized, growing 12 percent in 2003 after falling 5 percent in 2002. This has had a favorable employment effect, particularly in industry, where the number of manufacturing workers in the formal sector increased 9.3 percent in the first trimester of 2004 compared with 2003.[8]

In Brazil, the crisis and devaluation of 1999 had little effect on urban unemployment, which increased slightly, from 7.6 percent in 1998 to 7.8 percent in 1999. Yet urban unemployment steadily increased from its 1990 level of 4.3 percent, and other labor market indicators, such as the percentage of workers in the informal sector and the percentage with social security coverage, also worsened. Manufacturing's share in employment fell from 16 percent in 1992 to 14 percent in 1999, when the country devalued; its share has since recovered to 15 percent in 2002.[9]

The experiences of Argentina, Brazil, and Mexico underscore the importance the real exchange rate has on employment in the tradable sector. Devaluation, however, has a less positive effect on the countries' debt levels, as devaluation of a national currency makes dollar-denominated loans more costly to service.[10] In Mexico, the late-1994 devaluation and subsequent bailout caused its outstanding debt as a percentage of GDP to increase from 33 percent to 58 percent; in nominal dollars the debt increased from US$140 billion in 1994 to US$166 billion in 1995 (see Figure 3.4). By 2002 the Mexicans had reduced their debt to US$134 billion, 22 percent of the value of its GDP.[11] The reduction stemmed from an aggressive strategy on the part of the Mexican authorities to replace the external debt component with domestic debt, through the development of a domestic debt market for longer-term instruments. The government also continued making debt repayments equivalent to above 3 percent of GDP following the 1995 crisis. As a result of these efforts, maturities have lengthened and interest rates have come down. These efforts, coupled with an appreciation of the Mexican peso in the early 2000s, lowered the debt-

60

Figure 3.4   Outstanding Debt in US$ Millions and as Percentage of GDP, 1993–2002

Argentina

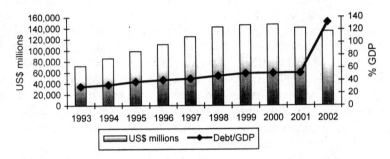

Brazil

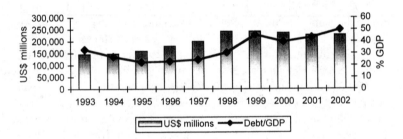

Mexico

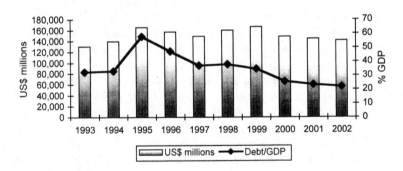

Source: ECLAC, various years.
Note: Data include IMF debt.

to-GDP ratio. The reduction in debt led to an upgrading of Mexico's invest-ment-grade rating in the early 2000s (Blázquez and Santiso, 2004).

In Brazil, the debt burden jumped to the 40 percent range following its economic crisis, reaching 50 percent of GDP in 2002, despite government ef-forts that reduced the nominal level of debt from its high of US$242 billion in 1998 to US$235 billion in 2003. As in Mexico, the Brazilian government has made an aggressive effort to run high primary surpluses in order to prepay debt, but devaluation and high interest rates have maintained the high debt level. Moreover, low GDP growth has meant a worsening in the debt-to-GDP ratio.

As in Mexico and Brazil, the debt-to-GDP ratio in Argentina skyrocketed after the devaluation, to 132 percent of GDP in 2002. In nominal terms, the debt has fallen slightly, from a peak of US$147 billion in 2000 to US$140 bil-lion in 2003.

Tight Monetary Policy, Fiscal Restraint, and Loose Exchange Rates

The economic crashes removed the constraint of maintaining a fixed exchange rate, but the high debt-to-GDP levels and fears of renewed inflation have meant that monetary and fiscal policy remain restrictive. Price stability contin-ues to be the central concern of macroeconomic policy, embodied in the cur-rent policy of inflation targeting. The other principal objective is debt sustain-ability. The restrictive bias in macroeconomic policy, particularly in Brazil and Mexico, has hurt employment creation. High interest rates have lessened do-mestic investment, while shrunken public resources have meant less spending on public and social infrastructure. The countries continue to maintain their capital accounts open, which as explained earlier limits a country to control-ling either its exchange rate or its interest rate. And although the exchange rate is no longer fixed, there are limits to its flexibility, since the countries must guard against excessive currency devaluation, which can fuel inflation as well as increase the cost of servicing the debt, as much of the debt is in dollars but national income is in local currency.[12] As a result, many of the same macro-economic constraints still impede the policy choices of Argentina, Brazil, and Mexico.

Inflation Targeting, High Interest Rates, and Low Investment

Brazil, Mexico, and more recently Argentina have adopted inflation targeting as their policy tool for controlling inflation.[13] Inflation targeting entails having the central bank preannounce a rate of inflation to be met for the year and center-ing bank policy on achieving this goal.[14] Thus, the central banks of Argentina,

Brazil, and Mexico do not consider employment when deciding on policy. Though the governments are concerned about job creation, the newly independent central banks have made inflation control their sole mandate. Indeed, in the 2001 report of Mexico's central bank, the only mention of employment policy was the perceived need to reform the labor market (Banco de México, 2002). If employment targeting replaced inflation targeting as the policy mandate of the central banks, the policy tools of the banks would have to change, but in doing so the countries could ensure that employment gains its prominence as a central component of economic policy (see Box 3.1).

Since adopting inflation targeting in 1999, Mexico has set descending targets starting from 10 percent in 2000 down to 3 percent in 2003. Brazil's target for 1999 was 8 percent, dropping steadily to 4 percent in 2004. Argentina, in agreements with the IMF, set inflation targets of 7–11 percent in 2004, 5–8

Box 3.1
What If the Central Banks Pursued Employment Targeting as Opposed to Inflation Targeting?

If macroeconomic policy were driven by employment targets as opposed to inflation targets, the policy goal of making employment the center of economic policies would be explicit. Employment targeting would be subject to an inflation constraint to ensure responsible policymaking, but by making employment creation an explicit goal, the livelihoods of workers and society would be improved. Targets could be set depending on the specific needs of the country. Thus it could be an unemployment rate target, an employment rate target—perhaps more appropriate, because it encourages labor force participation—or a target that considers formal sector employment rates or female employment rates. The targets need not be exclusive; for example, there could be an employment target for the whole economy that also includes targets to increase female employment.

Achieving an employment target would require that central banks expand their policy tools beyond the short-term interest rate. Depending on the mechanism that the bank believes is the most effective way to generate employment, the portfolio of tools used would vary. For example, if ensuring a stable and competitive exchange rate was believed to be the best way to increase employment, then the central banks would need to be willing to control the money supply through the use of credit allocation mechanisms such as quantitative credit controls, interest rate ceilings, and reserve requirements on bank deposits. But the central bank could also take a more direct approach with credit allocation by setting quotas that banks and other financial institutions would have to achieve in lending for employment generation. Alternatively, the central bank could establish differential reserve requirements—for example, by imposing low reserve requirements on loans for activities that would generate employment. Even more direct, the central bank could lend to a development bank that specializes in loans for employment-generating activities (Epstein, 2005). These policy tools could then be complemented with other government macroeconomic policies, particularly fiscal policies that stimulate demand.

continues

Box 3.1   Continued

Employment objectives in central bank policy are not new. The US Federal Reserve is subject to the Humphrey-Hawkins Full Employment and Balanced Growth Act of 1978, which specifies policy goals as full employment, balanced growth, and price stability and sets interim targets of 4 percent unemployment and 3 percent inflation (Galbraith, 1999). The act has been instrumental in ensuring that the Federal Reserve pursue its dual mandate, making it one of the few central banks in this era of inflation targeting that considers employment. But during the 1950s, 1960s, and 1970s, central banks throughout the developing world actively used a wide range of policy tools to promote economic growth and development, including credit allocation policies, support for development banks, and regulations devised to support development lending (Epstein, 2005). Though economic growth rather than employment generation was the goal, these policies had a more beneficial effect on raising incomes and improving livelihoods than did the current policy of inflation targeting.

---

percent in 2005, and 4–7 percent in 2006 (Prat-Gay, 2003). Mexico has had somewhat greater success at reaching its announced targets than has Brazil: inflation descended from 9 percent in 2000 to 4 percent in 2003 in Mexico, compared with increasing from 6 to 11 percent during the same period in Brazil. Brazil's less successful performance mainly stems from its more pronounced exchange rate movements following the 1999 devaluation. Yet even if the Brazilian and the Mexican governments have not always met their inflation targets, making an explicit commitment to inflation control "has worked as an important coordinator of expectations and generated a more stable inflation scenario" (Minella et al., 2004, p. 131). Thus, as an inflation-reduction policy it is successful. But this success has come at a price, since the policies implemented to restrain inflation often involve raising interest rates, which deters investment and, as a result, labor demand.

Furthermore, it is not clear why inflation targeting has become the central macroeconomic policy after the demise of exchange-rate anchoring, since there is no empirical evidence that shows that an economy with an annual rate of inflation of 10 percent performs worse than an economy with annual inflation of 3 percent. Indeed, recent studies on inflation have shown that "inflation rates need to be quite high—in the 15 to 40 per cent range—before they become prejudicial to growth" (Islam, 2003, p. 11). What is undesirable, and should be avoided, is inflation that is continuously accelerating, or that fluctuates unpredictably from year to year (Diaz-Alejandro, 1985). In contrast, inflation that is fairly predictable but moderate may be better to live with than excessively restrictive policies and low inflation, if the former can allow space for economic growth.[15]

Interest rates are determined endogenously, based on the base rate set by the central banks, but they are also affected by exogenous factors, such as the country's risk premium. If a government issues a bond to raise external financing, investors will assess the rate of return according to the interest rates offered as well as concerns of credit risk—both of the country itself as well as the overall risk sentiment in international capital markets.[16] Thus, countries with a high-risk premium are forced to offer higher interest rates, yet this has the adverse effect of increasing the cost of debt, the debt burden, and ultimately the perception of risk. It also raises domestic interest rates, making it more expensive for domestic banks to borrow from abroad, thus increasing the cost of credit available domestically.

Brazil, Argentina, and to a lesser extent Mexico have endured high real interest rates, which have negatively affected private investment and, as a result, economic growth and job creation. The situation is particularly severe in Brazil, where the real prime lending rate in 2002 was 42 percent (see Table 3.3). Although the real lending rate in Mexico, relative to Brazil, seems comparably low, the interest rate has also been used as a policy tool to retain capital flows, for instance in 1999, when Mexican real lending rates reached 13.3 percent following the Brazilian crisis. Since then, Mexico has been able to lower its interest rate as a result of an improvement in its credit risk rating. Argentina's low real interest does not reflect the current external conditions, as the country is blocked from international markets after having declared a moratorium on its debt in December 2001.

The high interest rates in Argentina, Mexico, and especially Brazil have aggravated the already difficult process that firms face in obtaining financing. In a business environment survey in 1999–2000, 73 percent of Argentine firms, 84 percent of Brazilian firms, and 71 percent of Mexican firms reported high interest rates as a major obstacle for the operation and growth of their business (World Bank, 2000). Another important obstacle is the lack of access to credit. Credit markets in the countries are skewed toward the largest firms, with small enterprises, particularly micro enterprises, sidelined. In Mexico in the late 1990s, for example, nearly 20 percent of private claims belonged to the largest twenty private firms listed on the stock exchange, whereas only 13 percent of urban micro enterprises received any credit, despite employing significant portions of the labor force (López de Silanes, 2002). Indeed, access to financing is often mentioned as an impediment to firm development. In Mexico in 1999–2000, 65 percent of small firms and 53 percent of medium-sized enterprises reported financing as a major obstacle, as did 52 percent of small firms and 46 percent of medium-sized firms in Argentina. In Brazil, financing was less of an obstacle, with 30 percent of small firms and 42 percent of medium-sized firms reporting it as an impediment (World Bank, 2000).[17] Though there is discussion of the need for bank restructuring in the region and some programs have been developed to support small-firm financing, these efforts will likely face impediments unless lending rates are brought down.[18]

Table 3.3 Real Interest Rates, 1994–2002

Country	Real Interest Rate	1994	1995	1996	1997	1998	1999	2000	2001	2002[a]
Argentina	Deposit rate	2.9	11.1	7.1	6.4	7.0	9.6	10.0	15.2	-1.8
	Lending rate	4.8	16.9	10.3	8.7	10.0	12.7	12.7	23.2	8.2
Brazil	Deposit rate	79.5	26.6	16.3	19.1	27.0	15.3	10.9	9.1	4.0
	Lending rate	n/a	n/a	n/a	69.9	83.2	65.4	48.0	46.4	42.3
Mexico	Deposit rate	2.8	-9.1	-1.4	-0.5	-4.4	-1.3	-1.7	-0.1	-2.2
	Lending rate	9.1	4.0	8.2	8.0	7.9	13.3	9.4	8.6	4.0

Source: ECLAC, various years.
Notes: a. Preliminary data.
n/a = data not available.

The rigid inflation-control policies have aggravated financing difficulties, affecting investment. Over the past several years, Brazil's economic growth has been stagnant, at around 2 percent annually, yet the country set an inflation target of 4 percent for 2003. Investment contracted 7.5 percent that year; urban unemployment increased by 0.8 percentage points.[19] Similarly, in an attempt to meet its 2004 inflation target of 4 percent, Mexico's central bank raised interest rates eight times during the course of the year, despite it being the first year of modest economic growth after three years in which real economic growth averaged just 0.6 percent.

Restrictive Fiscal Policy

Controlling public spending is integral to keeping inflation in check and is also necessary for funding debt payments. Yet like a restrictive monetary policy, restrictive fiscal policy reduces aggregate demand, hampering job creation. Because of the large debt repayment burden, the countries have to run primary fiscal surpluses to service the debt, yet this means that the government is taking in more money domestically than it is spending, which is contractionary. Furthermore, fiscal policy has been procyclical, which aggravates downturns, since spending is reduced when the economy goes into recession. If fiscal policy could be designed to be countercyclical, then it could cushion economic slumps. Moreover, by controlling spending better during boom periods and using the saved revenues during downturns, the countries could lessen economic volatility. As mentioned earlier, a more stable rate of economic growth favors employment by preventing the firm deaths that are associated with sharp falls in GDP.

Mexico, and more recently Argentina and Brazil, have made efforts to bring their budgets into balance by running primary surpluses to finance debt repayment. Mexico has run a primary surplus since 1983 (including interest payments, the government has run an overall budget surplus three times between 1983 and 2001). In Argentina, based on data from the Economic Commission for Latin America and the Caribbean (ECLAC) from 1994 to 2002, the country ran a positive operating surplus every year except 1996, with an average surplus of 0.8 percent of GDP for the eight-year period; overall, the budget deficit was 1.8 percent of GDP. Similarly, Brazil has had positive primary balances since 1998, averaging 3.6 percent of GDP during 1999–2002. Nevertheless, interest payments continue to swallow a large share of government outlays, averaging 8 percent of GDP during 1999–2002 (Giambiagi and Ronci, 2004). Besides the objective of meeting debt repayments, deficit control is fundamental to the governments' objective of keeping inflation in check. Indeed, Mexico, and Brazil and Argentina for the most part, would meet the fiscal criteria under the Maastricht Treaty, whereby the general government debt-to-GDP ratio has a ceiling of 60 percent and the government financial deficit-to-GDP ratio has a ceiling of 3 percent.[20]

Although the governments must meet debt service obligations, there are arguments for and against running a large primary fiscal surplus to lower the debt. The Brazilian debt problem has been compared to the Italian debt problem of the late 1990s, with the important difference that the Italian debt was primarily domestic-currency denominated, whereas 60 percent of Brazilian debt is either indexed to the exchange rate or foreign-currency denominated.[21] In 1997 the Italians ran a primary surplus that exceeded 6 percent of GDP, which may have sent an important signal to which financial markets responded by permanently lowering the cost of debt (Favero and Giavazzi, 2002). Mexico has also followed this general policy and for the most part it has proved successful, as debt-to-GDP ratios have fallen and the country risk rating has improved. It is therefore argued that maintaining a restrictive policy stance, involving large primary surpluses to service debt payments, will encourage financial markets to lower interest rate spreads, facilitating debt repayment in the medium to long term. The flip side to this argument is that running a fiscal surplus is a contractionary policy, as government expenditures are an important component of aggregate demand. Though a higher primary surplus may send such a strong signal to investors to alter the cost of debt, it is not certain that this will work, particularly since other variables affect financial markets, some of which are exogenous to Brazil's management of its economy. As a result, the strategy, which is currently being pursued by the Brazilian government, may have a positive impact on investor confidence, but the outcome is by no means guaranteed. It is certain, however, that a contractionary fiscal policy will reduce the rate of growth of the economy.

For this reason, some Brazilian economists have proposed lowering the current fiscal surplus target of 4.25 percent to 3 percent, so that the government can dedicate these funds to investment projects.[22] The Brazilian government has also requested from the IMF that spending on infrastructure not be counted as government outlays but rather as investment. If this were allowed, it would give the government more fiscal space, allowing it to invest in public infrastructure. Infrastructure projects that use labor-intensive production methods would have the added benefit of reducing unemployment in the country. Moreover, by fixing a primary surplus target without considering economic cycles, countries run the risk of aggravating downturns, since there is no built-in mechanism to provide relief.

During the 1980s, public sector spending in Mexico averaged 36.7 percent of GDP, but the lack of sufficient revenues meant that the government ran a public deficit that averaged 10.9 percent of GDP. During the 1990s, to achieve macroeconomic stability, the deficit fell to an average of just 0.7 percent of GDP, but because revenues were not expanded, this meant that public spending dropped to an average of 23 percent of GDP (see Figure 3.5).[23] As a result of the drop in public sector spending, the World Bank expressed concern that "the supply of public goods today is far below optimum levels," particu-

Figure 3.5   Deficit Control Through Reduction in Public Spending, Mexico, 1980–2000

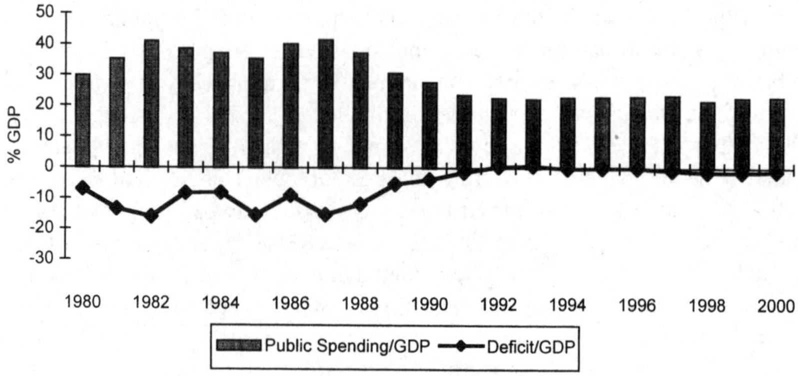

Source: Guigale et al., 2001.

larly given the pressing need to improve basic infrastructure as well as improve access and quality of educational and health services (Guigale et al., 2001, p. 152).

In Argentina and Brazil, total government spending also fell in the 1990s compared with the 1980s. During the 1980s, government spending in Argentina totaled 33 percent of GDP, falling to 29 percent of GDP in 1990–1997. In Brazil, government spending in the 1980s equaled 24 percent of GDP, falling to 18 percent in 1990–1997.[24] The 1990s also saw a shift in public spending, toward social spending (education, health, social security, and housing), reflecting the view of the Washington Consensus that governments should not be involved in productive activities, but rather concentrate on education and health (Stallings and Peres, 2000). As a result, social spending as a share of total government spending increased in all three countries, though the overall drop in spending has meant that governments are cutting much-needed public investment, rather than finding other ways to accommodate debt payments. Moreover, spending has remained highly procyclical (Mostajo, 2000).

Yet looking at the revenue side of fiscal budgeting shows that there is significant room, particularly in the case of Mexico, for increasing revenues to finance debt repayment or public investment. In the three countries, tax revenues as a percentage of GDP are far below the OECD average of 37 percent. Brazil is closest to international comparison, with tax revenues of 27 percent of GDP in 1996, approaching the US average of 28 percent for that year. Mexico, however, is at the bottom of the OECD ranking, with tax revenues of 11 percent of GDP in 1996; it collects much less than Argentina, and substantially less than Brazil (see Table 3.4).

Table 3.4 Tax Revenue as Percentage of GDP, Argentina, Brazil, and Mexico Compared to the OECD, European Union, and United States, 1992, 1996, and 2000

	1992	1996	2000
Argentina	19.3	18.3	n/a
Brazil	24.7	26.5	n/a
Mexico[a]	13.3	10.8	10.6
OECD	35.6	36.6	37.1
European Union (15)	40.0	41.2	41.5
United States	26.6	27.9	29.7

Sources: Shome, 1999; OECD, 2004.
Notes: Data are for general government, which is a consolidation of central, local, and state government, including social security.
a. Mexican data include social security but do not include contributions from PEMEX, which in 2000 amounted to 3.2 percent of GDP.
n/a= data not available.

Although taxes can potentially hurt aggregate demand by taking income away from individuals and firms, if this additional revenue is used for much-needed public investment, the externalities gained from the public spending will likely outweigh the income loss of the taxpayers. Moreover, taxes can be designed to lessen the demand loss. For example, M. Guigale and colleagues (2001) point out that the base of the Mexican income tax could easily be expanded by taxing the income of foreigners, as US tax law allows credit for taxes paid abroad. Thus this potentially revenue-generating tax would not discourage foreign investment.

The value-added tax (VAT) accounts for roughly 45 percent of revenues in Argentina and Brazil and almost 30 percent in Mexico. The other sources of tax revenue are income taxes (personal and corporate), social security taxes, excise taxes, and trade taxes. Although the VAT is the most important source of revenue, all three countries suffer from a low collection rate for VAT taxes. Tax evasion and administrative problems are widespread and have been magnified with the growth of the informal economy (Shome, 1999). In Mexico, it is estimated that tax evasion contributes to a loss in revenues equal to 2 percent of GDP on the VAT and 3 percent of GDP on the income tax (OECD, 2004).[25] In Argentina, tax evasion has been found to be commonplace.[26]

Conclusion

Job growth—particularly formal sector job growth—continues to be of great concern to workers and policymakers in Argentina, Brazil, and Mexico. Job creation is fundamentally dependent on the rate of economic growth, yet there has been little consideration about the importance of generating jobs when deciding on macroeconomic policy. As a result, the tools of macroeconomic policy— monetary, fiscal, and exchange rate policy—have not been best used to promote job creation. Instead, price stability has been the overarching goal since liberalization in the late 1980s and early 1990s. While controlling inflation is important, it should not come at the expense of lost competitiveness, economic stagnation, unemployment, and underemployment. Rather it should be considered along with policies that boost economic welfare.

This chapter has reviewed the course of macroeconomic policymaking and performance since the countries opened their capital and current accounts to external liberalization. Two different six-year spans, the economic opening of the three countries in 1985–1991 and the economic crashes of 1995–2001, mark their volatile economic experience. During the precrash period the countries maintained a fixed exchange rate that resulted in a loss of export competitiveness and a negative trade balance. The countries had to rely on capital inflows to finance the imbalance, causing sharp appreciations in the real exchange rate. As a result, the brunt of adjustment costs were forced onto the labor market, in the form of increased unemployment in Argentina, and declining real wages in Mexico and Brazil.

In the postcrash period, the countries have regained their competitiveness, as exchange rates are now flexible, but macroeconomic policy continues to be restrictive because of the need to finance debt repayments and the adoption of inflation targeting. To provide a greater space for macroeconomic, particularly fiscal, policy, it is necessary for governments, along with the international community, to consider alternative forms of debt repayment that do not hamper economic growth. Other policy objectives—such as maintaining a competitive exchange rate and lessening volatility with countercyclical fiscal policy—should also be pursued, to promote a more stable and prosperous environment for economic growth and job creation. In Chapter 8 we review, in detail, policy recommendations for making employment a central objective of macroeconomic policy, including the possibility of instituting employment targeting.

Notes

1. Data from International Monetary Fund (IMF), *International Financial Statistics* database.

2. Capital inflows force a central bank to buy currency reserves, which in turn devalues the local currency, causing inflation.

3. See Stallings and Weller, 2001, for a discussion of the debate.

4. Although labor costs are just one of many indicators of competitiveness, the increases in dollar prices as a result of appreciation applies as well to the overall cost of the good, and thus gives an indication of its international competitiveness.

5. In Chapter 4 we analyze in detail the evolution and composition of exports and their effect on employment.

6. The US-IMF bailout made tesobono convertibility a loan condition. An alternative option would have been for Mexico to redeem tesobonos in pesos and impose controls to deter dollar flight. This option is allowed under Article 6 of the IMF charter, but was not pursued (Pieper and Taylor, 1998).

7. An important control instituted was the "corralito," a mandatory freeze on the withdrawal of bank deposits. Because of the dollar shortage following the crash, the corralito system was designed to contend with the shortage of dollars and thus allowed the purchase of "bank" dollars, but not "liquid" dollars. This meant that depositors could use their money for checks and credit card payments, but they could not retire funds from the banking system. This money constraint further contracted economic activity, particularly in the informal sector, which relies on cash transactions.

8. Output data from Ministerio de Economía y Producción, April 2004; employment data from Instituto Nacional de Estadística y Censos (INDEC; National Institute for Statistics and Census), *Encuesta Industrial Mensual.*

9. International Labour Organization (ILO) data from country household surveys processed by SIAL-Panama.

10. Even if the amount of debt in absolute terms were to not change substantially, by having dollar-denominated debt measured in proportion to gross domestic product (GDP), a currency devaluation will automatically increase the debt-to-GDP ratio for the simple reason that the country's GDP valued in dollars has fallen, even if in absolute, nominal currency terms it has not.

11. The debt-to-GDP ratio is about 13 percentage points higher if liabilities arising from bank restructuring obligations and debtor support programs are included (OECD, 2002; Blázquez and Santiso, 2004).

12. Another drawback to devaluation that is less discussed is its possible contractionary effects, since devaluation redistributes income to richer groups which spend less on consumption (Krugman and Taylor, 1978).

13. Argentina announced in 2003 that it would officially adopt inflation targets beginning in 2005, yet the country has already established inflation targets as part of its negotiations with the IMF.

14. Inflation targeting is a relatively new trend. The first country to adopt it as an explicit policy was New Zealand, in 1990. Many countries have since followed suit, including Australia, Canada, Finland, Israel, New Zealand, Spain, Sweden, and the United Kingdom.

15. It is argued correctly that inflation has a negative effect on the income of the poor, but the relationship between inflation and average income of the poor is substantially smaller than the relationship between economic growth and average income of the poor. For example, a 1 percent increase in inflation leads to a 0.01 percent drop in the poor's income, but a 1 percent increase in per capita GDP leads to a 0.94 percent increase in the poor's income (Islam, 2003).

16. Risk premiums for all three countries jumped abruptly with the financial crises of the past decade. For example, the Tequila crisis caused Argentina's country-risk rating to jump from under 500 points in 1994 to 1,800 in 1995 as measured by JP Morgan's emerging bond index plus (EMBI+). This shock also caused Brazil's rating to jump to around 1,400 in 1995. Similar jumps occurred in the ratings of Mexico and Brazil at the time of the Argentine default. Brazil's country-risk rating was further aggravated by the presidential elections of 2002 (causing the index to reach 1,513 in December of that

year), and continues to be high as a result of the elevated debt-to-GDP ratios (Frenkel, 2004; data from JP Morgan EMBI+).

17. The problem of access to finance can also be seen at the individual level, where many residents are simply excluded from credit markets. For example, 57 percent of Brazilians in 2002 and 74 percent of Mexico City residents in 2003 had no bank accounts (Ruiz Durán, 2004).

18. Chapter 6 describes some of the various micro- and small-firm credit programs that exist in the three countries.

19. Growth and investment data based on ECLAC, 2004e; unemployment data calculated by author from the Brazilian Geographical and Statistical Institute's monthly urban unemployment series. Because of a change in methodology, total urban data were missing for January and February 2003; thus the calculations are based on the average of March–December (11.7 percent in 2003; 12.5 percent in 2004).

20. With the devaluation in late 2001, Argentina's debt-to-GDP ratio jumped from 52 to 132 percent. However, it continues to meet the public deficit criteria. With a debt-to-GDP ratio reaching a height of 50 percent, Brazil meets the ratio criteria, though it has exceeded the public deficit criteria several times in the 1990s, most recently in 1998, when it ran a public deficit of 7.1 percent of GDP.

21. Data on the structure of Brazilian debt from Palley, 2004.

22. See website of Desemprego Zero (http://www.desempregozero.org.br) for a variety of articles on this topic.

23. Author calculations based on data given in Guigale et al., 2001.

24. Brazilian data are for the central government; Argentine data are for the national federal public sector. Author calculations based on data given in Mostajo, 2000.

25. CIDE, 1999, cited in Guigale et al., 2001.

26. In a 1997 survey of Argentine taxpayers, 82 percent of respondents reported a willingness to take risks and evade the value-added tax in a standard transaction of $10,000. In comparison, in a similar survey taken in Chile in 1998, 75 percent of respondents reported that standard tax evasion was very risky. This suggests that boosting compliance among Argentine taxpayers requires stronger enforcement (Bergman, 2003, p. 604).

4

Trade Liberalization, Export Dynamism, and Employment Growth

During the 1990s, Argentina, Brazil, and Mexico undertook fundamental reforms of their economic development model. Inspired by the Washington Consensus, they all opted—albeit in varying degrees—in favor of a more liberal system. Three main policy shifts occurred: (1) from import-substitution policies involving trade barriers and capital controls toward export-oriented growth strategies involving elimination of trade barriers and open capital markets; (2) from a prominent role of the state in economic affairs toward a diminished role by handing over many assets and initiatives to the private sector; and (3) from more expansionary policies toward policies that primarily targeted price stability. The policy design and outcomes of the first two shifts are investigated in this chapter, while the third is discussed in Chapter 3. Export orientation was also accompanied by efforts toward regional integration: Argentina and Brazil created the Mercado Común del Sur (Mercosur; Southern Cone Common Market) with their neighboring countries, Paraguay and Uruguay, while Mexico reinforced its trade links with the United States and Canada through its membership in the North American Free Trade Agreement (NAFTA).

According to traditional international economic theory, economic liberalization is expected to result in increasing trade, accelerated technological change, efficiency gains, and growth. It is argued that a more efficient allocation of resources will, in the long run, lead to increased welfare and will have a positive impact on employment as well as on poverty and inequality,[1] even though negative employment effects in specific sectors may occur in the short run. The economic disengagement of the state through privatization and deregulation is expected to stimulate investment and growth in the private sector, while liberalization and privatization are expected to help the domestic economy improve its competitiveness and better integrate into the world market. Stronger competition, new financial resources, and transfer of technology are believed to push the economy toward higher value-added production and toward its strongest comparative advantages. In addition, production and exports will shift toward tradable goods, as they seem to be more dynamic than non-tradable goods. All this should yield sound economic and employment growth.

But did these expectations hold true? This is the main question of the chapter, which describes the trade liberalization process as well as the general patterns of trade in Argentina, Brazil, and Mexico. The chapter also assesses the export performance by sector and attempts to evaluate sectoral labor market impacts.

Trade Liberalization and Regional Integration

Argentina was the first of these countries to start a trade liberalization program, during the mid-1970s and then again during the mid-1980s, initially on a unilateral basis, then deepening it in 1986 with its neighboring country, Brazil, through an economic cooperation and integration agreement.[2] This agreement was reinforced in 1988 by the Treaty on Development Integration and Cooperation,[3] which contained important sectoral protocols for a list of product categories.[4] In 1989, over 60 percent of tariffs were eliminated (Estevadeordal, Goto, and Saez, 2000). The country proceeded with further liberalization thereafter, with the exception of the car industry. In 1990, import licensing requirements were removed and tariffs were made uniform, to 21 percent, and progressively reduced further thereafter, as described in Table 4.1.

Brazil launched a major tariff reduction program in 1991, which envisaged annual tariff reductions to reach fixed final target rates by 1993. Later, the range of tariffs was further reduced, nontariff barriers (NTBs) were removed, and the average rate was lowered. Table 4.1 shows that drastic reductions were already achieved in Argentina and Brazil even before the inception of Mercosur, and continued after this regional agreement came into effect, in terms of both tariffs and NTBs. The late 1990s, however, saw some setbacks[5] due to economic crisis, and specific industries, such as auto, sugar, and telecommunications, benefited from above-average tariff rates. But the over-

Table 4.1   **Evolution of Average Unweighted Import Tariffs, 1987–2001 (percentages)**

	1987	1990	1991	1992	1995	1997	1998	2001
Argentina	27.0	20.5	12.2	11.8	10.5	11.3	13.5	11.6
Brazil	51.0	32.2	25.3	21.2	11.1	11.8	14.6	12.9
Mexico	11.3	11.1	13.1	13.4	13.1	12.6	13.3	16.2

Source: Author calculations based on figures derived from databases of the World Trade Organization, the Inter-American Development Bank, the World Bank, and the United Nations Conference on Trade and Development.

all trend was toward further liberalization. Nevertheless, the Mercosur countries still have a relatively high level of trade protection compared with countries belonging to the OECD: in 2001, the average tariff for the European Union (EU) was 3.9 percent; for the United States, 5.1 percent; and for Japan, 4.0 percent. At the sectoral level, OECD countries have high protection—directly or indirectly—for specific agricultural and semimanufactured products, where they have lost competitiveness on the world market, and low protection for high-technology products, where they are strongly competitive. The trend in Mercosur countries, and to a lesser extent Mexico, is the opposite: low protection for primary products and high protection for industrial products, as their comparative advantage lies mainly in low-value-added products.

After liberalizing trade bilaterally, Brazil and Argentina decided to create a common market of the Southern Cone of the Americas, Mercosur, to which they invited Uruguay and Paraguay. Both countries already had bilateral agreements with Uruguay. The main goals of Mercosur were to foster trade, enhance productive and technological changes in key sectors through investment flows, and promote cooperation in key areas such as transport, energy, and technology. The major pillars of Mercosur are the free movement of goods and services, but also of productive factors, the establishment of a common external tariff (CET), as well as the harmonization and coordination of economic policies[6] and legislation among member countries. Its final objective is more ambitious than that of NAFTA, and it aims to follow, to some extent, the model of the European integration, with a strong emphasis not only on the economic but also on the social, political, and cultural dimensions. Its final goal is the establishment of a common market. Despite this ambitious goal, Mercosur has as yet—in contrast to the EU—few supranational bodies and institutions; instead, governance has been mainly intergovernmental. This is particularly true for labor market governance (see Chapter 6).

In addition to being a free trade zone, Mercosur is also a customs union, in that the member countries agreed in Ouro Preto in 1994 to a CET, which implied substantial overall external tariff reductions (Baumann, 2001), but also some tariff increases for specific products of each member country. In this context, the CET contains a national list of exceptions for specific products (mainly automobiles, sugar, capital goods, informatics, and telecommunications) proposed by each Mercosur member. In general, the trend is to reduce the CET and the list of exceptions. The list of sensitive products was introduced to facilitate structural adjustment and help place the sectors involved in a competitive position within the region by the end of a specified period. The CET is characterized by tariff escalation, meaning that products in the same sector, but at different stages of production, have different tariff levels. A form of managed trade applies to the automotive sector, whereby it benefits from local content provisions.[7]

Mexico has followed a similar path of trade liberalization, but a different regional integration strategy. After being badly hit by an economic crisis in 1982, it changed its economic policy drastically, from an import-substitution to an export-oriented development strategy, and it progressively liberalized its trade regime. It accorded special attention to its relationship with its main trading partner, the United States, initially through bilateral agreements in the 1980s and subsequently by a further deepening of relations with the formation of NAFTA in 1994. This agreement included, for the first time, a developing country and two industrialized countries (Audley et al., 2003). NAFTA's objectives are mainly limited to the liberalization of trade between its members (United Nations Conference on Trade and Development [UNCTAD], 2003b). It is basically an economic agreement; even migration is not adequately covered in the treaty. Mercosur, on the other hand, aims at socioeconomic, political, and cultural integration, although this process is still in its early stages. Moreover, Mercosur is a process of integration among similar countries of the South with similar production patterns, and thus few complementarities. In addition, the national markets have relatively low demand elasticity.

However, the regional market, being less competitive, serves as a trial or apprenticeship stage for future integration at the global level, as it entails fewer social adjustment costs. NAFTA, on the other hand, has implied the integration of an emerging economy, Mexico, with a powerful and very competitive country, the United States, but also Canada. Despite strong competition from US exporters, Mexico has nevertheless benefited from a high degree of complementarity of its production structure vis-à-vis that of its northern partners in terms of goods and services and production factors, with special emphasis on the labor force. It also received privileged, permanent, and secured access to the richer countries' markets, which have a high demand for their exported goods. As a result, Mexico became a destination for large inflows of foreign direct investment (FDI), through which it also acquired know-how and technology aimed at closing the technology gap. Mexico attracts the interest of not only its northern partners, but also other industrialized countries in Europe and Asia by virtue of its role as an export platform to the United States.

NAFTA resulted in significant US tariff cuts for a number of agricultural products and most Mexican manufactured goods, particularly textiles and apparel, and smaller cuts on footwear, chemicals, miscellaneous manufactures, and transport equipment. Mexico also undertook dramatic tariff cuts on all agricultural and livestock products and all manufactured products of its NAFTA partners. Some sensitive agricultural products such as corn and beans are still excluded, but Mexico allowed a substantial above-quota, tariff-free import of corn that caused a negative employment impact on rural workers (see Table 4.4). Tariff rates with NAFTA, covering about 90 percent of Mexico's trade, are thus very low (WTO, 2002), but unweighted average import tariffs increased slightly, though continuously, with the rest of the world (from

11 percent in the late 1980s to 16 percent in 2001). This means that its trade with the rest of the world was not facilitated during this period.

Trade by Origin

In Chapter 3 the surge in trade is noted, with a disproportionate rise in imports compared to exports in the region. The analysis of trade flows by region and country in Table 4.2 shows the growing importance of trade with partners of regional trade agreements.

Even though we can already consider NAFTA and Mercosur as "natural" trading blocs among neighboring countries with historically strong ties, the agreements signed in the 1990s, as well as general trade liberalization, gave an additional boost to trade with their neighbors.[8] In Mercosur, intraregional trade increased strongly until 1995 (20.3 percent) and then declined steadily to 17.7 percent in 2002, because of the economic crises in Argentina and Brazil. Within NAFTA, intraregional trade has been increasing constantly, from 41 percent in 1990 to 56 percent in 2002. In 2002, 91 percent of Mexico's trade was with its NAFTA partners, while 22 percent of Argentina's trade was with its Mercosur partners,[9] and only 5 percent of Brazil's was with its Mercosur partners due to its economic crisis. The United States is increasingly important for Mexican

Table 4.2   Destination and Origin of Imports and Exports, 1990–2002 (percentage shares of total)

	Imports		Exports	
	1990	2002	1990	2002
Argentina				
Latin America and Caribbean	33	37	27	42
United States	20	20	14	12
European Union	27	23	31	20
Asia	12	11	10	11
Brazil				
Latin America and Caribbean	18	18	11	19
United States	20	22	25	26
European Union	22	28	32	25
Asia	11	16	17	14
Rest of the world	30	17	15	17
Mexico				
Latin America and Caribbean	4	4	6	3
United States	67	63	70	89
European Union	17	10	13	3
Asia	8	18	7	1

Source: Author calculations based on UNComtrade.

trade, accounting for 89 percent of its exports and 63 percent of its imports. Europe's share has declined quite dramatically. Trade with other Latin American countries does not have much relevance for Mexico, Brazil, and Argentina, except perhaps trade links between Brazil and Mexico. Industrialized countries, mainly those of Europe and the United States, are crucial trading partners for Argentina and Brazil, although recently, as Table 4.2 shows, new partners have emerged, particularly China, as a destination for agricultural products mainly from the two big Mercosur countries (see Box 4.1).

Box 4.1
China's Increasing Role in the World Economy: Threat and Opportunity

The emergence of China as a dominant player in the world market has important implications for Argentina, Brazil, and Mexico. Between 1990 and 2003, China's share in global FDI flows increased from 2 to 6 percent (Inter-American Development Bank, 2005). Its share in global trade flows has expanded even more so, with China accounting for 12.4 percent of world imports and 13.1 percent of world exports between 1990 and 2002 (Dussel Peters, 2004b). Since the 1980s, China's growth rate has been around 8 percent, whereas Argentina lost 0.1 percent and Brazil grew by only 0.8 percent and Mexico by 1.1 percent. China's strong growth in gross domestic product (GDP) stems from a concerted industrialization policy of specific economic zones, tied to its policy of increased geographic integration—the integration of Hong Kong and Macao into Greater China—as well as its accession to the World Trade Organization (WTO) in 2002. The 2005 elimination of the Multifiber Agreement presents additional trade opportunities for China.

The implications of China's boom are threefold for Argentina, Brazil, and Mexico. The strong growth of China's GDP has led to a rise in demand for consumption goods, but also for intermediary goods for production. As a result, Argentina and Brazil have had a strong increase of exports to China, Argentina by 143 percent and Brazil by 80 percent in 2002–2003 (Economic Commission for Latin America and the Caribbean [ECLAC], 2004c). Brazil has had a trade surplus with China since the 1990s, whereas Argentina started to have a trade surplus with China in 1995. The exports have been mainly primary or semiprocessed goods, among them soya beans, food products, pulp, seamless tubes, and iron ore, and in the case of Brazil also some industrial products such as auto parts and small aircrafts (Gutiérrez, 2003). China, however, has specialized in exports of more varied goods and of goods with more technological content. In the automobile industry, there has also been a rise in intraindustrial trade. For example, Volkswagen Brazil and Volkswagen China cooperate in the production of the car Gol (ECLAC, 2004c). Recent trade negotiations between Brazil and China have resulted in an increase in mutual FDI flows. Some examples are Embraer, which invested in Avic 2, a Chinese air company, in 2002, and Vale do Rio Doce and Baogang Metallurgic, which announced a joint venture in 2002. These are positive signals for a consolidation of economic ties.

continues

Box 4.1   Continued

But while Argentina and Brazil have mostly benefited from China's boom, Mexico has not been as fortunate, as China is an important competitor on the world market. Contrary to Argentina and Brazil, which have a high complementarity with China (they export goods that China needs and vice versa), Mexico and China specialize in similar products that are highly labor intensive, particularly textiles and clothing, electronics, and auto parts. Already at the beginning of 2000, a large number of maquiladoras closed in Mexico, only to reopen in China (see Chapter 5).

Also, Mexico's exports are strongly oriented toward the US market, but there it faces increased Chinese competition, especially in textiles and clothing. In 2003, China surpassed Mexico as the second most important exporter to the United States. Mexico is one of the potential losers of the phasing out of the Multifiber Agreement (see Ernst, Hernández Ferrer, and Zult, 2005). Mexico's international competitiveness in textiles and clothing is rather low, as shown by the fact that total costs of production, besides labor costs, are significantly higher in Mexico than in China (Dussel Peters, 2004b). Nevertheless, wages per hour are over five times higher in Mexico than in China. The emergence of China as a major car exporter is another source of concern for car producers in Mexico who export to the US market.

The third effect of China's emergence as a major exporter is related to the internal market. Argentina, Brazil, and Mexico have increasingly imported consumption goods from China, mainly clothing, footwear, plastic, and rubber products (Gutiérrez, 2003), and personal computers in Mexico (Dussel Peters, 2004b). As a result, Mexico's trade balance with China is negative and has increasingly deteriorated, from US$342 million in 1993 to almost US$9 billion in 2003.

China's importance in the world economy will continue to increase, and the best strategy for Argentina, Brazil, and Mexico is to encourage trade and economic ties, mutual public and private investment, and diversified exports to China, including higher technological goods (see also Martinez, 2004a). Closer ties may help resolve conflicts in areas of competition and increase the benefits of new trade opportunities.

The difference in importance of intraregional trade between Mexico on the one hand and Brazil and Mercosur on the other is due to various reasons, including an earlier start at trade liberalization by Mexico, the evolution of a favorable exchange rate, and an expansionary phase of the US economy. One important aspect not mentioned so far concerns the economic complementarities between the countries, not only in the labor markets, but also with regard to specialization. A high degree of trade complementarity means that a country's exports are of goods that the receiving country does not produce, and vice versa. A low complementarity means that the two countries export similar goods. A high trade complementarity is a sign of strong potential to develop interindustry trade. E. Dussel Peters (2000a) found a high degree of complementarity between Mexico and its NAFTA partners, while trade complementarities between Argentina and Brazil are rather low, compared to their complementarity with EU countries.[10] Low complementarity, due to limited industrial diversity and development as well as similar specialization in primary and low processed products, has meant limited trade in terms of quantity and diversity (Ernst, 1997).

Briefly, intraregional trade is important, indeed extremely important, for Mexico, and it has been fostered by regional integration through NAFTA. For Argentina and Brazil, trade relations outside the regional setting, especially with industrialized countries, are crucial because of low intraregional complementarity.

Export Specialization and Employment

In order to evaluate the effect of trade liberalization on employment, we undertake the following analysis of the relationship between export specialization and employment, based on a comparison of data on (1) the share of specific products in exports, (2) the import content of exports,[11] (3) the labor intensity of specific product groups (see Appendix Table 4.B), (4) employment by product group, (5) wage growth, as well as (6) the share of those product groups in total manufacturing employment.[12] This analysis will help pinpoint those sectors that have benefited from the policy shift to trade liberalization as opposed to those that have encountered problems and have lost ground. It will also provide an overall picture of the impact of trade liberalization on sectoral employment.

Historically, primary products, especially agricultural and food products, have constituted the highest proportion of Argentina's major exports and are still dominant (73 percent in 2003 according to ECLAC, 2004e). This pattern has not changed significantly since the 1980s (77 percent in 1980 and 71 percent in 1999), but the composition of products has changed, notably an increase in vegetable oils and soya products (ECLAC, 2003e). Also, petroleum products have emerged as one of the leading exports since the early 1990s as a result of new discoveries. These products have low to medium labor intensity. The largest export item, processed food, experienced positive but below-average employment and wage growth; however, its employment share is relatively important within the manufacturing sector, at 9.4 percent over the period 1995–2000 (see Table 4.3). Argentina has only one highly labor-intensive sector among the seven main export sectors: tanning and dressing of leather. But while exports have grown, the sector has experienced negative employment and wage growth. The country has maintained capital-intensive sectors among its main export sectors, which benefited from special treatment throughout the import-substitution industrialization (ISI) period. All these sectors experienced a negative trade balance during the 1995–2000 period, and, besides other chemical products, which performed well, had below-average (basic chemicals) or even negative employment and wage growth rates (motor vehicles). Argentina's exports are strongly concentrated. According to ECLAC,

Table 4.3 Main Manufacturing Exports and Their Labor Market Impact, 1995–2000 (percentages)

Product Group	X Share	M in X	Labor Intensity	Employment Growth	Wage Growth	Employment Share
Argentina						
Food processing and production	27.0	0.9	Medium	2.6	5.1	9.4
Manufacture of motor vehicles	7.2	-0.3	Medium	-5.8	-2.7	2.7
Tanning and dressing of leather	3.6	0.9	High	-2.4	-2.0	1.7
Manufacture of basic chemicals	3.5	-1.9	Medium	-1.7	7.3	1.6
Manufacture of other chemical products	3.2	-1.6	Low	7.5[a]	14.3[a]	6.1
Total manufacturing average				3.9	7.5	
Brazil						
Food processing and production	12.2	0.8	Low	2.1[a]	-1.0[a]	5.3
Manufacture of basic iron and steel	7.7	0.8	Medium	-4.2	-7.3	2.1
Manufacture of motor vehicles	5.3	-0.3	Medium	-4.5	1.7[a]	2.3
Manufacture of other food products	5.0	0.9	Medium	-1.2	-1.5[a]	8.0
Manufacture of paper and paper products	4.5	0.5	High	-2.6	-4.5	2.8
Total manufacturing average				-0.9	-3.1	
Mexico						
Manufacture of motor vehicles	15.0	0.8	Low	6.6[a]	0.1[a]	3.1
Manufacture of televisions and radios	7.7	0.6	Low	9.8[a]	0.9[a]	0.1
Manufacture of office, accounting equipment	6.0	0.5	Low	17.8[a]	4.2[a]	0.6
Manufacture of other electrical equipment	4.5	0.6	Low	11.5[a]	3.7[a]	0.8
Manufacture of wearing apparel	3.8	0.5	Low	4.4[a]	-6.1	1.5
Total manufacturing average				3.5	-5.1	

Source: Author calculations based on WITS; and UNIDO, Indstat 4, Revision 3.

Notes: Ranking according to exports (four-digit level) in value (current US$). "X share" indicates the share of product group exports in total exports (Xi / $Xtotal$, where Xi indicates exports of a product group, such as food processing and production, and $Xtotal$ indicates total exports of a country). "M in X" shows the share of product group imports (M) in product group exports (X): $[X - (M / X)]$. "Labor intensity" is calculated for each country based on employment-output elasticities. "Employment growth" indicates average annual growth. "Wage growth" indicates real average annual wage growth in constant US$: Argentina, 1995–1999; Brazil, 1996–1999; Mexico, 1995–2000. "Employment share" indicates the sector's share in total manufacturing employment: Argentina and Brazil, 1999; Mexico, 2000.

a. These industries performed better than the average for manufacturing.

the ten leading exports constitute 54.3 percent of total exports, and all of these exports are from the primary sector.

Brazil's leading exports have generally constituted a mix of primary and, to a lesser extent, secondary semiprocessed products. Nevertheless, there has been an evolution from roasted coffee as the leading export product in 1980, to iron and ore in 1990 and aircraft in 2001, but a return to a primary product as the leading export product, soya beans, in 2003 (ECLAC, 2004e). As in Argentina, most of the leading products in Brazil are of medium labor intensity. Processed food products are also among Brazil's main exports, but contrary to Argentina, they are less labor-intensive and the sector employs fewer workers. Together with other major food products, they constitute 13.3 percent of the manufacturing sector. Both sectors have negative, but above-average, wage growth. Processed food has shown positive employment growth figures, while other food products have shown negative employment growth. Automobiles, another leading export industry, experienced an employment decline of 4.5 percent during the period 1995–2000, though the industry imported more than it exported.[13] At the same time, real wages increased by 1.7 percent for the remaining work force. While the primary sector in Brazil is almost as important for exports as it is in Argentina (49 percent in total exports in 2003, slightly up from 48 percent in 1990), Brazilian exports are more diversified, with primary products accounting for only 34 percent of total exports.

Contrary to Mercosur countries, Mexico shows clear, strong growth in its manufactured exports. While in the 1980s petroleum and gas and agricultural products dominated exports, the leading exports in 2001 were machines, transport equipment, and telecommunications. And while Argentina's and Brazil's main exports have a medium level of labor intensity, Mexico's, in general, besides the maquiladora sector (Ghose, 2003), are concentrated in low labor-intensive products with relatively high value added. However, those exports contain a high level of imported inputs, as the relatively low levels of net exports demonstrate (see Table 4.3). In general, these industries experienced above-average wage and employment growth. Nevertheless, the share of the leading exports in total industrial employment is rather low, apart from motor vehicles with a 3.1 percent share over the period 1995–2000.

Mexico has indeed succeeded in changing its specialization from primary[14] to manufactured goods, which comprised nine of the ten leading exports in 2003, even though crude petroleum again became the leading export good. Manufacturing exports experienced above-average wage and employment growth for the period under analysis, but also low labor intensity. The importance of manufacturing exports for employment creation and wages, even though positive, is therefore relatively limited. The exception is the maquiladora industry, which saw a strong increase in production and strong employment growth during the second half of the 1990s (see Chapter 5). However, the country's exports have a high proportion of imported inputs, and the maquila export sector in particular has developed few links with the rest of the economy and thus few positive multiplier effects.

In summary, export orientation has produced disappointing employment results in the Mercosur countries, but has had a fairly positive impact on the labor market in Mexico. And contrary to expectations of traditional economic thinking, countries with a relatively high number of working poor, and thus an abundance of cheap labor, have not succeeded in specializing in high labor-intensive products, apart from Mexico's maquiladora industry. The recent return of primary goods as the leading export products in Brazil and Mexico is an indication that the countries have not yet succeeded in diversifying their exports sufficiently. A more detailed analysis of the international competitiveness further reveals the nature of specialization in these countries and its implications for employment. A simple analysis of exports could be misleading, as high export levels do not necessarily mean that a country is in a favorable position on the world market. It could even be in deficit if the import value exceeds the export value. The specialization index adopted here is therefore based on the principle of the revealed comparative advantage (RCA) developed by Bela Balassa. This specialization index is then compared with the change in the import share of the destination market within a competitiveness matrix. This matrix shows whether or not a country is specialized in dynamic exports with regard to the market of destination. This kind of specialization would be promising for the future development of trade, production, and thus employment. In this matrix, the horizontal axis shows the change in percentage of imports (see Figure 4.1).

Products that experience a positive change over time in the market's import share are called *dynamic goods,* meaning that their share in the market of destination increased between the base year and the final year of analysis. Imports of this commodity increased faster than total imports of all commodities or the commodity average of import growth. Products with a negative change over time in market share are termed *stagnant goods,* which means that the share of a stagnant commodity on the import market has decreased over time. Imports of this commodity have seen a slower rate of growth than total imports of all commodities, or the commodity average of import growth. A *rising star* is therefore a dynamic commodity in the destination market of the export in

Figure 4.1 Competitiveness Matrix

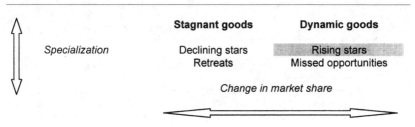

which the country under consideration is specialized, while a *declining star* is a stagnant commodity in which the country is specialized, as described below. *Missed opportunities* are dynamic commodities on the world market in which the country has lost its specialization, while *retreats* are stagnant products worldwide, with declining specialization in the country under analysis.

This is best illustrated by an example. The iPod is a dynamic good on the world market; it is exported by the United States, and is a rising star for that country, but a missed opportunity for France, for example, as the latter is not specialized in the export of this product. The traditional Walkman, on the other hand, has lost its importance on the world market and has become a stagnant good. For a country like China, which still exports Walkmans, it constitutes a declining star, while for Germany, which is not specialized in this product any more, it has became a retreat.

Interesting observations can be made from an analysis of the total number of product groups in each category of the competitiveness matrix listed in Table 4.4. Between the periods 1985–1995 and 1995–2000, the number of rising stars declined considerably, from 277 to 89, for all three countries taken together, while the number of retreat products increased considerably, from 109 to 246, as did the declining stars.[15] In the regional setting, the evolution has been more favorable, with more products in the category of rising stars and fewer in the category of declining stars, but also with a higher number of missed opportunities. This means that specialization within the region was fairly positive compared to the world market.

Table 4.4   Evolution of Number of Products Within the Competitiveness Matrix, 1985–1999

Argentina		Brazil		Mexico	
1985–1990	World	1985–1990	World	1985–1990	World
65	99	64	71	77	106
46	32	39	62	24	25
1995–2000	World	1995–2000	World	1995–2000	World
101	29	96	35	70	25
70	35	76	29	100	26
1995–2000	Mercosur	1995–2000	Mercosur	1995–2000	NAFTA
64	47	73	41	68	27
59	56	48	63	90	43

Source: Author calculations based on ECLAC, 2003f.
Note: This table follows the pattern of Figure 4.1: for each set of four numbers, top left = declining stars, top right = rising stars, bottom left = retreats, bottom right = missed opportunities.

Declining and rising stars are of particular interest when analysing the labor market, as they show the country's actual specialization, contrary to missed opportunities and retreats. Table 4.5 lists these product categories and their labor market impact. Between 1985 and 1995, Argentina specialized exclusively in agricultural and food products (see Appendix Table 4.A) and between 1995 and 2000 in refined petroleum products, but also in a higher-value industry, motor vehicles, which featured among the rising stars. Nevertheless, Argentina's economic opening up led to the strengthening of its specialization in primary products and to medium-technology products.[16] An analysis of its specialization vis-à-vis the regional and less competitive Mercosur market, which also includes Paraguay and Uruguay, shows that, almost exclusively, agricultural and food products have dominated Argentina's specialization (Ernst, 2005b). In general, those sectors have a low to medium level of labor intensity and reveal an above-average employment performance, with the exception of motor vehicles.

Between 1985 and 2000, Brazil, like Argentina, specialized in primary products and in slightly processed primary products such as food products (coffee) and iron and steel vis-à-vis the world market. Their employment results have been rather mixed. Whereas nickel (rising star) and oil seeds (declining star) showed above-average employment and wage performance, spices (rising star), coffee, and iron ore (both declining stars) had negative results. The new specialization in aircraft manufacturing has been the most striking phenomenon during the past few years. It is a sector of low labor intensity, but high in value added and technology, and has enjoyed strong employment growth (74.3 percent) and real wage growth (85.4 percent). However, it directly employs only 0.3 percent of manufacturing workers. Nevertheless, it has positive indirect employment effects in the region of São José do Campos, where it is concentrated (see Table 4.5). Unlike Argentina, which exports low-processed goods to its neighboring countries, Brazil specializes in manufactured product groups in intraregional Mercosur trade (see its rising and declining stars in Table 4.5). Its textiles and motor vehicles, which are its leading specializations of exports toward the region, are industries of high and medium labor intensity respectively. However, in general, these industries have displayed a relatively poor performance with regard to employment and real wages, with the exception of motor vehicles (which showed above-average wage growth).

Mexico, on the other hand, reinforced its specialization in manufactured exports in the 1990s to the world market but also with NAFTA, dropping its specialization of primary products and semiprocessed primary products. Its sectors of specialization are of low or medium labor intensity, with the exception of two declining stars, fuelwood and sulphur, that are of high labor intensity, as are the maquiladora industries in general (Palma, 2003; Mortimore, Buitelaar, and Bonifaz, 2000). As for wages, the results are mixed. While

Table 4.5   Rising and Declining Products in World and Regional Markets, and Their Employment Impact

Declining Stars				Rising Stars			
Wage Growth	Employment Growth	Labor Intensity			Labor Intensity	Employment Growth	Wage Growth
			Argentina				
			Trade with the World				
∧	∧	Medium	Fixed vegetable oils	Essential oils, perfumes	Medium	n/a	n/a
∨	∧	Medium	Feeding stuff for animals	Petroleum products, refined	Low	∧	∧
∧	∧	Medium	Maize (corn), unmilled	Motor vehicles	Medium	∨	∨
			Trade with Mercosur				
∧	∧	Medium	Maize (corn), unmilled	Wheat and meslin, unmilled	Medium	∧	∨
∧	∧	Low	Milk and cream	Cereals, unmilled	Medium	∧	∧
∨	∨	Low	Nonferrous base metal waste	Margarine and shortening	Medium	∧	∧
			Brazil				
			Trade with the World				
∨	∨	Medium	Iron ore and concentrates	Spices	Medium	∨	∧
∧	∨	Medium	Coffee and coffee substitutes	Aircraft	Low	∧	∧
∧	∧	Low	Oil seeds and oleaginous fruit	Nickel	Low	∧	∧
			Trade with Mercosur				
∨	∨	High	Cotton fabrics, woven	Made-up articles of textile materials	High	∨	∨
∧	∧	Low	Cutlery	Motor vehicles	Medium	∨	∧
∨	∧	High	Footwear	Other artificial fibers for spinning	High	∨	∨

continues

Table 4.5 Continued

	Declining Stars				Rising Stars		
Wage Growth	Employment Growth	Labor Intensity	Declining Stars	Rising Stars	Labor Intensity	Employment Growth	Wage Growth
			Mexico				
			Trade with the World				
>	>	Low	Radio-broadcast receivers	Motor vehicles	Low	>	>
>	0	Low	Railway vehicles	Undergarments	Low	>	<
>	>	Low	Rotating electric plant	Furniture and parts	Medium	<	<
			Trade with NAFTA				
<	<	High	Sulphur and unroasted iron pyrites	Railway vehicles	Low	0	>
<	<	High	Fuelwood	Undergarments	Low	>	<
>	>	Low	Radio-broadcast receivers	Telecommunications equipment	Medium	<	>

Source: Author calculations based on ECLAC, 2003f, at the three-digit level.

Notes: Period of analysis: 1995–2000. "Wage growth" indicates real wage growth calculated in constant US$. "Employment growth": Argentina, 1993–1999; Brazil, 1996–1999; Mexico, 1994–2000. "Labor intensity" denotes ">" for growth rate above average compared with the manufacturing sector, "<" for below average. n/a = data not available.

motor vehicles, radio-broadcast receivers, and undergarments showed above-average employment growth, undergarments showed negative wage growth. Furniture, fuelwood, sulphur, and telecommunications equipment showed negative employment growth, although telecommunications equipment showed a positive real wage growth. Real wages also grew faster in the maquiladora industries, but they were still significantly lower than in other manufacturing industries.[17]

In brief, Argentina and Brazil have remained specialized in low-value and low to medium labor-intensive primary and semiprocessed products, creating little employment (International Labour Organization [ILO], 2005). However, Brazil has a comparative advantage in some manufactured goods (e.g., motor vehicles, textiles), especially in its trade with its Mercosur neighbors. Nevertheless, with the exception of some successful industries, the Mercosur countries are increasingly distant from the most dynamic flows of international trade, such as high-technology products.[18] Mexico has continued to deepen its specialization in manufactured goods. According to Dussel Peters (2003), Mexico is better positioned, as 60 percent of its exports in the late 1990s were considered to be of a medium to high technological level, compared to only 20 percent in the 1980s. However, these industries depend heavily on imports of intermediate goods, which represent more than 80 percent of the total export sales, and which account for a larger proportion of the value added (e.g., knowledge, research). The local value added of maquila exports decreased from a gross production value of 37 percent in 1974 to just 20 percent in 1997. This implies that those apparently high-technological products are assembled by a relatively low-skilled labor force. A closer look at the missed opportunities reveals that all three countries may have the potential to specialize in hitherto unexploited, relatively high value-added product categories; for example, all three in the production of internal combustion piston engines, Argentina also in auto parts, Brazil in some textile categories, and Mexico in electrical equipment.[19]

In general, the increasingly worsening specialization of Argentina, Brazil, and Mexico is an issue that future trade and industrial policies should address. The employment and real wage performance of their export products, although slightly positive, remains mixed. Outward orientation has not led to an export specialization with strong employment growth. Economic restructuring has led to a concentration in low value-added and capital-intensive manufactures, with low to medium labor intensity, contrary to expectations of traditional trade theory.

Though trade in services is an important component of total trade in Argentina, Brazil, and Mexico, its relative importance has for the most part declined. According to UNCTAD (see http://stats.unctad.org/), in Argentina the share of trade in services fell from 21 percent in the 1980s to 18 percent in the 1990s; in Mexico, it fell from 19 to 11 percent. In Brazil, however, the share of trade in services increased from 8 to 13 percent. All three countries have a negative trade in services balance, mainly because of higher transport and travel imports, but also royalties, government services, and other business services. Besides travel and transport, commercial services improved significantly in all three countries, which was strongly related to economic opening. Besides that, Mexico saw a strong increase in communications, other business services, and computer and information services, Brazil in financial and other business services, and Argentina in computer and information services and government services. The category of finance, insurance, and business services had a strong contribution to employment, and even of good quality, especially in Argentina, but also in Brazil and Mexico during the 1990s (see Chapter 2). Recently, the three countries and mainly Brazil have demonstrated dynamism in its exports of service-intensive technology and qualified work, but also of some nontraditional services, such as transport, travel, and insurance. Trade in services in the region is often linked to FDI and intrafirm trade, especially in finance and business services, which are explained in Chapter 5.

Imports, Increased Competition, and Impact on the Labor Market

The economic opening of a country tends to encourage imports. Increased imports lead to greater competition in the local market, thus putting a strain on local producers, who either disappear or adjust to the new context. However, it also helps enterprises to become more competitive through the use of imported components in their production.[20] The most successful companies often apply modernization or rationalization measures that affect employment negatively. This section, in analyzing the effect of increased imports on employment in Argentina, Brazil, and Mexico, shows that the direct impact of imports on employment was small over the period 1995–2000, but that increased competition contributed to a rise in productivity, which had a negative employment impact.

Table 4.6 analyzes the employment impact on specific products at the three-digit level of the Standard International Trade Classification (SITC) that have had high import penetration, according to an indicator that compares net imports with domestic absorption. Within these industries, we then look at output, employment, and wages to assess the labor market impact of increased import competition.

With the exception of two food industries in Mexico, most of the goods exposed to import competition were higher value-added goods such as medical appliances, electronic valves, or special-purpose machinery. Contrary to major export sectors, which had a low to medium labor intensity, industries exposed

Table 4.6 Industries Most Exposed to Imports and Evolution of the Labor Market, 1995–2000

Country	(X – M) / (Y – X + M) (ranking)	Output Growth	Labor Intensity	Employment Share	Employment Growth	Wage Growth
Argentina	Electronic valves, tubes, etc.	3.1	Medium	0.6	*4.1*	*7.3*
	TV, radio receivers, assorted goods	0.4	High	0.4	-2.9	2.2
	Medical appliances	8.9	Medium	0.8	*5.1*	*6.9*
	Special-purpose machinery	1.9	Medium	2.3	3.3	3.9
	Electric motors, generators	6.6	Medium	1.0	1.1	*6.0*
	Total manufacturing	1.7		100	3.9	4.1
Brazil	Processing of nuclear fuel	-4.4	Medium	0.9	-9.0	*2.0*
	Electronic valves, tubes, etc.	-1.5	High	0.5	-2.5	-8.2
	Medical appliances	5.7	Medium	0.8	-2.5	-0.6
	Optical instruments, photo equipment	13.8	Medium	0.2	*1.1*	*4.0*
	Artificial fibers	12.3	High	0.1	-0.3	-4.0
	Total manufacturing	4.0		100	-0.9	-3.1
Mexico	Electronic valves, tubes, etc.	14.7	Low	0.1	*4.1*	*7.0*
	Processed meat, fish, fruit, vegetables	-2.4	Medium	3.0	1.8	*-4.1*
	Special-purpose machinery	3.4	High	0.9	6.2	*-1.5*
	Dairy products	5.8	Low	1.2	3.1	*-1.1*
	General-purpose machinery	4.8	Medium	1.4	6.6	-2.0
	Total manufacturing	3.7		100	3.5	-4.4

Source: Author calculations based on data from UN Comtrade, UNIDO, Indstat4, Revision 3.

Notes: The indicator $(X – M) / (Y – X + M)$ shows net imports $(X – M)$ divided by domestic absorption $(Y – X + M)$, or how much has been consumed domestically. This indicator demonstrates which industry has been most exposed to import competition. Table 4.6 lists the five industries most exposed to import competition for each country. Labor market indicators are calculated as in Table 4.5. Italic employment and wage values show above-average values. Output growth rates are annual average values at constant market prices, wages are real: Argentina, 1995–1999; Brazil, 1996–1999; Mexico, 1996–1999.

to imports had a mostly medium to high labor intensity and were therefore slightly more important for employment. Yet their share in total manufacturing employment was not significant, with values of less than 1 percent over the period 1995–2000, besides special-purpose machinery in Argentina (2.3 percent) and food products in Mexico (together 4.2 percent). Nevertheless, the labor market impact of economic opening was mixed and strongly depended on each specific industry. In Mexico these industries experienced good output and, for the most part, employment growth, and negative, but above-average (–4.4 percent) wage growth, excepting electronic valves. In Argentina and Brazil, even though these industries largely had good output and wage growth, employment growth was for the most part less favorable compared to the rest of the manufacturing sector. It was either negative, especially in Brazil, or lower than the average of the manufacturing sector.

What explains the relatively good labor market performance of sectors that faced the highest import penetration? First, during the period of analysis, the sharp increase in imports following trade liberalization came to an end, which may imply that in those sectors, employment may also have declined in the first half of the 1990s. However, this cannot be confirmed, since employment figures (where available for the first half of the 1990s) do not show a sharp decline. A more convincing argument is that during 1995–2000 the three countries had relatively good growth rates, apart from the crisis years in Mexico (1995) and Brazil (1998–1999) and an economic slowdown in Argentina (at the end of the 1990s). However, these crises were accompanied by or were the result of currency devaluations in Mexico (1994) and Brazil (1999), reducing the relative price bias in favor of imports. One obvious argument is that increased imports are not always bad for production and consumption, or for employment. Imports of intermediary products may help introduce new technologies and increase productivity. Furthermore, although increased productivity has a labor-conserving component, it also leads to higher efficiency in the domestic economy, thus having a positive impact on production, welfare, and employment.

Overall, trade liberalization led to increased imports, especially of medium to high labor-intensive goods with relatively high value added and technology, compared with exports. The labor market impact of increased competition on manufacturing was mixed, with both positive and negative benefits for employment. Agriculture, on the other hand, suffered significantly from cheap imports. Rural workers were the main losers in Mexico; they were strongly affected by cheap corn imports, as well as by grains and oilseeds from the United States. As a result, corn prices fell and so did rural incomes. According to Mexico's National Institute for Statistics, Geography, and Informatics (INEGI; Instituto Nacional de Estadística, Geografía e Informática),[21] about 1 million jobs were lost during the period 1993–2002, which spurred emigration (Papademetriou, 2003). This phenomenon was not the result of the lack of complementarity between the two countries. Mexico was self-sufficient in corn; indeed, corn was a crucial product of subsistence and domestic farming. Rather, the US farmers only managed to export the product to Mexico thanks to high government subsidies and to Mexico's permission of a substantial above-quota, tariff-free import of corn, a policy failure with implied high and unnecessary social costs.

In order to understand better the importance of trade compared to other variables, we deepen our analysis by using a *growth-accounting approach*. This method takes a simple accounting framework to decompose or isolate the contribution of relevant variables to employment. Doing so enables an understanding of whether and how much import penetration led to job losses compared with other variables, such as labor productivity, domestic consumption, or absorption, and the domestic coefficient. Domestic absorption represents domestic utilization for final private consumption. The domestic coefficient is the share of domestic output in domestic absorption (see Ernst, 2005b).

The accounting approach confirms the previous analysis that the direct effect of trade, particularly imports, on employment was low during the period 1995–2000. All countries generally experienced a slight increase in import competition and a rather low offsetting effect of export expansion. In terms of net jobs, increased import competition cost Argentina 43,000 jobs, or –1.03 percent of total employment; Brazil, 287,000 jobs, or –0.44 percent; and Mexico, 269,000 jobs, or –1.64 percent. The figure is relatively low for Brazil, but significantly higher for Argentina and Mexico. If net imports are considered, the situation is even reversed in the case of Argentina (20,000 jobs created) and Brazil (216,000 jobs created) and mitigated in the case of Mexico (which still suffered from 224,000 jobs lost). A strong rise in domestic absorption— even outpacing the productivity increase—is the main explanatory variable, which was rather high in Argentina and Brazil and low in Mexico. Industries that suffered the most from import competition were footwear, basic chemicals, and motor vehicles in Argentina, basic chemicals, special-purpose machines, and medical appliances in Mexico, and electric motors and television and radio-broadcast receivers in Brazil. However, other industries benefited from increased imports, such as sawmilling, publishing, and medical appliances in Argentina, and man-made fibers (still negative, but less so with the help of imports), general and special-purpose machines, and medical appliances in Brazil. Exports can have an offsetting impact on employment in specific sectors, such as in the automobile sector in all three countries, but this effect was rather low.

As the growth-accounting approach could not find a significant negative and direct impact of imports on employment, other more indirect channels may explain the disappointing employment figures. Many economists have pointed out that imports bring about higher competition in the domestic market, forcing domestic producers to improve their productivity through greater availability of high-quality inputs, technology acquisition via imports or exports, import discipline, and higher turnover. This phenomenon implies the exit of the least efficient firms and the expansion of the most efficient ones. In Brazil and Mexico during the 1990s, productivity gains in manufacturing were positive. Import discipline may have played an important role in this regard (López-Córdova and Mesquita Moreira, 2003), as increased competition through imports forced companies to improve efficiency in firm management, raise output, and increase their scale efficiency. Productivity growth in a low-economic-growth context may provide another explanation for the negative impact of imports on employment. An analysis of the relationship between the rate of growth of imports and labor productivity shows that the correlation between both variables for the whole economy was rather insignificant for Argentina and Brazil, but high for Mexico at 0.8. At the sectoral level, even though Argentina and Brazil had low productivity values in manufacturing, they were significantly above average: 0.2 in Argentina and 0.3 in Brazil, but they are well below Mexico's level of 0.6. ILO research (1999) covering the first half of the 1990s confirmed a close relationship between economic opening and productivity in all three countries. In Mexico a certain time lag was observed between both variables (Laos, 1999), in Argentina (Frenkel and González Rozada, 1999) sectoral differences and the importance of the business cycle were stressed, and in Brazil a strong surge of productivity in tradables was observed (Amadeo and Melo Filho, 1999).

Implications of Trade Liberalization for Domestic Companies

The new outward-oriented development strategy and a more globalized world market led to the abandonment of old methods of organizing production and to a change in business behavior. This section shows how local companies reacted to the changing environment. Small and medium-sized enterprises (SMEs) experienced serious difficulties integrating into the global economy, which led to negative employment and wage figures. For example, in the 1990s, SMEs accounted for only about 10 percent of the exports of Argentina and Brazil, compared to 56 percent of the exports of Taiwan (China), and 53 percent in Italy (ILO, 2005).

During import-substitution industrialization, firms would typically carry large inventories of spare parts, had a high degree of vertical integration and a reduced level of specialization, and were oriented toward the domestic market. Since opening their markets, Latin American enterprises have learned to apply new organizational principles of flexible manufacturing and just-in-time and zero-defect methods, adapting them to their own needs and circumstances. They have increasingly begun resorting to outsourcing of intermediate inputs and subcontracting of production services. Integration has become less vertical and production has a higher import content per unit of product (Benavente et al., 1997). Efforts at technological adaptation have thus become less necessary; new technology has entered the country through imported inputs, which have become cheaper due to the reduction of import tariffs, specific regulations allowing tax exemptions (Ferraz, Kupfer, and Iootty, 2004), and exchange rate appreciation. Increased imports have led to a decline in the ratio of domestic value added to the value of the goods (Kosacoff, 2000a), in particular for exports (ECLAC, 2004b). This has had a negative effect on local producers of intermediary and final goods, whose production was replaced by imports (Dussel Peters, 2004a). Cheap imports of capital goods have also aggravated the trend toward the substitution of labor by capital. The industries which suffered most in Argentina, Brazil, and Mexico due to increased import competitiveness were footwear, wearing apparel (with the exception of Mexico), furniture, capital goods, machinery and equipment, as well as printing (Kosacoff, 2000b). Increased outward orientation has also generated new opportunities for export industries, not only in the maquiladoras, as mentioned earlier, but also in specific manufacturing sectors promoted during the ISI period, and more recently in agricultural products, which have benefited from exchange rate devaluation.

As a result, current production patterns are technologically more complex and closer to global technological standards of production, but, on the other hand, less intensive in the use of local technical knowledge and local equipment. Proactive strategies, aimed at high rates of increase in production and related productivity, were implemented in Argentina only in the early 1990s. In general, many companies in Argentina, for example, applied defensive restructuring strategies in order to keep up with the increased competitive pace (Bisang, 2000). This generated a surge in productivity mainly through a reduction of the work force. Companies invested less in new plants, and undertook more reorganization and rationalization of existing productive structures through the introduction of new technologies and investment in information technology (Bonelli, 2001). In Mexico, on the other hand, where companies applied more aggressive regimes that sought out strategic domestic and foreign markets, labor productivity increased at a slower pace (Haar, Leroy-Beltrán, and Beltrán, 2004; Ramos Francia and Chiquiar Cikurel, 2004). As a result, there was a lower rate of decline in employment, also because of different labor market institutions. For example, contractual clauses guaranteeing employment have been much more common in Mexico than in Argentina (Katz, 2000a). It has also been observed that there is a certain convergence toward the standards of productive efficiency in developed countries, but all in a context of strong growth of structural unemployment, trade imbalances, and unequal distribution of the benefits of technological modernization. The productivity increase in Argentina and Brazil was fragmented and only strong in some specific sectors. Moreover, the surge in informal activities in Brazil, and to a lesser extent in Mexico, had a negative impact on productivity growth (ECLAC, 2004b).

The 1990s experienced fundamental changes in the structure of business organization. The new economic environment, less regulated and more competitive, acted as a powerful selection mechanism and enhanced business concentration. Public companies' share in the economy strongly declined as a result of privatization. In all three countries, national branches of transnational corporations (TNCs) and big national companies increased their presence in the economy and became the most dynamic with regard to exports. For example, in Brazil, market participation (sales) of public enterprises declined from 44.6 percent in 1991 to 24.3 percent in 1999, TNCs' participation increased from 14.8 percent to 36.4 percent, while national holdings remained static (Ferraz, Kupfer, and Iootty, 2004).

The losers in the new outward-oriented strategy have clearly been SMEs, which are extremely important for employment. In 2002, they accounted for 70 percent of total employment in Argentina, 60 percent in Brazil, but only 48 percent in Mexico. The new scenario led to strategic uncertainties about future positions in the market; companies had to face new and stiffer competition, were dependent on new intermediary agents (e.g., suppliers), and needed cooperative arrangements with other firms, among others, to increase the scale of production (Yoguel, 2000). Besides higher productivity gains in larger companies than in SMEs (Katz, 1998), access to credit was the major obstacle for SMEs. While large national companies (Bisang, 2000) and TNCs had access to either international or national credit, it was almost impossible for SMEs to obtain credit from the local market, not only because of high real interest rates but also because commercial banks steadily reduced their credit to the productive sector between 1990 and 2003 in Mexico, Argentina, and Brazil. Banks' lending policies have favored ability-to-pay criteria of the traditional kind instead of being supportive to firms in their business projects (Dussel Peters, 2004a; Yoguel, 2000). While big companies were able to begin modernizing their product lines, local subcontracted firms could not pursue modernization, as they were less export-oriented. Moreover, new foreign investors often had their own supplier network, which meant fewer new opportunities for local suppliers (Alarcón and Zepeda, 2004).

An interesting but still rare phenomenon of the 1990s is industrial clustering among firms. The synergistic effect of forward and backward linkages of clusters helps exploit respective comparative advantages and thus increases competitiveness. Clusters can be found in natural resource–based sectors, such as the grape and mango cluster in Petrolina and the apple cluster in Santa Catarina, Brazil, or the software industry in Blumenau and the electronic industry in Guadalajara, Mexico. Most clusters can be found in the context of complex production systems. In these clusters, and mainly in the Mexican maquiladoras such as automobiles and electronics, the first-tier supplier, a foreign company, generally specializes in high-technology activities. Local second and third suppliers are often trapped in the low value-added segment.[22] Brazil provides two interesting examples of clustering. First is the metalworking cluster in Espirito

Santo, in which small and large local companies have cooperated successfully and have managed to upgrade production in specific niches.

Second is the aeronautics cluster in São Paulo, which has successfully established backward and forward linkages around the leading firm, the aircraft manufacturer Embraer, and thus helped second- and third-tier subcontractors to upgrade. Aircraft, which represent high value-added goods including high technology, have become one of the most important Brazilian exports, and Embraer has even started to invest heavily in production plants abroad, including in China. This cluster, which created important backward linkages through subcontracting relationships and a focus on horizontal integration, is certainly a Brazilian success story, even though it has contributed to only 0.3 percent of direct employment in manufacturing. Nevertheless, direct employment increased by 97 percent between 1995 and 1999, creating 4,000 new jobs between 2000 and 2002 (Bernardes, 2001; data from Embraer). Moreover, there are multiplier effects on manufacturing in this region and the local economy as a whole, especially in traditional services, like social activities or education, but also transport and infrastructure. Its recent success can be explained by a deep restructuring process as a result of privatization. However, it is also a very specific sector that depends largely on government support—not only in Brazil, but also in OECD countries—such as public purchase, export promotion, or direct and indirect support of technological innovation.[23] It also includes an increasingly high share of imported components in its aircraft production;[24] in the early 1990s, components of Brazilian origin constituted 40–80 percent of production depending on the aircraft model. This is to a large extent the result of the high labor share in the value of an aircraft varying between 30 and 50 percent of total costs (Frischtak, 1992). Embraer, however, has tried to develop local competencies in the framework of its "learning strategy" (Bernardes, 2001). In some cases, industrial clustering was the result of private initiatives, which were then further promoted by the public sector. In other cases, the state took the first step to enhance industrial clustering (Pietrobelli and Rabellotti, 2004).

FDI and Trade

The 1990s were characterized by a general trend toward greater market opening, which created a favorable environment for increasing trade and FDI flows.[25] Industrial policies were fairly neutral and supportive of this trend. The involvement of foreign companies can help boost trade in goods and services of the host country, since foreign investment in general spurs imports of intermediary and capital goods, and in Latin America, TNCs have also become the leading export firms.[26]

Figure 4.2 illustrates the evolution of exports, imports, and FDI flows. The closest link between all three variables, and thus the strong interdepend-

Figure 4.2a   Exports, Imports, and FDI, Argentina, 1990–2003

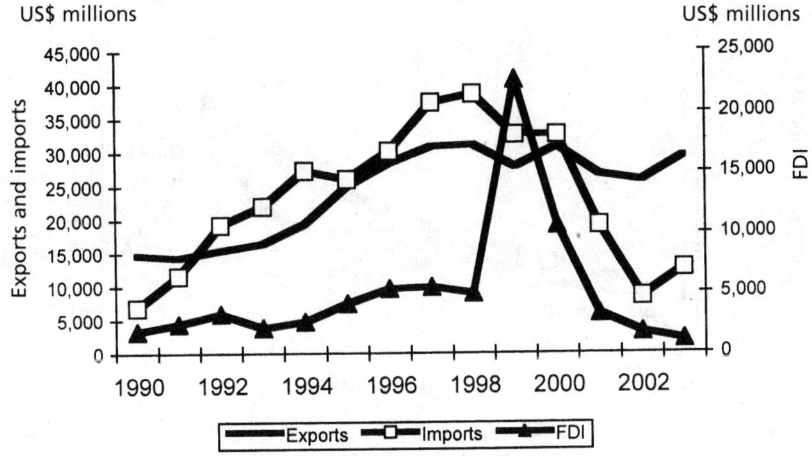

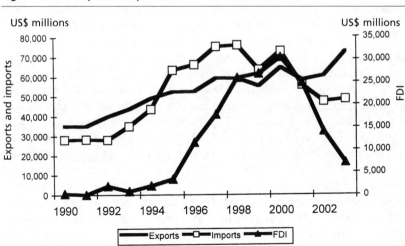

Source: ECLAC, 2004e.

ence between trade and FDI, can be observed in the case of Mexico. The looser links in Argentina and Brazil can be explained by the fact that a large part of foreign investment in the 1990s went to nontradables such as utilities and finance. It is interesting to observe that, since 2000, declining FDI inflows

Figure 4.2b   Exports, Imports, and FDI, Brazil, 1990–2003

Source: ECLAC, 2004e.

Figure 4.2c   Exports, Imports, and FDI, Mexico, 1990–2003

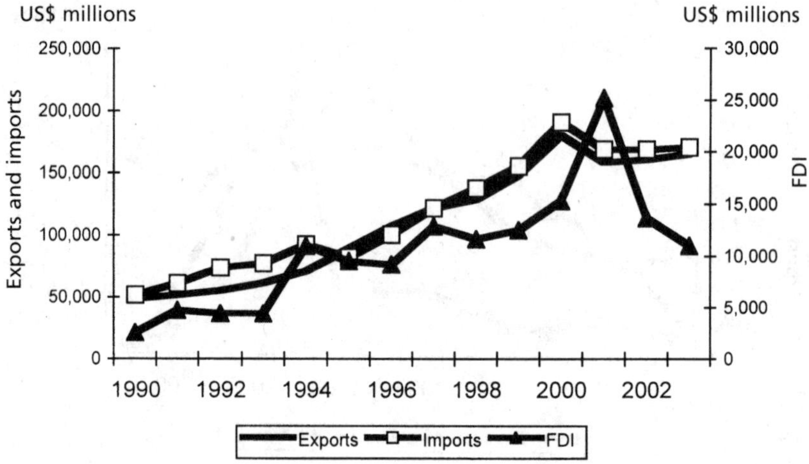

US$ millions   US$ millions

Source: ECLAC, 2004e.

have not been followed by declining exports and imports. Since 2003, exports
in particular have shown promising results, which were partly due to a favorable exchange rate in Argentina and Brazil. Nevertheless, the "export boom"
is highly concentrated in specific agricultural goods (e.g., soybeans), to specific countries, in particular China, and is therefore rather fragile. Intrafirm
trade has been playing an increasing role, not only in Mexico's assembly
plants, but also, to a lesser extent, in Brazil and Argentina (e.g., Kulfas, Porta,
and Ramos, 2002). In Argentina, for example, 60 percent of TNCs' exports
and 80 percent of their imports were intrafirm transactions (Kosacoff, 2000c).
In the case of Mexico, a large part of imports were reexported after being
processed, such as in textiles, confectioneries, and chemicals (León González
Pacheco and Dussel Peters, 2001). Due to special sectoral agreements, the automobile industry has been extremely important in terms of intraindustry trade
for all three countries (Asociación Latinoamericana de Integración/Associação
Latinoamericana de Integração [ALADI], 2000). In Mexico, other main areas
of intraindustry trade have been machinery and equipment and electrical
equipment (Dussel Peters, 2000a). As TNCs contributed to higher exports and
even higher imports, they had a generally negative impact on the trade balance, in particular in Argentina and Brazil, but a positive one on the capital-
account balance. All three countries also received increasingly foreign-di-
rected investment in traded services. The most striking flows went into
packaging and commercial services in Argentina, research and development
production in Brazil, and software development in Mexico.

Conclusion

Even though trade liberalization and regional integration caused a strong increase in trade and led to a better integration into the world economy for Argentina, Brazil, and Mexico, it did not have the expected positive impact on production and employment during the period of analysis. Instead, there was a steep
rise in imports in the region, but not a similar degree of export dynamism, in particular in Argentina and Brazil. Constant exchange rate appreciation was a major
macroeconomic variable hampering an export drive, as explained in Chapter 3.
Only Mexico experienced an export surge in manufacturing production and employment during the second half of the 1990s, mainly due to the booming
maquiladora sector. However, the maquiladora industry did not develop significant links with the rest of the economy. Even for the more sophisticated exports,
it did not generate value-added upgrading, since the import content of exports
also rose significantly. Moreover, the maquiladora industry has declined significantly since 2000, thus reducing formal job creation in Mexico drastically. The
opening of the domestic market to highly subsidized US agricultural products
had a disastrous impact on employment in agriculture and represented another
setback of trade opening. This shows that sequencing and targeting of economic
opening is crucial for avoiding high social adjustment costs.

Of concern is the decline in specialization of dynamic products vis-à-vis
the world market and the remaining specialization in primary or semiprocessed primary products, in particular in Argentina, but also in Brazil. Even
though strong exports in these goods may have a positive impact on macroeconomic variables such as the trade balance, currency reserves, and public
revenue from export taxes, this type of specialization is not very promising for
the future development of the country and may strengthen the marginalization
of Argentina and Brazil in the world market. Indeed, these exports have high
price vulnerability and create very few good quality jobs. In addition, few new
production plants have been created in Argentina and Brazil as a result of economic opening, which led more to the restructuring of existing manufacturing
plants. This process did not therefore create many new jobs, as it did not focus
on sectors with high labor intensity.

The direct impact of imports on employment in the manufacturing sector
was both positive and negative, depending on the industry, during the second
half of the 1990s. Its indirect impact, however, was negative (see Table 4.7).
Greater competition in the domestic market and imports of technology led to industrial restructuring and to a rise in labor productivity in the traditional industrial sectors, in particular in Argentina and Brazil. This resulted in a general decrease in demand for labor in manufacturing, but also to a wage shift in favor of
skilled workers, as illustrated clearly in the automobile sector of Argentina and
Brazil. Nevertheless, there was also a strong link between trade and FDI. Chapter 5 analyzes the importance of FDI for employment.

Table 4.7   Summary of Trade and Labor Market Variables

Variable	Argentina	Brazil	Mexico
Tariff reduction	Very strong	Very strong	Strong
Export increase	Strong	Strong	Very strong
Import increase	Very strong	Very strong	Very strong
Intraregional trade increase	Strong	Strong	Very strong
Specialization in dynamic exports	Declining	Declining	Declining
Labor intensity of major exports	Strong	Strong	Low positive
Employment impact of exports	Mixed	Slightly declining	Low positive
Wage impact of exports	Mixed	Low positive	Slightly positive
Direct employment impact of increased imports	Mixed	Mixed	Mixed
Indirect employment impact of increased imports	Declining	Declining	Slightly declining

Appendix Table 4.A   Competitive Matrix Compared with World and Regional Markets, 1985–2000

Argentina

1985–1990 World

Vegetable oils	Meat and edible meat offals, fresh
Meat and edible meat offals, preparations	Fish, fresh, chilled, dried, frozen
Fuelwood	Cereal and flour preparations
Cereals, unmilled	Leather
Oil seeds and oleaginous fruit	Crustaceans and molluscs
Dyeing and tanning extracts	Special transactions and commodities

1995–2000 World

Vegetable oils	Essential oils, perfumes
Feeding stuff for animals	Petroleum products, refined
Maize (corn), unmilled	Motor vehicles
Meat and edible meat offals	Residual petroleum products
Tea and maté	Internal combustion piston engines
Cotton	Parts and accessories of motor vehicles

1995–2000 Mercosur

Maize (corn), unmilled	Wheat and meslin, unmilled
Milk and cream	Cereals, unmilled
Nonferrous base metal waste	Margarine
Vegetable oils	Leather
Vegetables, fresh, chilled, frozen	Edible products and preparations
Fish, fresh, chilled, dried, frozen	Textile yarn

continues

Appendix Table 4.A   Continued

Brazil
1985–1990 World

Iron ore and concentrates	Pig iron, spiegeleisen, sponge iron
Coffee and coffee substitutes	Ingots and primary forms of iron/steel
Tin	Silk
Fruit, preserved and fruit preparations	Footwear
Feeding stuff for animals	Manufactures of leather
Meat and edible meat offals	Meat and edible meat offals

1995–2000 World

Iron ore and concentrates	Spices
Coffee and coffee substitutes	Nickel
Oil seeds and oleaginous fruit	Wood manufactures
Feeding stuff for animals	Internal combustion piston engines
Ingots and other primary forms	Made-up articles, of textile material
Dyeing and tanning extracts	Essential oils, perfumes

1995–2000 Mercosur

Cotton fabrics, woven	Made-up articles, of textile materials
Cutlery	Road motor vehicles
Footwear	Other artificial fibers for spinning
Iron ore and concentrates	Meat and edible meat offals
Coffee and coffee substitutes	Tin
Tea and maté	Margarine and shortening

Mexico
1985–1990 World

Sulphur and unroasted iron pyrites	Equipment for distributing electricity
Lead	Television receivers
Coffee and coffee substitutes	Radio-broadcast receivers
Silver, platinum	Crustaceans and molluscs
Internal combustion piston engines	Telecommunications equipment
Petroleum oils, crude	Stone, sand, and gravel

1995–2000 World

Radio-broadcast receivers	Motor vehicles for transport
Railway vehicles and equipment	Undergarments
Rotating electric plant and parts	Furniture and parts
Television receivers	Equipment for distributing electricity
Meters and counters	Electric power machinery
Vegetables, fresh, chilled, frozen	Internal combustion piston engines

1995–2000 NAFTA

Sulphur and unroasted iron pyrites	Railway vehicles and associated equipment
Fuelwood	Undergarments
Radio-broadcast receivers	Telecommunications equipment
Meters and counters	Television receivers
Vegetables, fresh, chilled, frozen	Equipment for distributing electricity
Electrical apparatus, electrical circuits	Rotating electric plant and parts

Source: Author calculations based on ECLAC, 2003f.
Note: This table follows the pattern of Figure 4.1.

Appendix Table 4.B   Labor Intensity per Country: Five Lowest and Highest Labor-Intensive Product Groups in Manufacturing

Low Labor Intensity	High Labor Intensity
Argentina	
Knitted and crocheted fabrics and articles	Tanning, dressing, and processing of leather
Wearing apparel, except fur apparel	Domestic appliances
Printing and related service activities	Railway and tramway locomotives and rolling stock
Refined petroleum products	Office, accounting, and computing machinery
Furniture	Coke oven products
Brazil	
Aircraft and spacecraft	Coke oven products
Recycling of nonmetal waste and scrap	TV and radio receivers and associated goods
Recycling of metal waste and scrap	Artificial fibers
TV and radio transmitters; line communication apparatus	Beverages
Electric motors, generators, and transformers	Building and repairing of ships and boats
Mexico	
Appliances for measuring, testing, navigating, etc.	Tobacco products
Made-up textile articles, except apparel	Builders' carpentry and joinery
TV and radio receivers and associated goods	Processing and preserving of fish
Railway and tramway locomotives and rolling stock	Fertilizers and nitrogen compounds
Tanks, reservoirs, and containers of metal	Wooden containers

Source: Author calculations based on UNCTAD, FDI database (http://www.unctad.org/templates/page.asp?intitemid=1923&lang=1) and UNIDO, Indstat, Revision 3.

Notes

1. See also Martinez, 2004a, 2004b, on the expected positive outcomes of trade liberalization.

2. Programa de Integración y Cooperación Económica/Integração e Cooperação Econômica.

3. Tratado de Integración y Cooperación para el Desarrollo/Integração e Cooperação para o Desenvolvimento.

4. Specific key sectors, either agricultural or capital-intensive industries, were promoted as a step toward harmonization and coordination of policies and rules and the reduction of trade barriers between these countries.

5. For example, the introduction of a statistical tax, an increase in the list of exceptions, and tariffs for some key industries such as the car industry (from 35 percent to 70 percent in 1995).

6. Although macroeconomic coordination, in particular, has been a problem between Argentina and Brazil due to economic crisis, devaluations, and different business interests (discussed in more detail in Chapter 3).

7. The CET has a tariff structure of eleven levels, ranging from 0 to 20 percent (Estevadeordal, Goto, and Saez, 2000).

8. A closer look at the enterprise level shows that the regional market plays an important role, especially for small exporting firms. In 2001, 46 percent of the exports from Argentina and 23 percent from Brazil went to Mercosur and Chile, while these destinations accounted for only 33 percent and 13 percent of the exports of large exporting companies in Argentina and Brazil respectively (ILO, 2005).

9. Figures for 2000 were even higher: Argentina, 32 percent; Brazil, 14 percent.

10. The complementarity index based on the revealed comparative advantage (RCA) index developed by C. Ernst in 1997 shows a value of 0.57 between Argentina and the European Union and of 0.62 between Brazil and the European Union, while trade complementarity between Argentina and Brazil is much lower, with a value of 0.47.

11. The difference of exports minus imports divided by exports $[(X - M) / X]$ shows the importance of the import content of exports, as economic opening has often led to an increase in the import content.

12. For example, take the case of tanning and dressing of leather in Argentina between 1995 and 2000. Employment in this sector, which is highly labor intensive, declined by 2.4 percent and wages by 2.0. Both values are inferior to average manufacturing employment, which increased by 3.9 percent, and wages, which increased by 7.5 percent, which means that this sector was severely affected by the new economic setting. The employment share of tanning within manufacturing employment was 1.7 percent on average. Tanning had a share in total exports of 3.6 percent and has a low input of imported goods with a value close to 1 (0.92).

13. $[(X - M) / X]$ is negative, as −0.31.

14. While primary exports represented 88 percent of total exports in 1980, the proportion decreased to 57 percent in 1990 and to 19 percent in 2003, according to ECLAC, 2004e.

15. A calculation of the evolution of the market share for each category confirms the trend toward the declining importance of rising stars in Argentina, Brazil, and Mexico.

16. Primary products: 42 percent of total exports in 1990 and 46 percent in 2001; medium-technology industries: 12 percent in 1990 and 16 percent in 2001. See International Labour Organization (ILO), 2005.

17. In addition, labor market institutions have been biased against wage increases. The government applied a policy to prevent a strong rise in the minimum wage and to control its influence on many other wages. Unionization and collective bargaining were repressed through weak labor laws. In the maquiladoras, protection contracts were signed with "ineffective" trade unions (Polaski, 2003; see also Chapter 6).

18. Just 12 percent of total exports in Brazil and 3 percent in Argentina were located in the high-technology sector (ILO, 2005).

19. Other missed opportunities with regard to the world market, 1995–2000: Argentina: parts of motor vehicles, residual petroleum products (and textile and leather toward Mercosur market); Brazil: essential oils, perfumes, textile made-up articles (tin, meat, and margarine toward Mercosur market); Mexico: equipment for distributing

electricity, electric power machinery (television receivers and electric plants toward NAFTA).

20. Example of high import dependency of exports: 78.6 percent of exports containing temporarily imported goods in Mexico between 1990 and 2003 (Dussel Peters, 2004a).

21. This figure also includes fishing, forestry, and trapping (Instituto Nacional de Estadística Geografía e Informática [INEGI], 2002).

22. There are some positive signs, such as Delphi in the automotive sector in Juarez, which developed a local engineering center and where local suppliers managed to produce higher value-added goods.

23. According to the Brazilian Aeronautics Industry Association, a cooperation program for high technology between North and South turned out to be quite successful in this regard.

24. An increase in imports by an annual average of 55 percent between 1995 and 1999.

25. See Chapter 5 for more details on FDI.

26. In Argentina, the participation of TNCs in the external trade of the major industries in 1998 was as follows: telecommunications—exports: 100 percent, imports: 98.7 percent; automobiles—exports: 98.9 percent, imports: 97.9 percent; pharmaceutical products—exports: 69.9 percent, imports: 76.3 percent (Kulfas, Porta, and Ramos, 2002).

5

Foreign Direct Investment and the Creation of Quality Employment

For many developing countries, attracting foreign direct investment (FDI) has been a key aspect of their outward-oriented development strategy, as investment is considered a crucial element for output growth and employment generation. FDI is seen to complement scarce domestic financial resources. It is also expected to help modernize production by transferring know-how and technology, while increasing domestic productivity and improving international competitiveness. FDI should also facilitate integration into the world market, domestic participation in globalized production, and the creation of forward and backward linkages with the domestic economy. In so doing, it will have a multiplier effect on the whole economy and could thus be a key element in spurring growth. On the negative side, skeptics argue that FDI can adversely affect domestic investment or lead to an increasing dependence on foreign interests, which are difficult to control. In addition, it can lead to uncontrolled competition between countries and even between regions within the same country in terms of offering fiscal incentives to attract investment.

New trends have reinforced the importance of private investment. As a result of the move toward neoliberal policies, the state's role as an active economic player declined. Private investment, both domestic and foreign, has come to be viewed as the driving force of the economy. With financial and trade liberalization, it is expected that there will be a reorientation toward the tradable sector and in particular to those activities that are based on the comparative advantage for developing or emerging countries, presumably the abundance of low-skilled labor. As a result, the role of private enterprises as investors and contributors to employment has grown in importance.

General Evolution, Origins, and Reasons for FDI

Evolution of FDI Stocks and Flows

Especially in the later part of the 1990s, FDI boomed in Argentina, Brazil, and Mexico, by far the largest recipients of FDI in the region. FDI inflows were significantly higher between 1990 and 2003 than in the 1980s, according to recent data from the United Nations Conference on Trade and Development (UNCTAD) (see http://stats.unctad.org/fdi/eng/reportfolders/rfview/explorerp.asp): they were four times higher in Mexico, which began trade and financial liberalization earlier, six times higher in Brazil, and over ten times higher in Argentina, which had the most comprehensive privatization program during the 1990s. Among developing countries, only China received more investment. An increasing part of FDI inflows came from countries belonging to the OECD, which have traditionally dominated these flows (see Ernst, 2005a).

As Figure 5.1 illustrates, Mexico was the first country to see a significant increase in its FDI inflows: between 1993 and 1994, on the eve of the creation of the North American Free Trade Agreement (NAFTA), its FDI increased from US$4 billion to US$11 billion. After a short break, due to the Tequila crisis mainly in 1995, it rose again, but FDI has slowed down since 2000, with the exception of 2001.[1] The lower FDI levels since 2000 can be explained by the recession in the United States, its main investor, the elimination of sectoral incentives, the reduction of public investments, and the crisis of the "maquila-

Figure 5.1   FDI Inflows, 1990–2003

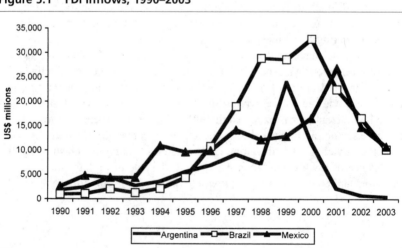

Source: UNCTAD, 2004.

dora model," which will be discussed later (Máttar, Moreno-Brid, and Peres, 2002).

Argentina, like Mexico, started to significantly increase its FDI in the early 1990s. The recovery of internal demand, a comprehensive privatization program, but also the launch of the Mercado Común del Sur (Mercosur; Southern Cone Common Market), contributed to the first wave of FDI inflows, from US$1.6 billion in 1989 to US$4.4 billion in 1992, and to a second rise from 1995 to 2000, with a peak in 1999 (US$23.9 billion) due to the purchase of the petroleum company Yacimientos Petrolíferos Fiscales SA (YPF) by the Spanish company Repsol. The economic crisis, which began in 2001, led to a sharp decline in FDI, to just US$478 million in 2003. The debt default, the resulting economic recession, and a price freeze for specific service sectors led to loan cuts by transnational corporations (TNCs). In addition, a few investors left the country (UNCTAD, 2003b).

Brazil, compared with the two other countries, was a late starter with regard to economic reforms, which is also reflected in the timing of FDI inflows. Such inflows only began to take off after the introduction of the Real Plan in 1994 and the resulting macroeconomic stabilization, peaking in 2000 at US$32.8 billion. However, in 2003 they fell sharply, to US$10.1 billion. The main reasons for this decline were the world recession in 2000 and 2001, which also affected Argentina and Mexico, Brazil's poor economic performance, an unstable political and economic environment, the crisis in Argentina, and the impending national elections. The decline of FDI in all three countries also represents a normalization of flows, after an exceptional FDI boom as a result of privatization and financial and trade opening.

Figure 5.2 shows the overall trend of inward FDI stocks, ignoring short-term fluctuations. Data on stocks represent the accumulation of foreign investment in the country, while those on flows only show how much new FDI went into the country in the period under analysis. The graph shows a constant increase in stocks in all three countries in the 1990s. Argentina was the big winner, with a stock almost nine times higher in 2000 than in 1990, but then the stock decreased sharply, in part due to the devaluation. In absolute terms, Mexico experienced the most impressive surge in FDI, while Brazil also significantly increased its stock by over six times. Brazil, as a late reformer, experienced a remarkable jump in its FDI stock beginning in 1997, which then slowed down and regained a strong increase in 2002 and 2003. Mexico had the highest level of FDI stock in 2003 (US$166 billion), closely followed by Brazil (US$128 billion); Argentina had the lowest level (US$35 billion). Calculated per capita, Mexico led with US$1,600, followed by Argentina with US$924 and Brazil with US$755.

Mexico's strong increase in FDI stocks was driven by investment from its NAFTA trade partners,[2] the United States and Canada, which increased their FDI to Mexico by over five times between 1992 and 2002. But Mexico's out-

Figure 5.2   Inward FDI Stocks, 1990–2003

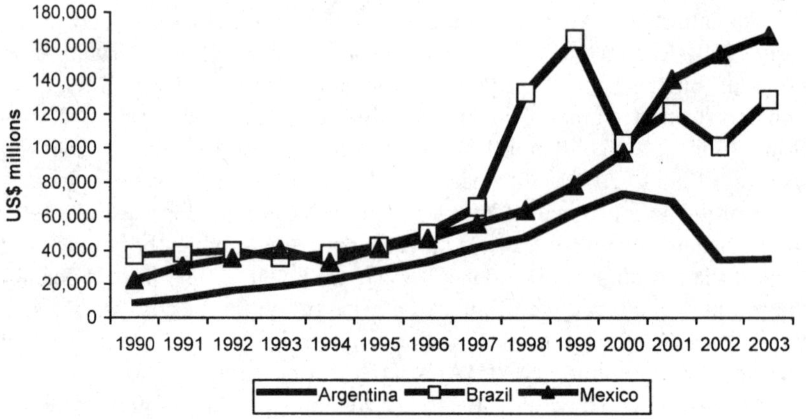

Source: UNCTAD, FDI database (http://www.unctad.org/).

ward flow of FDI stocks to the United States also increased significantly, from a low of US$575 million in 1990 to US$7.9 billion in 2002. Much of this is accounted for by the integration of the Mexican automobile industry into an already deeply integrated North American automotive industry spurred by the creation of NAFTA. European investment is mainly concentrated in automobiles, electronics and electrical products, chemical products, food, beverages and tobacco, and some services such as finance and retail trade.

In Argentina and Brazil, overall figures show that interregional FDI, mainly from the United States and Europe, is much more important (about 50 percent) than regional FDI (15 percent) compared to Mexico. In this regard, it should be stressed that Spain "recovered" its former regional influence and became the most important European investor, mainly in services, particularly financial services. Nevertheless, there have been some interesting developments within Mercosur, where sectoral agreements have benefited some sectors, such as the automobile industry (see Box 5.1).

Transnational corporations are the main providers of FDI and are thus an important source of employment. The transnationality index (TNI) reveals the importance of TNCs in a domestic economy taking into account the production potential stemming from FDI inflows and the outcome of that investment. Table 5.1 clearly shows that the three countries have a high TNI compared with other countries. This is especially true for Brazil and Argentina, where TNCs are more important than in India, France, or even China. Mexico has a lower but still high TNI, of 11.6 percent. Nevertheless, in terms of employment share, TNCs are not as important in Argentina, Brazil, and Mexico as they are in China (UNCTAD, 2002). Data for China and India suggest that

Box 5.1
The Automobile Industry

In the 1990s, in all three countries, the automobile industry benefited from a specific industrial policy. Brazil and Argentina had already entered into a sectoral agreement even before the inception of Mercosur that provided for a system of compensation, which was then extended to all Mercosur countries. The compensation system was strengthened in 1994 through the Protocol of Ouro Preto and slightly revised later. It stipulated the gradual elimination of tariffs among the member countries and the establishment of a common external tariff, and permitted the use of investment incentives. The main purpose was to secure a balanced exchange in the automobile sector between Argentina and Brazil and to provide a certain level of import protection (Bonelli, 2001). The special regime did not, however, provide any specific clause to foster local suppliers. The regional agreement was complemented by special provisions at the national level. Since 1991, Argentina's motor vehicle industry has been governed by a special regime that increases the import content to 40 percent, allows the import of vehicles for assembly firms if exports exceeded imports, and sets an import quota for cars not produced locally. Brazil also designed its own regime in 1995 with similar provisions. Additionally, in 1996, a new regime offered fiscal incentives for Brazil's less developed regions, which resulted in 70 percent of new investment going to these regions between 1996 and 2001, such as Ford in Bahia (Bonelli, 2001).

These sectoral regulations contributed immensely to attracting foreign investors interested in exploiting the regional market. Argentina, in particular, became more attractive to investors as a result of the enlarged Mercosur market, as the companies could produce on a much larger scale. As a consequence of the special Mercosur regime, and in line with the new strategies adopted by the existing TNCs, Argentina began to specialize in a small number of upper-grade models, while Brazil concentrated on mass production of a lower class of cars. Consequently, there was a spectacular rise in production, by 400 percent between 1990 and 1994, partly also due to a rise in domestic consumption (Kosacoff, 2000b).

The new interest in the automobile industry also led to deep restructuring related to changes in TNCs' strategies. On the one hand, new trends leaned toward less vertical integration and toward the external provision of parts and accessories. There was also less plant engineering. Assembly of imported components, rather than of locally integrated production, began to characterize the sector (Benavente et al., 1997). On the other hand, the lean production system led to a closer relation with first-tier suppliers. "Improved manufacturing practices were diffusing throughout the production chain" (Posthuma, 2004, p. 52), causing the technological upgrading of suppliers. TNCs played an active role in this integration process. Intraindustry and, in particular, intrafirm trade became important, and ties between the TNC branches in Argentina and Brazil were strengthened (Economic Commission for Latin America and the Caribbean [ECLAC], 2001), which resulted in greater imports of car components. In many instances, already-existing firms regained control over production in Argentina, and new firms arrived in both countries. Production plants underwent a major rationalization and modernization process, but still faced problems of scale economies; this led them to create new plants conforming to international production standards. In general, the international competitiveness gap was reduced in this sector in terms of the product

continues

Box 5.1 Continued

quality and efficiency levels (Ferraz, Kupfer, and Iootty, 2004). The economic crisis and lower consumption in both countries since 1999 led to a fall in production, by 24.5 percent in Argentina between 1993 and 2000, and by 10.0 percent in Brazil, and to the transfer of some activities from Argentina to Brazil (see Ernst, 2005a). The restructuring and modernization process increased the productivity of the sector, but it had a negative impact on the labor market. Employment in this medium labor-intensive sector declined by 10.9 percent in Argentina and by 11.3 percent in Brazil, and real wages fell by 48.6 percent in Argentina and 7.2 percent in Brazil between 1993 and 2000.

There are many similarities but also important differences between employment development in the sector in Mexico and in Argentina and Brazil. In Mexico, between 1960 and the late 1980s, the automobile industry benefited from active and interventionist policies within the framework of its import-substitution industrialization (ISI) strategy, but in the 1990s, policies were more passive and liberal: import quotas for assembly plants were removed, the use of inputs from maquiladoras in export models and those destined for the local market were facilitated and FDI in auto parts was promoted. The sectoral policy sought to find convergence with the corporate strategies of the assembly plants. Within NAFTA, tariffs and local content requirements were expected to be reduced to 0 percent by 2004, but also within its trade agreement with the EU, strong reductions were foreseen. Mexico also signed a new agreement with Brazil to guarantee better access to the Brazilian market and vice versa (ECLAC, 2004b).

As a result of these policies and easier access to the North American market, Mexico attracted many investors including some from Asia and Europe. According to UNCTAD (see http://www.unctad.org), 21.2 percent of all manufacturing investment went to the automobile sector between 1999 and 2003, and output grew by 50.1 percent between 1995 and 2000. In the second half of the 1990s, however, there was a stark contrast with the Mercosur countries in terms of the labor market impact. Employment in the Mexican automobile sector rose by 29.3 percent and real wages by 15.6 percent between 1996 and 1999. The main reason for this may be found in the higher level of greenfield investments in Mexico and increased exports to the United States market.

In general, strong investment, attracted by the larger regional market and promoted by sectoral policies, has led to the modernization of the industry, higher productivity, and competitiveness. It has helped the countries adjust to the conditions of a more open market, but their domestic markets still face problems of scale, quality, and price. Even though the market-seeking argument is still relevant for investors, the industry has become more outward oriented, not only in Mexico, which serves as a hub or export platform for sales to North America, but also in Mercosur, where the automobile sector still depends heavily on the economic situation in the region. This industry, which had experienced special and continuous support for decades, has maintained its importance not only for manufacturing, but also for employment and development in general. It also demonstrates that even in a Washington Consensus–inspired environment, specific industrial policies or sectoral policies play an important role in developing the industry and, through this, in Mexico at least during the 1990s, in boosting employment in manufacturing.

Table 5.1   Importance of FDI for Employment in Transnational Corporations, Selected Countries

Country	Transnationality Index	Employment Share (%)
Argentina	16.6	8.0
Brazil	17.2	5.0
Mexico	11.6	7.0
India	2.9	4.1
China	14.4	9.5
France	9.4	4.2

Source: UNCTAD, 2002.

Notes: "Employment share" refers to transnational corporations' employment as a percentage of total employment. The transnationality index, developed by UNCTAD, is a composite index of the following elements: (1) FDI inflows as a percentage of gross fixed capital formation, average for the period 1997–1999; (2) inward FDI stock as a percentage of GDP; (3) value added of foreign affiliates as a percentage of GDP; and (4) employment of foreign affiliates as a percentage of total employment.

workers are employed in sectors of higher labor intensity than in the Latin American countries.[3]

FDI and Domestic Investment

As there was a strong increase in FDI during the 1990s, one important question concerns whether foreign investment crowded out domestic investment. If it has no impact whatsoever, any increase in FDI should be reflected in a rise in total investment. If FDI crowds out investment by domestic companies, the rise in investment should be smaller than the rise in FDI. Recent studies from J. Weeks (2000) and M. Agosin and R. Mayer (2000) show that Asia, the least liberal region toward FDI among developing regions, had the strongest crowding-in effect, while Latin America, with the most far-reaching liberalization of FDI rules in the 1990s, has not benefited from crowding-in effects, but suffered from crowding-out.

This is apparent if we compare overall domestic investment to FDI. Despite the large surge of foreign financing in the 1990s in Argentina, Brazil, and Mexico, overall domestic investment did not increase. In Argentina, domestic investment averaged 17 percent of gross domestic product (GDP) during 1990–2001; in Brazil and Mexico, it was slightly higher, at 20 percent of GDP (see Figure 5.3).[4] Another drawback to the surge in capital inflows was that domestic investment was volatile and became strongly correlated with FDI. This was especially true in Argentina, where fluctuations in foreign participation in investment and total investment-to-GDP had an astoundingly high correlation of 90 percent during 1990–2001. In Brazil and Mexico the relationship was strong, but not as dramatic, with correlations of nearly 60 percent in

Figure 5.3　Investment as Percentage Share of GDP, 1990–2003

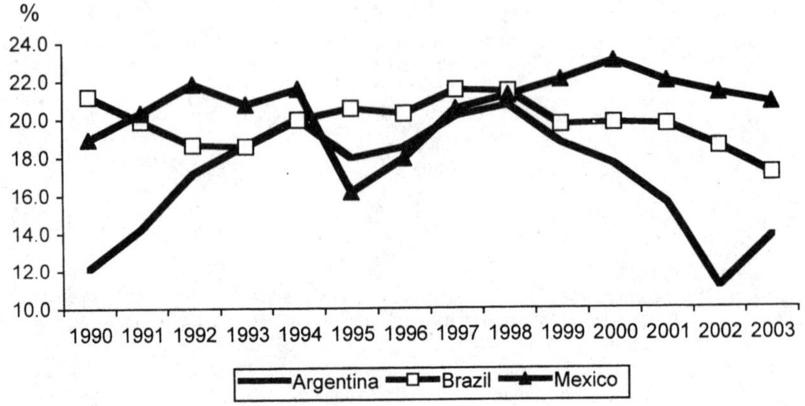

Source: World Bank, *World development indicators*, various years.
Note: Gross fixed capital formation is used as a proxy for domestic investment.

both countries. The high sensitivity to fluctuations in foreign investment also shows a crowding out of national investment during this period.

Reasons for FDI Inflows

The economic determinants of FDI have been classified by standard FDI theories as market-, resource-, and efficiency-seeking. The main considerations of market-seeking investors are market size and per capita income, market growth potential, including access to regional and global markets, country-specific consumer preferences, and the structure of the markets. Generally, market-seeking investment is *horizontal*. It means that a large part of the production chains is based within the country, implying important backward and forward linkages and technological spillovers. The local plant only delivers its products to the local market. *Market-seeking* FDI is still the dominant form in Argentina, Brazil, and Mexico.[5] Economic recovery through macroeconomic stabilization and the potential offered by an enlarged regional market have fostered FDI in manufacturing, especially in automobiles in Mercosur countries, in chemicals in Brazil, and in food, beverages, and tobacco in all three countries. New opportunities in services as a result of deregulation and privatization were also responsible for large FDI flows to finance, retail trade, telecommunications, and, to a certain extent, utilities (UNCTAD, 2004; ECLAC, 2002; see also Box 5.2). In general, market-seeking TNCs also contributed to an increase in intraregional, intrafirm trade.[6] Market-seeking investment can be found in industries of different labor intensity, but the majority of them are of medium labor intensity, such as automobile production in the Mercosur countries.

Box 5.2
Deregulation and Privatization of
State-Owned Enterprises

One of the important drivers of FDI was the privatization of economic assets that were formerly owned and managed by the state. The privatization of state-owned enterprises (SOEs) was expected to reduce the role of the state and in the belief that this would improve the efficiency of the companies concerned. Privatization was mainly concentrated in public utilities (electricity, gas, water, transport), energy (petroleum, natural gas, mining), telecommunications, and banking (ECLAC, 2001; Inter-American Development Bank [IADB], 2002d). Major foreign investors were from Europe, in particular Spain, and the United States (Anuatti-Neto et al., 2003). Privatization was supposed to have a multiplier effect and hence attract investments in other sectors of the economy.

Mexico began divesting government holdings through privatization in the 1980s, with major efforts beginning in 1987, while in Argentina the bulk of sales of state-run enterprises began in 1992 after the introduction of the Convertibility Plan (Correa, 2001; Kosacoff, 2000b). When privatization slowed in Argentina and Mexico during the second half of the 1990s, Brazil's privatization initiative expanded considerably. It overtook Mexico as the largest recipient of FDI in the region, propelled mainly by deregulation with respect to privatization (Ernst, 2005a). Between 1998 and 2000, privatization in Brazil accounted for about 20 percent of its total FDI (UNCTAD, 2001).[7] By 2002, the privatization boom had largely ended, leaving the three countries with few assets left to sell.[8]

While major privatizations have already been completed, their impacts on the economy and on public opinion are still being felt in all three countries. Public opinion polls reveal that an average of 63 percent of Latin Americans feel their countries have not benefited from privatization (Lora and Panizza, 2002). A major reason for this is that in many cases employment suffered. Operational efficiency output and industrial productivity, however, increased in some cases, providing higher profits for the investors (IADB, 2002d; Katz, 2000b). In Argentina, the privatization of the national telecommunications company led to job losses affecting 15,000 workers. In Mexico, on the other hand, the transfer of telecommunications from the public to the private sector was arranged under a framework agreement that guaranteed the protection of the work force, which was the result of an effective social dialogue in this sector. Different labor market institutions thus had different outcomes for labor in the two countries, which clearly illustrates the importance of the institutional aspect (Katz, 2000a). But even the preparations for privatization through rationalization and modernization measures led to job losses, as in the case of the YPF, which reduced its work force from 50,000 in 1989 to 12,000 in 1992 (Ernst, 1996). Another negative and unexpected effect of privatization was that instead of abolishing state monopolies, these were often just replaced by private ones, or at least by private oligopolies, often without a significant increase in efficiency. As a result, in some sectors, such as telecommunications in Argentina, service quality has generally improved, but prices have increased, causing further problems for impoverished workers (IADB, 2002a). But also in some cases, FDI in utilities failed to meet agreed standards (UNCTAD, 2004). Moreover, the expected technological transfer to national companies within the framework of privatization was rather disappointing (Gerchunoff, Greco, and Bondorevsky, 2003).

Resource-seeking investors are mainly attracted by the availability of cheap raw materials. This form of investment has been significant only in Argentina, where it is largely in petroleum, gas, and minerals (ECLAC, 2001), sectors of low labor intensity and thus making a limited contribution to job creation. These TNCs contributed to export growth, and since they imported few products, they had a positive impact on the balance of payments (Chudnovsky and López, 2002).

Efficiency-seeking investors are mainly concerned with the cost of labor or environmental resources and assets, adjusted for productivity, or other input costs such as transport and communications. This form of investment (as well as resource-seeking investment) is in general *vertical*. It means that the parent company locates each stage of production in different countries and regions where it can benefit from differences in factor costs. The production plant primarily produces for the world market or the market of origin of the investor. This has been observed on a large scale only in Mexican manufacturing, mainly in automobiles and auto parts, electronics, and apparel, which generated significant employment during the 1990s due to high levels of investment. US, Japanese, and European Union investors were motivated mainly by an efficiency-seeking strategy aimed at drawing benefits from cheap and appropriately qualified labor and the modernization of production processes to assemble various goods for US and Canadian markets (ECLAC, 2002). Rather than applying exclusively one of these strategies, firms usually combine them and, as the process is dynamic, a market-seeking FDI might in fact become later an efficiency-seeking FDI.

Different strategies have different implications for employment. On the one hand, previous periods have shown that locational advantage is very important for market-seeking FDI, attracting investment flows even under difficult economic and political conditions. This type of investor generally has a particularly strong interest in the efficient functioning of the internal market, including the labor market. Growth of employment and real wages is important in contributing to an increase in internal demand, which implies that the foreign producer finds a growing number of domestic consumers of goods produced for the host-country market. On the other hand, resource- or efficiency-seeking investments aim at tapping the best resources the country has to offer with a view to export goods and services, or with the aim to integrate some production processes into the investor's international production chain. The competitiveness of the exported products, the exchange rate, and external demand are of major interest to this kind of investor.

A new, favorable, rules-based investment framework or set of fiscal incentives was sometimes used as a strong argument for attracting FDI inflows in the early stages (i.e., for the first two to three years after the change in rules) (Christiansen, Oman, and Charlton, 2003). However, this is certainly not a sufficient condition to ensure constant and high FDI inflows. Often, high labor costs are believed to be a strong disincentive for foreign investment inflows. However, in major international indicators[9] that measure the investment attractiveness of a country, absolute labor costs do not appear to be a major variable.[10] In general, they seem to be a minor consideration in investment decisions. Nevertheless, they may be a stronger consideration in specific industries, where labor costs are a major share of production costs. However, the evolution of labor costs does not depend on the labor market alone, but also on other variables, such as exchange rate appreciation. Since 2000, Mexico has seen a strong outflow of maquiladora investment in low-end products such as the garment industry to countries with lower costs, which resulted in job losses of 20 percent in this industry between 2000 and 2004 (Lapper, 2004).

Nevertheless, developing countries play a rather passive role in the distribution of international financial resources; access to these resources is largely determined by exogenous factors. FDI was attracted to Mexico for reasons related to the economic conditions of the US rather than the Mexican economy (Palma, 2003). Investment flows increased significantly during the 1990s because of a favorable international environment, but from 2000 onward the recession in major source countries of FDI had a reverse effect. Second, general trust in developing countries is crucial. The second half of the 1990s saw other developing and emerging countries suffer from the contagion effects of financial crises originating in Mexico, Southeast Asia, and the Russian Federation. Third, the three countries are in competition mainly with other developing countries such as China, especially for efficiency-seeking FDI. Sound domestic policies often contribute, but are not sufficient, to attract FDI (Baumann, 1998, 2001).

Generally, it is not just one element alone that leads to the increase or decline of FDI inflows; it is normally a combination of various factors. And last, but not least, companies have strategic reasons to invest in a country. They might adopt an aggressive strategy to compete against a rival company in order to capture an important share of the market, because the market is strategic and has a high growth potential, or they might use a defensive strategy to defend their market share in the economy where they have invested, sometimes even at high costs in the short run. Often, the mere announcement of a regional trade agreement leads to an increase in FDI in anticipation of an enlarged market and more favorable trading prospects (Lederman, Maloney, and Serven, 2003), even before the actual implementation of the agreement.

In brief, FDI flows remained mainly market-seeking, although efficiency-seeking considerations have been gaining ground, especially in Mexico. In all three countries, privatization, economic recovery, and enlarged regional markets were the major internal attractions for FDI. While FDI contributes to development and better integration into the world market, external factors, which cannot be influenced by the three countries, also played a significant role. The greater dependence on external financing and the lack of influence on investment decisions increase the external vulnerability.

Types of FDI Inflows

Portfolio Versus Productive Investment

Portfolio investment flows are mainly short-term flows, responsive to international differences in interest rates and exchange rates. A high level of portfolio investment does not directly lead to the generation of new productive assets and thus to job creation. It is often guided by a speculative logic that is attracted mainly by the prospect of short-term gains, and not necessarily by economic fundamentals. Portfolio investment helps countries increase capital in their respective economies and may thus provide additional financial resources for economic activities. However, for employment growth it is more interesting to receive investment directly related to productive activities that may lead to the creation of new jobs. In Brazil, until 1994, when the Real Plan was introduced, portfolio investment constituted almost 60 percent of all foreign investment. As a result of effective inflation control, and of an increased interest in productive investment, the share of portfolio investment in total investment then declined to 10 percent, and even to negative figures in 1998, whereas FDI increased considerably in the second half of the 1990s (Baumann, 2001; Baer and Borges Rangel, 2001). In Argentina, portfolio investment reached a peak between 1992 and 1994, followed by a sharp decline (Petrocella and Lousteau, 2001).

In Mexico, short-term capital flows represented 93 percent of all capital inflows in 1993. But they collapsed in 1995 as a consequence of the Tequila crisis (Máttar, Moreno-Brid, and Peres, 2002; Lederman, Maloney, and Serven, 2003). Since then, portfolio investment has not reached the levels of the early 1990s. All three countries saw large inflows of portfolio investments when investors had the most to gain from arbitrage on interest and exchange rate differences. These speculative activities, which gained in importance in the region as a result of globalization of the financial markets, contributed to destabilizing these economies rather than building up productive assets.

Mergers and Acquisitions Versus Greenfield Investment

Greenfield investment concerns investment in new production facilities and installations, which may imply significant job creation. Mergers and acquisitions (M&As), on the other hand, involve two or more already-existing firms being regrouped into one firm, which is not prone to creating new employment. Indeed, M&As often involve rationalization measures leading to job losses. These forms are rarely perfect substitutes, but in developing countries with a more advanced industrial sector, the acquisition of a local firm can represent, to a certain extent, a realistic alternative to greenfield investment (Agosin and Mayer, 2000).

Table 5.2 shows that foreign participation in M&As increased at a higher rate in these three countries than in other developing countries. M&As were frequent in Argentina (82.3 percent of total FDI in 1997–2002), and also in Brazil (58.5 percent). In both countries, M&As have been the main source of FDI growth (Chudnovsky and López, 2002; Ferraz, Kupfer, and Iootty, 2004). Mexico, with 42.6 percent, had a significantly lower level of M&As in total FDI than did the other two countries.[11] Nevertheless, even in Mexico the percentage was higher than that of India and remarkably higher than that of China, which attracted a much higher share of greenfield investments than M&As.

The reasons behind the large number of M&As were the relaxation of regulations relating to foreign portfolio investment and direct investment and the privatization of state assets in Argentina and Brazil, and to a lesser extent in Mexico (UNCTAD, 2000; Garrido, 2001). These factors helped foreign firms gain market access and improve market concentration (market-seeking argument), in particular in attractive services, such as telecommunications, power generation, trade, and financial services (Baumann, 1998; Máttar, Moreno-Brid, and Peres, 2002; Bonelli, 2001; Garrido, 2001). Moreover, foreign firms were actively involved in M&As in automobiles and electronics. Among the ten largest privatization deals involving foreign firms worldwide, two took place in Argentina, the petroleum company YPF and Argentina airports, and two in Brazil, Telebras and Telesp (UNCTAD, 2000). M&As increase in frequency in relation to the level of development of a country and are highest in the industrialized world. Since Argentina, Brazil, and Mexico are generally considered to be among the more industrialized of the developing countries (so-called emerging or middle-income countries), this would also explain the wave of M&As they experienced. The M&As were often part of a strategy to modernize and rationalize existing productive structures such as in the automobile industry or in the banking system.[12] Moreover, given the slow growth environment, investors were not inclined to add new productive capacities.

Table 5.2   Average Share of Mergers and Acquisitions in FDI Inflows, 1991–1996 and 1997–2002, Selected Countries (percentages)

Country	1991–1996	1997–2002
Argentina	38.9	82.3
Brazil	44.1	58.5
Mexico	15.6	42.6
China	2.6	4.4
India	15.3	39.1
Developing countries	17.4	34.5

Source: UNCTAD, 2000.

The general assumption that high levels of FDI will lead to a strong increase in production and employment is misleading. It is not the level of FDI that matters, but the kind of FDI (see Table 5.3). Only strong vertical greenfield FDI in the maquiladora sector created significantly new production plants and employment. However, it did not have a multiplier effect on the rest of the economy. Major FDI flows did not lead to the establishment of new production units; rather, they merely resulted in a change of ownership through privatization and M&As. Rationalization and modernization measures were often the consequence of, or sometimes a preliminary step prior to, a change of ownership, which resulted in job losses, but also, and in general, contributed to a rise in competitiveness. Market-seeking investment is still an important motive for FDI in all three economies, but it did not help create much employment in the 1990s, mainly because of rationalization measures in capital-intensive and some service activities. However, recent reforms could place these industries in a better position for future development and for exporting outside the region.

Sectoral Evolution of FDI and Its Labor Market Impact

A major concern for a host country should not just be the volume of FDI it may receive, but in which sectors it enters and what benefits it brings to the domestic economy in terms of employment and wages (for more details, see Ernst, 2005a). FDI inflows during the 1990s are compared with output and employment growth, wage growth, and the labor intensity of specific sectors. Labor

Table 5.3   Types of Foreign Investment and Their Dimension and Importance for Employment

Investment	Importance of Investment for Employment	Importance of Foreign Investment Inflows		
		Argentina	Brazil	Mexico
Portfolio	Insignificant	Medium	Medium	Medium
Foreign direct investment	Medium	High	High	High
Privatization	Mixed	High	Medium	Insignificant
Horizontal investment	High	High	High	Medium
Vertical investment	Medium	Insignificant	Insignificant	High
Mergers and acquisitions	Mixed	High	High	Medium
Greenfield investment	High	Medium	Medium	High
Resource-seeking	Insignificant	High	Insignificant	Insignificant
Market-seeking	Medium	High	High	High
Efficiency-seeking	Medium-high	Insignificant	Insignificant	High

Note: "Importance of investment for employment" refers to the importance of this type of investment for the creation of new employment.

intensity of economic growth is simply defined as employment growth divided by output growth.[13] In Brazil, for example, aircraft manufacturing has the lowest employment-output coefficient, while ship repairing has the highest.

Figure 5.4 illustrates sectoral distribution of FDI since the 1990s. It shows that Argentina is the only country with sizable investments in primary resources, with a share of 37 percent of accumulated FDI flows in 1990–2002 and an increase of FDI inflows of over 900 percent between 1993 and 2000.[14] This is mainly due to the creation of a special regime for that sector (Petrocella and Lousteau, 2001), its deregulation and privatization, and recent oil discoveries.

The service sector received the most FDI inflows in the 1990s, mainly in Argentina and Brazil. Major FDI inflows to Argentina and Brazil, as in Mexico in the 1980s, went to utilities (electricity, gas, and water) as a result of deregulation and the privatization of state-run companies.[15] These sectors traditionally are of low labor intensity, and this was exacerbated by rationalization measures. Another important receiver of FDI inflows was the financial sector, which was liberalized during the 1990s and opened to foreign capital. This sector experienced a large number of M&As instead of greenfield investments. Moreover, bank restructuring also led to rationalization measures that resulted in labor-shedding. All these reasons explain why high FDI inflows were related to disappointing employment growth in services.

FDI in manufacturing also saw a boom in the 1990s, even though its share in the total FDI flows fell slightly.[16] Nevertheless, since 2002, the share of manufacturing FDI has started to rise again (UNCTAD, 2004). Within the manufacturing sector, as shown in Table 5.4, the capital-intensive industries, promoted

Figure 5.4   Sectoral Distribution of FDI: Share of Sum Values, 1992–2002

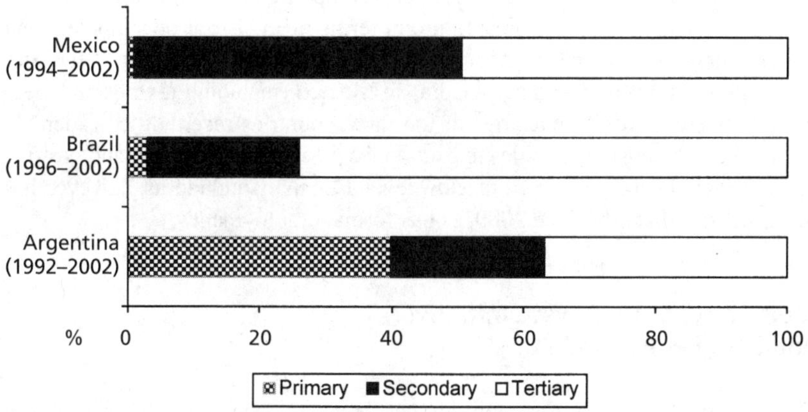

Source: UNCTAD, FDI Country Profiles (http://www.unctad.org/).

Table 5.4   FDI Inflows and Their Employment and Wage Impact by Sector, 1993–2000

Sectoral FDI	Argentina	Brazil	Mexico
Primary sector	Very strong	Insignificant	Insignificant
Employment impact	Insignificant	Insignificant	Insignificant
Services	Very strong	Very strong	Very strong
Employment impact	Positive	Negative	Positive
Industry	Strong	Strong	Very strong
Employment impact	Positive	Negative	Positive
Wage impact	Positive	Slightly positive	Slightly positive
Automobiles	Strong	Strong	Very strong
Employment impact	Negative	Negative	Positive
Wage impact	Positive	Positive	(not available)
Labor intensity	Medium	Medium	Low
Chemicals	Very strong	Very strong	Strong
Employment impact	Positive	Positive	Negative
Wage impact	Positive	Insignificant	Positive
Labor intensity	Low to medium	Low to medium	Low to high
Food, beverages, and tobacco	Strong	Very strong	Strong
Employment impact	Positive	Negative	Negative
Wage impact	Positive	Insignificant	Insignificant
Labor intensity	Low/medium	Low to high	Low to high

through the ISI period, mainly automobiles and chemical products as well as food, beverages, and tobacco, received major FDI inflows. All these industries are characterized on average by low to medium labor intensity. The employment results were rather mixed, but these sectors experienced strong growth in productivity and a positive evolution of real wages.[17] Industries formerly promoted during the ISI period and benefiting from sectoral agreements maintained their importance in the region. Their increasing competitiveness and export orientation are a positive sign for their future in terms of industrial development and employment once the period of modernization and consolidation has been successfully completed. The maquiladoras in Mexico (including textiles and electronics) were the only industries of the three countries receiving considerable FDI in labor-intensive activities to experience positive employment and positive growth of real wages, albeit from a low level. FDI in maquiladoras, however, has declined significantly since 2000, as has formal employment.

Less State, More Private Initiative: Industrial Policy and FDI

The role of the state in the economy has changed, from actively protecting a large part of the domestic productive sector to creating the environment for private activities. Now the state is expected to provide safety nets for workers exposed to the rough winds of private business. The state's role is to guide economic activities, providing the productive sector with information, advisory services, and other forms of support.[18]

The industrial policies of the 1990s tended to offer favorable conditions to enterprises to promote industrial development and international competitiveness. The main goal of this new policy was to attract investment through a new, more liberal framework of rules and priority given to macroeconomic stabilization (see Chapter 3). An enlarged regional market through regional agreements and trade liberalization was seen to enhance competitiveness, quality, and productivity in the economy. Sectoral or vertical policies lost their legitimacy, with some exceptions such as the automobile industry, and were more difficult to implement within the new ideological framework. Import protection was not considered in the new outward-oriented development strategy, and fiscal restraints did not leave much space for significant state interventions. Horizontal policies[19] were implemented to deal with market failures through financial instruments, such as credits for capital goods in Argentina, textiles in Brazil, and cinematography in Mexico, but also through the provision of fiscal incentives in activities such as forestry in Argentina, electronics in Brazil, and publishing in Mexico. However, in Brazil, much more than in Argentina and Mexico, government policy has consistently sought to actively promote industrialization (Bonelli, 2001), even though the role of the state has diminished as a consequence of deregulation, privatization of public enterprises, and trade liberalization. Nevertheless, Brazil dismantled the protection of its industry at a slower pace and to a more limited extent, and it was more cautious in privatizing public companies.

At the regional level, NAFTA has adopted a fairly liberal stance; it does not envisage anything similar to a common industrial policy, besides the maquiladora regime, which was introduced in the 1960s (see Box 5.3). Mercosur, however, does not have much more to offer in this regard. Little progress has been made in the field of harmonization of industrial and technological policies. The Grupo Mercado Común (Common Market Group), which has a working subgroup (number 7) on industry,[20] has not yet defined a global industrial and technological strategy for the subregion. In general, the lack of effective tools for the coordination of industrial policies has hindered the potential impact of sectoral arrangements to coordinate industrial restructuring, such as in textiles or chemicals. However, specific sectoral agreements of relevance have been signed for the automobile, iron and steel, and sugar industries. Facilitating the creation of binational enterprises *(empresas bi-nacionales)* between Brazil and Argentina certainly had a positive, but not strong impact, especially in the first half of the 1990s.

In all three countries, active state intervention through vertical industrial policies was largely given up in the 1990s, with some exceptions, mainly the maquiladoras and the automobile industry. Macroeconomic stabilization as

Box 5.3
Mexico's Maquiladoras

The maquiladoras in Mexico are perhaps the most outstanding example of a proactive industrial policy during the 1990s, as they had a significant impact on the evolution of the manufacturing sector. In 1980, just 14 percent of Mexico's exports could be attributed to the maquiladoras (Buitelaar and Padilla Ruth Urrutia, 1999), but by 2002, this had increased to 50 percent, representing earnings of about US$80 billion—larger than Brazil's total exports (Palma, 2003; ECLAC, 2004c). In the 1980s, maquiladora output accounted for 10 percent of GDP, compared with 30 percent by the end of the 1990s (Dussel Peters, 2003).

Mexican policy to promote maquiladora-style assembly plants[21] is not new; it was launched much earlier, in 1965, as an industrial promotion program for the regions bordering the United States (Buitelaar and Padilla Ruth Urrutia, 1999), and was then extended to other areas of the country in 1971. Nevertheless, maquiladoras experienced a boom after the sharp devaluation of the peso as a result of the Tequila crisis, but also due to the creation of NAFTA. The major motivation to invest in this type of assembly plant in Mexico was cheap and abundant labor as well as geographical, historical, cultural, and institutional proximity to the United States. Maquiladoras mainly exist in electronics, car accessories, automobiles, apparel, and textiles. They were the principal source of export and production growth in manufacturing during the 1990s. In addition, they were mainly responsible for the surge in intraindustrial and even intrafirm trade between US firms and their branches in Mexico. The technological level of final products is relatively high.[22] Nevertheless, more than 80 percent of the exports depend on imported inputs, considered temporary imports (Dussel Peters, 2003). This strong dependence on imported inputs means that the sector still adds very limited value to the goods being produced. Thus gross output per employee has increased, but productivity, measured as value added per employee, has not.

This can be explained largely by the current maquiladora promotion scheme, which creates disincentives for the domestic production of intermediary products. Neither import taxes (up to 20 percent) nor a value-added tax (VAT) of 15 percent are imposed on imported goods under the regulation, and the profit tax has been reduced significantly. US companies are taxed only on the value-added component of the imported assembled goods, so that there is no incentive to establish linkages with Mexican industries, as domestic companies are subject to a VAT. This implies a price advantage of up to 50 percent for imported goods, which both positively and negatively affects domestic suppliers, and those outside the maquiladoras (Dussel Peters, 2003). The domestic suppliers who need imported inputs for their production benefit from the lower prices, but other domestic suppliers face tougher competition, as they do not get the same benefits. Thus, despite the enormous increase in production, the maquila economy continues to have few linkages with the rest of the Mexican economy.

Employment in the maquiladoras increased at an average annual rate of 13 percent between 1993 and 1999. As a result, employment tripled, from 446,000 employees in 1990 to almost 1.3 million in 2000, representing 5.6 percent of total employment. Manufacturing of electrical and electronic components accounted for 34 percent of employment in 1997, down from 40 percent in 1988. Automobiles maintained a constant share of 20 percent, while apparel increased its share from 9 percent in 1988 to 20 percent in 1997 (Buitelaar and Padilla Ruth Urrutia, 1999). Wages of maquila-dominated industries

continues

Box 5.3   Continued

are still significantly lower than the wage share of traditional ISI industries, even though the maquiladoras are closing the gap with above-average growth rates over the past decade. Moreover, maquiladora growth accounts for 50 percent of the increase in skilled labor (Lederman, Maloney, and Serven, 2003), as some plants use more skilled workers and provide more training for current employees (Carillo, 2003). The tremendous growth in the maquiladoras also caused large-scale migration, in particular from the southern parts of the country to plants located along the border with the United States.

A disturbing fact is the sharp decline of the maquiladoras since 2000 due to increased competition from China and other Central American and Caribbean countries (UNCTAD, 2003b). Between June 2001 and July 2002, 19,545 maquila firms either left the country for another country, such as China or El Salvador, or closed down (Palma, 2003). The number of enterprises fell from 3,700 to 2,800 and the number of workers by 220,000 between 2000 and 2004 (UNCTAD, 2004). Their main advantages, cheap labor and proximity to the United States market, have proved to be rather fragile in terms of attracting FDI inflows.

Briefly, the maquila program succeeded in creating employment with a relatively high share of female workers, though the quality of the jobs is generally low and wages have been low but increasing. Moroever, the maquiladora industries are characterized by low labor standards (Alarcón and Zepeda, 2004), and have been noted to obstruct unionization and violate existing labor laws (Altenburg, Qualman, and Weller, 2001).

The future of the maquila economy is tied to its ability to remain internationally competitive without relying on "low-road" development practices. To this end, second- and third-generation maquiladoras have recently moved away from simple assembly activities to manufacturing and knowledge-intensive design of products. In particular, the television and the auto-parts industries, with firms like Sony, Delphi, or Valeo, have moved toward high value-added, technology-intensive activities, implying an important component of research and development (Dussel Peters, 2003). This "high-road" competitive strategy, albeit involving only a limited number of industries so far, has the potential of going beyond low-cost competition and developing greater linkages with the domestic economy through more vertical production activities in the country (including design, development, and quality control).The rise in high-tech production also caused a higher demand for skilled workers (Moreno-Fontes, 2004).

well as trade and financial liberalization were the main elements of the outward-oriented strategy that shaped manufacturing in Argentina, Brazil, and Mexico.

Conclusion

The new outward-oriented development strategy of the 1990s and the increased globalization of production worldwide led to an FDI boom in the region. Many economists and decisionmakers believe that the opening of a country to international investment and trade will automatically improve trade and growth performance, but the reality of Latin America proved the opposite. In Brazil and Mexico, increased FDI has not stimulated total domestic investment. In Argentina, FDI had a positive impact on total investment, mainly in the second half of the 1990s, but it was volatile. Total domestic investment in 2002 was close to its level in 1990.

The impact of large FDI inflows on employment was also disappointing, which can mainly be explained by the form of investment. Most foreign investment went into services as a consequence of domestic market opening and privatization. A smaller share, particularly in Argentina and Brazil, went into the production of manufacturing tradables. Service FDI mainly came in the form of M&As, the result of privatization of public utility companies or bank restructuring, which did not create new productive assets; instead, they tended to use existing ones. In addition, decades of protection led to a slack labor force, which was reduced during the privatization and modernization process of the 1990s, so that the overall impact on employment was minimal or even negative.

Economic liberalization led to increased competitiveness in the manufacturing sector, the second most important destination of FDI inflows. As a consequence, restructuring strategies to increase productivity often involved rationalization measures and labor-shedding as in the service sector. In addition, FDI mainly went into low to medium labor-intensive sectors. Already-present manufacturing TNCs made little, if any, contribution to employment creation. Even though those "old" capital-intensive industries, such as automobiles and chemicals, were major recipients of FDI, these sectors experienced a decline in employment in the 1990s. Nevertheless, they experienced a rise in productivity and competitiveness as well as a further export orientation of their products, which are promising signs for the future. This trend shows that the maintenance of targeted sectoral support by the public sector to this industry, even during a period inspired by liberal policies, was crucial and helpful in the restructuring process. Moreover, wages in FDI-dominated sectors rose above average in the manufacturing sector, especially with regard to skilled workers, which was mainly related to increases in labor productivity.

In Mexico, contrary to Argentina and Brazil, the employment situation is much more favorable, as strong manufacturing FDI generated many new jobs. This positive trend, however, can be mainly attributed to the maquiladoras, which benefited from strong greenfield investments in labor-intensive industries. The maquiladora sector also experienced above-average wage rises, even though their level is in general still below the manufacturing average. However, their comparative advantage is rather fragile, as evidenced by net FDI outflows since 2000 and a subsequent decline of formal employment. FDI is also meant to create forward and backward linkages with domestic firms. In ISI industries, some linkages have been created, but mainly before the 1990s. Nevertheless, strong capital and import inflows caused an increased substitution of national suppliers in favor of international suppliers even in those sectors dominated by horizontal investment. Mexico benefited mainly from new vertical FDI in the assembly plants located on the border with the United States, which developed very few links with the rest of the economy.

Finally, the new outward-oriented strategy and the reduction of the role of the state as an active economic player, especially with regard to industrial policy, failed to attract enough FDI and to provide a significant contribution to employment. Strong foreign investment flows have also had the negative side effect of hampering domestic investment, particularly the competitiveness and investment potential of SMEs and micro enterprises, which are important employers. Moreover, the countries had a limited influence on FDI inflows, with investment decision depending on the country of origin, mainly OECD countries, and the investment decision of its companies. For example, FDI inflows decreased in 2000 in the region because of the recession in OECD countries and not because of a deteriorating investment environment in the three countries. FDI is crucial for the development of the region, for the integration into the world market and for employment, but so is domestic investment of local firms. A good balance between both has to be found in Argentina, Brazil, and Mexico.

Appendix Table 5.A   Average Wage in Specific Product Categories as Share of Average Wage in Total Manufacturing, 1993–2000

Argentina	1993	1999
Food, beverages, and tobacco	0.56	0.93
Chemicals and chemical products	0.40	1.94
Motor vehicles and other transport equipment	0.85	1.17
Brazil	1996	1999
Food, beverages, and tobacco	0.78	0.79
Chemicals and chemical products	2.25	2.29
Machinery and equipment	1.34	1.29
Electrical and electronic equipment	2.21	2.91
Motor vehicles and other transport equipment	1.69	1.87
Mexico	1994	2000
Food, beverages, and tobacco	0.56	0.58
Chemicals and chemical products	0.92	1.05
Motor vehicles and other transport equipment	0.81	0.82
Electrical and electronic equipment	0.55	0.57
Machinery and equipment	0.61	0.68
Other manufacturing	0.44	0.39

Source: Author calculations based on UNIDO, Indstat4, Revision 3; average share of wages per worker based on current domestic currency.

Notes: Real average annual wage growth in total manufacturing per worker in constant US$: Argentina, 7.5 percent; Brazil, –3.1 percent; Mexico, –5.1 percent. An increase in a share value can therefore mean an above-average and positive wage growth (e.g., motor vehicles in Brazil with 1.7 percent, compared to an average of –3.1 percent), or a below-average wage fall (e.g., food, beverages, and tobacco in Brazil with –1.0 percent, compared with the average of –3.1 percent). Both evolutions will lead to a rising wage share of this industry in total wages in manufacturing.

Appendix Table 5.B   Efficiency-Seeking, Resource-Seeking, and Market-Seeking Investment by Sector, 1990s

Sector	Efficiency-Seeking	Country	Resource-Seeking	Country	Market-Seeking	Country
Primary			Gas/petroleum	Argentina, Brazil		
			Minerals	Argentina		
Manufacturing	Automobile	Mexico			Automobile	Argentina, Brazil
	Electronics	Mexico			Agro-industry, food	Argentina, Brazil, Mexico
	Wearing apparel	Mexico			Chemical products	Brazil
Services					Finances	Argentina, Brazil, Mexico
					Telecommunications	Argentina, Brazil, Mexico
					Electrical energy	Argentina, Brazil
					National gas distribution	Argentina, Brazil, Mexico
					Retail trade	Argentina, Brazil, Mexico

Source: ECLAC, 2002.

Notes

1. The exceptional jump in 2001 can be explained by the merger of the Mexican bank, Banamex, with the American bank, Citigroup.

2. For more information, see Ernst, 2005a.

3. India, for example, has a low TNI combined with a high employment share, while the opposite is true for Brazil.

4. In contrast, in East Asia during the 1970s and 1980s, investment-to-GDP ratios exceeded 30 percent, resulting in sustained high growth rates (ILO, 2004a). In order for investment to be beneficial for development, it must not just be high, but also be continued. Typically, investment-to-GDP ratios should be in the 25 percent range for middle-income developing countries for an extended time period, five years at minimum (UNCTAD, 2003b).

5. See Annex Table 5.B.

6. See, for example, Chudnovsky and López, 2002, for Argentina.

7. Between 1991 and July 2001, the Brazilian federal and state governments collected US$ 67.9 billion in revenue from privatization.

8. However, the sale of the large Mexican insurer Aseguradora in 2002, to the US company MetLife for US$92 million, was a notable exception (see ECLAC, 2001).

9. UNCTAD's Inward FDI Potential Index Ranking is based largely on structural economic factors, such as GDP per capita, real GDP growth, inward FDI stock, exports as a percentage of GDP, number of telephone main lines and mobiles, commercial energy use, research and development expenditure, students in tertiary education, and country risk. According to the FDI Confidence Index of the Global Business Policy Council, the factors that have recently had the greatest effect on Brazilian FDI inflows are: (1) macroeconomic stability (69 percent); (2) consistent government support for promarket policies (53 percent); (3) regional stability (48 percent); (4) political and economic recovery in the Mercosur countries (31 percent); (5) progress on the Free Trade Agreement of the Americas (24 percent); (6) recovery of the US economy (22 percent); (7) security reforms (22 percent); (8) sustained market-based policies (13 percent); and (9) privatization of key industries (13 percent).

10. For more information, see Chudnovsky and López, 2002; Baumann, 1998; IADB, 2002b; Blomström and Kokko, 1997.

11. See also Dussel Peters, 2000b.

12. R. Bielschowsky (1999) refers to a "minicycle" of modernization, especially between 1995 and 1997. See also Posthuma, 2004.

13. Data, measured in local currency, concern the period 1996–1999 for the manufacturing sector in all three countries. The period is relatively short because of the lack of comparable and available data for a longer time period.

14. In terms of FDI stock, the share of investment in primary resources increased from 19.4 percent in 1992 to 34.5 percent in 2002.

15. In Argentina, for example, 67 percent of all capital involved in privatization came from abroad. Author calculations based on Kulfas, Porta, and Ramos, 2002.

16. The share of the secondary sector in total FDI stock declined in Argentina, from 37 percent in 1992 to 28 percent in 2001, and in Brazil, from 69.1 percent in 1990 to 33.7 percent in 2000, as FDI in services increased strongly. However, over the period 1990–2001 it saw a growth rate of 222 percent in Argentina, and of 34.9 percent in Brazil. As for FDI in services in Argentina, there were net outflows resulting from the crisis in 2002.

17. See Annex Table 5.A. For the 1990s, it reveals a general trend toward an increase in relative wages in industries that benefited most from FDI. A major contributory factor

was the productivity rise in those industries as a result of a greater use of modern machinery, but labor-shedding also played an important role (e.g., chemical industry).

18. Trade liberalization is not an industrial policy, but it nevertheless profoundly affected the industrial sector, as the latter became directly exposed to international competition and to international rules.

19. Horizontal industrial policies include a large set of trade, fiscal, and financial tools, targeted in general to the whole economy. They are supposed to have a "neutral" effect on the domestic economy, whereas vertical industrial policies are considered to be selective (see ECLAC, 2004b).

20. It looks at issues such as promotion of science and technology, encouraging quality and productivity, and harmonization of measures promoting specific sectors, as well as the respect of property rights.

21. Programa de Importación Temporal para la Exportación (PITEX; Temporary Imports for Exports Program).

22. In Mexico, technological upgrading was observed as a consequence of FDI inflows, especially in automobile assembly, auto parts, and nonelectrical machinery, which have been able to produce medium- to high-technological goods for export. However, in many cases national content was rather low and there was no integration with the rest of the economy. Technology and productivity spillovers to national companies did not take place (Zarsky and Gallagher, 2004). In Mercosur countries, a certain level of technology transfer and diffusion was observed in automobile production (Blomström and Kokko, 1997), but in general the technological specialization index fell in Argentina, from 0.12 in 1977–1980 to 0.07 in 1995, and in Brazil, from 0.25 to 0.23 over the same period, partly due to the disengagement of the state (Máttar, Moreno-Brid, and Peres, 2002; de Abreu Campanario and Muniz da Silva, 2003).

6

Employment Effects of Labor Market Regulations and Policies

The structural reforms undertaken by Argentina, Brazil, and Mexico beginning in the late 1980s and 1990s were far-reaching, covering a wide range of policies that formed part of the so-called Washington Consensus. Within these policy debates, both in Washington and in Latin America it was argued that for the economic reforms to be successful, it would be necessary for labor markets to be deregulated as well, so that firms could adapt to the changing competitive environment. This view, espoused by the World Bank in its 1995 World Development Report, *Workers in an Integrating World,* led to much reflection and debate by governments and social partners of the region, and in some countries led to significant overhaul of their labor legislation, particularly regarding employment protection regulation and the use of temporary or trial contracts.

Flexibilization of constraints, in particular, giving employers greater autonomy regarding the hiring and firing of labor and controlling labor costs, was among the reforms deemed necessary for the success of the new economic model. These labor reforms were expected to improve adaptability of enterprises to the new environment and thus external competitiveness and employment performance. The nature and scope of the labor reforms were determined by the importance that governments assigned to labor-cost cuts as a mechanism to adjust to countries' international repositioning, influence from opponent trade unions and political parties, pressure from employer and international financial institutions in favor of the proposed changes, and finally, the nature and degree of protection guaranteed to workers by preexisting laws.

The adverse labor market outcomes of the economic reforms, namely increased unemployment, informality, and poverty, in turn called for state intervention via employment and income maintenance programs—forms of state

This chapter is based on a background paper by Adriana Marshall, *Labour market policies and regulations in Argentina, Brazil and Mexico: Programmes and impacts,* Employment strategy paper, no. 2004/13 (Geneva, ILO, 2004), http://www.ilo.org.

intervention that had little precedent in the region. These new programs were to be modeled, in part, by the well-developed passive and active labor market policies that existed in Europe. This chapter examines some aspects of the labor policies implemented since 1990 in Argentina, Brazil, and Mexico, and the employment and unemployment compensation programs existing in these countries in the early 2000s, as well as certain of their labor market effects. Regarding labor regulations, emphasis is placed on employment protection reforms and on trends in nonwage labor costs.

Labor Market Regulations

The Debate on Labor Market Regulations

Labor markets are governed by the labor laws of a country, which are in turn influenced by international agreements, particularly International Labour Organization (ILO) conventions and regional agreements, if they exist (see Box 6.1). Collective bargaining agreements, custom, and practices also play a role in governing labor markets. Traditionally, the purpose of labor regulations has been to protect workers, viewed as the weaker party in employer–employee relationships. With economic opening in the 1990s, labor regulations have been modified—particularly in Argentina, but also in Brazil—with the aim of making the labor market more responsive to the economic challenges of globalization.

Reforms of labor market regulations in Latin America in the 1990s were motivated by the belief that constraints on employers' freedom to hire, use,

---

Box 6.1
Labor Market Provisions in Mercosur and NAFTA

Though the Mercado Común del Sur (Mercosur; Southern Cone Common Market) and the North American Free Trade Agreement (NAFTA) were founded principally as free trade agreements, they also contain labor market provisions, including institutional and legal arrangements that address the social dimension of integration.

Following the 1994 Protocol of Ouro Preto, Mercosur established several labor market bodies with important consultative functions. A technical-political tripartite organ that meets regularly is the Working Subgroup No. 10, previously No. 11 (ILO, 1999). It designs, manages, and implements labor guidelines and laws, providing proposals and recommendations for their harmonization among member countries. The main topics are labor regulations, labor costs, social security, occupational safety and health, professional training, migration, and labor inspection. Mercosur also convenes regular meetings of the labor ministers, thus acknowledging the importance of labor market topics for regional integration.

continues

Box 6.1 Continued

Mercosur has advanced in defining a minimum level of basic labor rights with important support from the member states. The Socio-labor Declaration (Declaración Sociolaboral), inspired by ILO conventions and the ILO Declaration on Fundamental Principles and Rights at Work, was adopted in 1998 and asserts basic labor rights of workers and employers such as freedom of association, the right to strike, elimination of forced labor, special protection of minors, nondiscrimination, and equal treatment with regard to labor market issues (ILO, 2003a). The Socio-labor Commission of Mercosur emerged from the declaration to promote the fundamental rights and improve their monitoring. To increase the involvement of employer and worker organizations in the integration process, the Consultative Social and Economic Forum was created. It has consultative functions and can give recommendations to the Grupo Mercado Común (GMC), the executive organ of Mercosur (ILO, 2003a). Member countries also approved the Multilateral Treaty of Social Security, which unifies existing bilateral treaties and consolidates the principle of equal treatment among nationals from each of the member countries. A recent milestone for labor rights was the Declaration of Mercosur, adopted at the Regional Employment Conference in Buenos Aires in 2004, which states that decent work should be at the center of Mercosur's development strategy.

NAFTA's social and political integration process is less ambitious, and consequently its sociolabor dimension is more modest. The North American Agreement on Labor Cooperation (NAALC) is the labor cooperation agreement, adopted on January 1, 1994, together with NAFTA. Its main objectives are to improve working conditions and living standards, to promote specific labor principles, to promote transparency in the administration of labor laws, and to stimulate cooperation on labor issues. In its introduction, the NAALC states that the protection of basic worker rights will generate competitive strategies of high productivity, thus providing a favorable environment for work and human development. The NAALC is also expected to ensure the enforcement of existing labor protections, but because it recognizes the sovereignty of countries over their labor legislation, there is no explicit mention of what provisions labor laws should entail. There is therefore no reference to common "minimum standards" (Martinez, 2004b). Moreover, the NAALC does not directly reference international labor laws, though it recognizes the basic elements of the ILO Declaration on Fundamental Principles and Rights at Work. However, the NAALC fails to guarantee free movement of labor and refers to national legislation on this issue.

The NAALC also lacks a permanent consultative body on labor issues. Though there is a commission on labor cooperation, in which the three labor ministers participate, it does not have permanent jurisdiction. Nevertheless, the NAALC can invoke economic sanctions—the suppression of the benefits of NAFTA—in the case of the noncompliance of the specific labor laws of the countries.

In sum, Mercosur has strengthened its labor provisions and institutions to better promote social and labor issues. Still, the Mercosur labor institutions lack decision-making power, making it difficult to address employment challenges such as regional differences in development, informality and poverty, as well as sectoral and geographical employment shifts. Though the NAALC has helped raise awareness and understanding of member countries' labor regulations, it is limited in its ability to guarantee labor rights and the improvement of working conditions and living standards.

and dismiss labor were adverse to employment, productivity, and ultimately economic performance. These views were akin to the debate in the OECD, where income maintenance programs were blamed for reducing the work incentive, contributing to the increase of unemployment, and being adverse to productivity growth. Questions surrounding the effect of labor protection systems on employment thus became the subject of intense debates, generating numerous academic and policy studies, dealing mainly with Europe and the United States. These controversies have since been reproduced with reference to Latin America.

Perhaps the most debated area has been the virtues and drawbacks of employment protection (i.e., regulations on contracts and dismissal). It has been argued that strong protection (stringent legal restrictions on the free utilization of individual and collective dismissals and of temporary contracts) inhibits employment growth and intensifies unemployment by stimulating labor substitution, by deterring employers from recruiting at times of economic expansion, and by fostering segmentation between the employed and the unemployed. It has also been blamed for encouraging the use of overtime and the growth of precarious and informal employment. Moreover, because stronger protection can moderate the fear of unemployment, these regulations have been held to undermine the work effort and collective labor discipline, and strengthen collective resistance to technological and organizational labor-saving innovation, all with adverse effects on productivity growth.

Seen more positively, it has also been argued that constraints on dismissals help to restrain unemployment growth during recessions and to stabilize labor demand in the longer term; that they encourage labor-saving innovation, stimulating productivity growth, helping to secure workers' commitment to enterprise success, inducing employers to provide and workers to acquire firm-specific training and skills, and favoring cooperative relations at the workplace. Empirical research has failed to settle the debate, as the findings have been ambiguous and often contradictory. With reference to Latin America, although several authors (Vega Ruíz, 2001) have dealt with the nature of regulations and reforms, empirical studies of the outcomes of labor regulations and labor policy reform have been sparse. Among these, A. Marshall (1994, 1996b) concludes that, although regulations affect employer practices (recruitment and dismissal), and in some cases worker behavior, this has had no effect on employment and productivity performances, whereas J. Heckman and C. Pagés (2004), by contrast, contend that job security provisions reduce employment and increase inequality. The effects of schemes of income maintenance for the unemployed have also been debated along similar lines of the deliberations in the OECD countries, even though the programs in Latin America were only incipient.

In relation to Latin America, however, it has often been argued that, despite the stringency of labor regulations and the constraints they may impose on employers, their impact is reduced by (1) high noncompliance, and (2) the tendency of workers to infrequently contest employer decisions, via the judiciary system, however arbitrary these decisions might be, because of discouragement due to extended lags in the labor courts, insufficient knowledge of protective regulations, or weak unions. One indication of the degree of noncompliance is the frequency of precarious wage employment relationships, which reflects how widespread "flexibilizing" practices are in spite of legal constraints. For this reason as well, it has been argued that generalized noncompliance and bottlenecks in applying the laws undermine the efficacy of legal labor protection; thus the laws should be made more compatible with the reality of evasion. In other words, fewer constraints could stimulate compliance.

Employment Protection Systems and Nonwage Labor Costs

At the end of the 1980s there existed some diversity in employment protection regimes among Argentina, Brazil, and Mexico, specifically concerning restrictions on dismissals and temporary contracts. Yet other areas of labor regulation were quite similar, such as regulations on working hours or maternity protection. Furthermore, there were small differences in the incidence of nonwage labor costs. Prior to 1988, protection was somewhat weaker in Brazil, but this was redressed that same year with reforms that improved layoff compensation. In Mexico, labor protection was in general stronger.

Of the three countries, the labor market reforms aimed at greater flexibility in the labor market during the 1990s were drastic only in Argentina. Still, by the early 2000s the changes had been partially reversed. In Brazil, as a result of the changes to improve protection established in the 1988 constitution,[1] some piecemeal reforms were made during the 1990s that relaxed constraints on the regulation of individual contracts. In Mexico, the many reform proposals emanating from the government, political parties, and employer organizations were never implemented.

Argentina. Reforms pursuing "external flexibility" and labor cost reductions progressed steadily in Argentina, even if there was partial withdrawal during elections or owing to negotiations with trade unions. In relation to employment protection, two stages may be identified: one, between 1991 and 1998, during which reforms in the direction of "flexibilization" were systematically deepened; and a second, from 1998 to 2000, during which progress was less unidirectional. Reforms dealt with temporary contracts and their associated social security costs (1991, 1995, 2000), dismissals (1991, 1998), and nonwage labor costs in general (1994). Officially, the rationale behind them was that, by facilitating flexible contracts and dismissals and by reducing nonwage labor costs, the reforms would stimulate employment creation as well as reduce noncompliance and precarious employment relations. From 1991 to 2004, eight reforms were pursued:

1. The Employment Law (Ley Nacional de Empleo) of 1991 reinstated a ceiling on layoff compensation, at three times the level of monthly earnings, and introduced "promoted" temporary employment contracts. The contracts were exempt, partially or totally, from payment of social security contributions, but subject to several restrictions. Of the four promoted contracts created by the 1991 law, three were targeted at specific groups. First, an employment promotion contract addressed unemployed workers, including those dismissed from the public sector due to administrative rationalization. It exempted employers from paying 50 percent of payroll taxes for the retirement and family allowance schemes, the national employment fund, and the healthcare scheme for the retired. Second, a youth promotion contract offered job experience to young workers (up to twenty-four years of age) with technical or professional skills. Third, a skills promotion contract was targeted at unskilled young workers looking for their first job. Under both the second and third contracts, workers were exempt from payroll taxes, with the exception of contributions to the healthcare scheme and the national employment fund. The fourth promoted contract was not targeted; rather, it allowed the use of temporary contracts for new employment. Its tax rebate was equivalent to 50 percent of social security contributions, the same contributions as in the employment promotion contract.

2. An across-the-board rebate of social security payroll taxes was decreed in 1993.[2] The reduction applied to employer contributions to the retirement scheme and the healthcare systems for active and retired workers, to family allowances, and to the employment fund. As a result of the decline in payroll taxes, government forgone revenues in 1996 were equivalent to 1.2 percent of gross domestic product (GDP) (Ministerio de Trabajo, Empleo y Seguridad Social [MTSS], 1996). According to L. Beccaria and P. Galin (2002), the average rate of employer contributions declined regularly until 1998–1999 and then rose again in 2001–2002.

3. In 1995, with unemployment peaking, the labor code was modified once again to introduce new contractual forms: the apprenticeship contract (minimum of three months, maximum of two years) for unemployed workers aged fourteen to twenty-five, with substantial nonwage labor cost reductions (Montoya, 1996), and a special temporary contract (minimum of six months, maximum of two years) applicable to workers older than forty, disabled workers, former soldiers of the Malvinas/Falklands war, and women. The special temporary contract granted a 50 percent rebate on payroll taxes except healthcare, and removed the requirement of severance pay at termination.[3] The 1995 reform also granted formal, separate status to part-time and trial-period contracts, though it limited trial periods to three months. Previously, part-time employment was allowed, with prorated payroll taxes and social benefits, but had no explicit legal status (Marshall, 1992).

4. Also in 1995, flexible measures were expanded for small firms by allowing them to modify, via collective agreement, dismissal regulations, in-

cluding a shorter advance-notice period. Small firms, with up to forty workers and sales not exceeding an upper limit established by an advisory committee, were exempt from complying with the requirements (in the law of 1991) that temporary contracts should be validated through collective agreements and be registered at the unified labor authority, and in certain cases were also exempt from paying compensation at termination.

5. The new labor code reform of 1998 eliminated the "promoted" temporary employment contracts created in 1991 and 1995. At the same time, modifications to advance notice and compensation reduced the cost of unfair dismissals by reducing the required number of days of advance notice for workers with up to three months of employment in the firm. Also, in the absence of notice, the law eliminated the obligation to pay the wage due from dismissal to the end of the month. The reform also imposed a stricter relation between period of service and dismissal compensation. These changes were made to reduce the cost of dismissal of workers with less seniority. According to the Ministry of Labor, dismissal costs of newer employees were to be reduced by more than 50 percent. Nevertheless, the cost of dismissal as a result of economic reasons was increased from one-half of the compensation for unfair dismissal to two-thirds (Beccaria and Galin, 2002).

6. In 2000, legislation on the trial-period contract was amended, making the contract fully subject to social security contributions and other mandatory benefits, but maintaining exemption from advance notice, expression of cause of dismissal, and compensation in case of contract termination at any time. However, there were restrictions on the use of trial contracts; for example, they were permitted only once for the same worker, and it was not acceptable to employ consecutively different workers under trial contracts for the same permanent job. The same law introduced incentives to the expansion of permanent employment, offering rebates on social security contributions if workers hired with trial contracts were subsequently incorporated with permanent contracts in addition to existing personnel. Rebates were larger if new contracts were for women heads-of-households, workers aged forty-five and over, or workers aged twenty-four or under. Wage subsidies were granted for contracts hiring unemployed female or older workers.

7. Given the dramatic social consequences of the crisis in the early 2000s, with open unemployment reaching over 21 percent in May 2002, an "emergency" measure taken in that year doubled compensation for unfair dismissal. It was expected that this would moderate unemployment growth. Other decrees limited layoffs due to force majeure or to lack or decrease of work (Beccaria and Galin, 2002).

8. In 2004, further reforms were introduced that established a minimum guarantee of severance pay for unjust dismissal at one month of salary, with a maximum of three months; limited trial contracts to three months; provided incentives to register employment in small and medium-sized firms with fewer

than eighty workers; stated that labor inspection would be strengthened to ensure compliance with the law; and widened the scope of social dialogue to encourage collective bargaining.

As a result, despite the drastic changes during the 1990s, the employment
regulations prevailing in the early 2000s were not dramatically different from
those that had existed prior to the economic reforms of 1991. The most important surviving changes are the reduced dismissal compensation for workers with
less seniority (though this was doubled in the 2002 decree), and the ability to
hire a worker on a trial contract for three months, but without the previous exemptions on social security payments. Also, specific, less protective regulations
for small firms remained and are important given that small firms account for a
relatively large share of employment. Furthermore, the ability to change regulations through collective bargaining has the potential for a more drastic impact.

Brazil. Reforms to labor regulations in Brazil, as in Argentina, were geared to
making the employment contract more flexible, though the changes were more
restricted than in Argentina, and most reforms were made only later in the
1990s. In 1994 a law was passed granting special conditions for small firms
with reference to holidays, prevention and sanitary conditions, and administrative formalities (Vega Ruíz, 2001), relatively minor aspects. But 1994 also
marked the passage of the Cooperatives Law, which permitted the creation of
cooperatives of workers to deliver services to firms without the constitution of
a work contract, with its recognized social and labor rights. The law made explicit that there is no employment relationship between cooperatives and their
members; firms do not contract workers, but their services, as in contracts of
rent. Salaries are normally paid below the legal minimum, and no trade unions
are involved (Cardoso, 2001). Though the law was originally put forward to
help landless peasants, it has been used increasingly by employers to avoid
their legal obligations with employees (Cook, 2000). Also in 1994, salaries
were deindexed from inflation, with the institution of free negotiation of
wages after almost thirty years of official wage policies. Workers' pay was
made even more flexible with a measure instituting their participation in profits. Finally, a new law also suspended the clause of the collective *dissidios*
(legal sentences in judicial arbitrations).

The year 1998 was one of major reforms. The "bank of hours" was instituted, making working hours more flexible. Allegedly created to avoid unemployment during economic crisis, the law permits the suppression of the payment of overtime (50 percent above legal working hours), giving employers
more control over the flux of work in production. Part-time work contracts
were legalized in the same year, permitting up to twenty-five hours per week
with lessened labor rights. Temporary suspension of labor contracts was also al-

lowed in 1998. Workers could have their contracts suspended for a maximum of one year and receive a benefit equivalent to unemployment benefits to participate in reskilling programs, at the end of which the employer could either hire the worker back or dismiss them. In 1998 another law instituted fixed-term contracts with reduced social rights. Firms with less than 50 employees could hire up to 50 percent of workers under the new legislation (25 percent in the case of firms with 200 workers or more). Responding to pressures from the labor movement, the law included the obligation of union representation in the hiring process. The federal government expected that the new legislation would create new jobs, formalize informal labor contracts, and create labor market efficiency, especially for micro and small firms. But fixed-term contracts did not thrive. In December 2001, only 3.4 percent of the formal work contracts were fixed-term, most of which were in the northeastern region.[4]

Mexico. Though there have been several projects under discussion in Mexico, the country has not reformed its labor law. Employer organizations have issued reform proposals since 1988. At that time, the proposals considered different aspects of flexibility, such as the regulation of employment termination in general and of layoff compensation in particular. Employer organizations again presented a proposal for reform in 1994, which this time included regulations on dismissals and temporary and other special contracts. There were also reform initiatives from the government and political parties, for instance from the Partido Acción Nacional (PAN; National Action Party) in 1996, addressing, among other things, dismissals (flexibilization through a seniority bonus that would replace all components of the existing compensation) and temporary contracts (creation of the apprenticeship contract with a trial period), and regulations on subcontracting and on weekly working time and overtime (de la Garza, 2002).[5]

Despite the absence of legal reforms in Mexico, many changes have been achieved through collective bargaining, some of which took place well before the 1990s.[6] From the analysis of collective agreements of both federal and local levels in the mid-1990s, E. de la Garza (2002) concluded that most of them guaranteed substantial functional flexibility, moderate numerical flexibility, and scarce wage flexibility, and that only a minority, possibly concentrated in large firms, had introduced new flexibilizing clauses during the first half of the 1990s. On the other hand, F. Herrera and J. Melgoza (2003) found, with reference to manufacturing, that deregulation was increasing, given that many central issues had ceased to be formally regulated. For example, the share of firms having written, formal instruments (collective agreements, specific accords, internal regulations of firms) addressing employment contracts, use of labor, and organization of production, had decreased by half between 1995 and 1999. Nonetheless, this process was less pronounced in large enterprises, but rather was concentrated in micro, small, and medium-sized firms, as well as in the maquiladora sector.

*   *   *

Working-time regulations experienced few changes, and only in Argentina and Brazil. In 2000, in Argentina, the ceiling on overtime was made more flexible, but overtime premiums were maintained (Beccaria and Galin, 2002). Moreover, throughout the 1990s, working-time flexibility clauses were introduced in many collective agreements. In Brazil, the 1988 constitution had permitted some flexibility in hours of work, and in 1998 there were new changes, as the "hours bank" (preexisting in some collective agreements) was legally recognized. This system makes it possible to reduce working hours at times of low activity, for 120 days, and to credit these unused hours to the worker, to be spent at times of high activity, with a ten-hour daily limit (Vega Ruíz, 2001).

Concerning nonwage labor costs, in Argentina, between 1991 and 1996, costs for workers with permanent contracts fell from 66 to 48 percent, relative to wages per hour. In 1998 the costs were similar, at 48 percent, as a result of declining employer contributions to social security (from 42 to 25 percent of wages) and, although less significant, the decline in work injury protection costs (from 3 to 2 percent) (Szretter, 1999). The 48 percent level occurred before the reduction of dismissal compensation, at the end of 1998.[7] In Mexico, social security reform, implemented in 1995, did not involve changes in the level of employer contributions, and therefore did not affect labor costs.[8] But before this reform, during the first half of the 1990s, according to V. Tokman and D. Martínez (1995), the incidence of nonwage labor costs had risen in 1990 as compared to 1980, and again in 1994–1995 as compared to 1990, due to the contributions to retirement and healthcare, and an additional payroll tax. Other contributory items remained constant. By 1995, total nonwage labor costs amounted to 47 percent of gross wages (27 percent in the case of contributions alone). In Brazil, according to estimates presented by M. Cacciamali (1999), nonwage labor costs represented some 48 percent of wages (27 percent social security, insurances, etc.; 21 percent wage supplements; an additional 1.3 percent and 2.6 percent corresponding to advance notice and penalty on dismissal are not included, as they are considered to be part of the firms' operational costs).[9]

Outcomes of Labor Reforms

The employment law of 1991 and the 1995 reforms in Argentina, as well as the unemployment package of 1998 in Brazil, were presented as policies devised to foster employment growth and reduce unemployment (Cook, 2000). In Argentina, some reforms were also aimed at reducing noncompliance. In

Mexico, labor legislation was not changed in the 1990s. Have the differential paths followed in relation to labor regulations and nonwage labor costs had visible impacts on comparative employment performances? Do employment structures demonstrate the effects of changes in labor regulations in Argentina and Brazil? We address these issues by looking at trends in the structure of employment in terms of contracts (importance of temporary contracts) and degree of compliance (share of nonprotected wage employment), as well as the general evolution of informal employment.

Temporary Contracts

Changes in the regulation of contracts in Argentina had some effects on the employment structure. The initial widening of possibilities for temporary contracts, as formulated in the 1991 national employment law, met with a modest response. Between 1992 and 1995, "promoted" contracts increased almost four times, but in 1995 they still amounted to 5,600 per month on average (data from MTSS). Nontargeted temporary contracts, permitted in the event of initiating new activities, accounted for most of the promoted contracts (55 percent in 1995), followed by employment promotion contracts (37 percent), whereas the two contracts involving a training component were seldom used (only 8 percent in 1995; data from MTSS). The limited success of these initial promoted temporary contracts has been attributed to the restrictions on their use stipulated in the same law, in particular the requirement for union consent, which made them scarcely attractive to employers.

By contrast, the contractual options provided by the 1995 law faced fewer restrictions and were supported by employers. Between 1996 and 1998, before the elimination of promoted temporary contracts by the reform of 1998, the share of temporary employment more than doubled, from 8 to 17 percent if trial contracts are included, and from 5 to 12 percent if they are not (see Table 6.1). At their peak in 1998, temporary agency contracts only represented about 2 percent of wage employment, whereas the share of trial contracts was about 5–6 percent (data from MTSS and Encuesta de Indicadores Laborales [EIL; Labor Indicators Survey]). Though just a small share of overall contracts, in terms of new recruitment, temporary contracts (including the trial contract) reached almost 80 percent of new contracts issued in 1997.[10] An additional indication of the extensive use of temporary contracts was the increase to almost 15 percent in 1997–98, compared with 10 percent in 1992, of the share of workers with tenure of up to three months.[11] There is no indication, however, that the introduction of temporary contracts created additional employment or reduced the number of nonregistered workers (Beccaria, 1999).

There was increasing union opposition to what was regarded as an "abusive" and spurious utilization of trial-period contracts, which, besides being used to screen new workers, were often employed as means to avoid dismissal

Table 6.1   Share of Temporary Employment in Wage Employment, Argentina and Mexico, 1996–2002 (percentages)

Year	Argentina[a]	Argentina[b]	Mexico
1996	8.2 Q3	4.8 Q3	n/a
1997	16.9 Q4	12.0 Q4	7.2
1998	15.3 Q3	9.4 Q3	10.0
1999	n/a	6.3 Q3	10.8
2000	n/a	5.0 Q3	11.2
2002	n/a	2.8 Q2	10.9

Source: Marshall, 2004.
Notes: Data for Argentina indicate the percentage of temporary contracts in establishments with ten or more employees in Buenos Aires. Data for Mexico indicate the percentage of *eventuales* (casual workers) insured at the Mexican Institute of Social Security.
a. Temporary contracts include fixed-term and trial contracts, and temporary agency work.
b. Temporary contracts include only fixed-term contracts and temporary agency work.
Q = quarter.
n/a = data not available.

compensation. Before the 1999 presidential election, the need to obtain union support and workers' votes forced the labor code reform of 1998 that eliminated the temporary contracts created in 1991 and 1995, although at the same time reducing the cost of dismissal. Following the 1998 reform, and with the persistent economic recession, the share of temporary contracts again went down substantially (to less than 5 percent in 1999 in the case of fixed-term contracts), while employment through temporary agencies continued to oscillate at low levels (1–2 percent or less; data from MTSS and EIL).[12]

No figures on temporary contracts are available for Brazil,[13] but data for São Paulo show that the share of workers with shorter tenure (up to six months) declined during the 1990s, from some 20 percent in 1991 to 14 percent in 2002 for protected wage employment, and from 60 to 49 percent for nonprotected wage employment, with corresponding increases in the average length of job tenure. The proportion of workers with up to two years of tenure (maximum permitted for fixed-term contracts) did not change. This finding may reflect simply the lack of new recruitment, but also suggests that the incentives for flexible contracts (relaxation of constraints on fixed-term contracts, regulation of part-time contracts) enacted in the second half of the 1990s did not affect the structure of wage employment, while the increased penalties on dismissal favored the lengthening of job tenure. The trends in job tenure are consistent with M. Cacciamali and A. Britto's (2002) findings that, in 1998, the clauses on flexible contracts that had been introduced in collective agreements represented a small proportion of all clauses dealing with forms of flexibility. They suggest that this might have contributed to expand informalization. This situation needs to be assessed in the light of the previous remarkably high degrees of turnover linked to workers' resigning in order to access severance funds, as well as the low penalty on dismissals before the 1988 constitutional reform. Nonetheless, Cacciamali and Britto (2002) also report that 68 percent of a sample of 2,200 Brazilian firms made use of some form of flexible contracts (primarily subcontracting, used by 56 percent of those firms), allegedly to reduce labor costs.[14]

In Mexico, use of temporary contracts continued by 2002 at its historical level of about 10 percent (see Table 6.1).[15] Within the manufacturing sector, the share of workers lacking indefinite contracts, such as subcontracted and part-time workers, did not increase during the 1990s, perhaps because low wage levels, training problems, and low union protection rendered these flexible employment forms unnecessary. Part-time and subcontracted workers together represented less than 2 percent of employment in 1999 (de la Garza, 2003a). Overall, firms did not make profound changes to their employment practices, possibly because contracts and labor relations were already very flexible (de la Garza, 2002). In any case, stability in the employment structure is consistent with the continuity of legal regulations.

Informal and Nonprotected Employment

Even when temporary employment was at its peak in Argentina—and despite the rebates on payroll taxes—nonprotected wage employment increased along with use of legal temporary contracts (see Table 6.2). Whereas in 1992–1995

Table 6.2   Share of Nonprotected Workers in Wage Employment, 1991–2002 (percentages)

Year	Argentina[a]	Argentina[b]	Brazil[c]	Mexico[d]	Mexico[e]
1991	23.2[f]	n/a	27.9	33.8	20.3
1995	23.6	30.7[g]	33.2	39.3	24.9
1999	30.9	33.2	37.2	40.3	23.6
2002	29.1	33.2	37.9	40.8	23.9

Source: Marshall, 2004.
Notes: Data are not comparable across countries, as concepts and methodologies differ.
a. Wage earners (excluding household services and, in 2002, beneficiaries of employment programs) without all social benefits (Buenos Aires-Cordoba-Rosario, EPH, INDEC).
b. Wage earners (excluding household services and, in 2002, beneficiaries of employment programs) with no social security contributions (urban areas, EPH, INDEC).
c. Wage earners without *carteira de trabalho* (formal work contract) (based on data in IPEA, *Boletim de mercado de trabalho: Conjuntura e análise* no. 22 [2003], Anexo Estadístico).
d. Wage earners without social benefits (INEGI: National Employment Surveys, urban areas).
e. Wage earners without social benefits (INEGI: Banco de Información Económica, forty-eight cities, National Urban Employment Survey).
f. 1992.
g. 1996.
n/a = data not available.

the wage employment share of nonprotected workers had been about 23–25 percent, it increased to some 31 percent after 1997.[16] Contrary to the expectations behind the reform, the offer of more flexible temporary contracts failed to stop the progress of noncompliance. Later, once the 1998 reform eliminated "promoted" temporary contracts, the proportion of workers with no social security contributions continued to rise, so that nonprotected employment, from representing 31 percent in 1996, rose to 33–34 percent in the early 2000s; and in the private sector, nonprotected employment rose from about 38 percent in 1996 to some 43 percent in 2002–2003 (all urban areas; Marshall, 2003).[17]

There are indications that the flexible contracts provided by the 1995 legislative reform were used by medium-sized and large firms to reduce nonwage labor costs, while the smallest firms relied on nonprotected employment to lower their payroll taxes (Marshall, 1998). By 2003, over 70 percent of wage employment in micro firms was not registered in the social security system, compared with 33 percent of wage employment in medium-sized firms and 14 percent in large firms (private sector; Marshall, 2003). Micro firms represented 33 percent of private sector employment in 2003, and accounted for 54 percent of nonprotected employees (data from Encuesta Permanente de Hogares [EPH; Permanent Household Survey] and Instituto Nacional de Estadística y Censos [INDEC; National Institute for Statistics and Census]). In part, micro businesses reflect the process of extensive subcontracting in certain sectors. For instance, the privatization of public utilities was followed by subcontracting of many activities previously undertaken by the state enterprise.[18] Between 2002 and 2003, there was a relatively substantial increase of nonprotected employment in the private sector, of about 4 percentage points, possibly stemming from the doubling of dismissal compensation in 2002.

In Brazil, nonprotected employment also rose, from 28 percent of waged workers in 1991 to 38 percent in 2002 (see Table 6.2). Though the sharp rise in informal employment may largely be explained by the decline in formal industrial employment as a result of economic opening, the labor market reforms of the 1990s appear to have been ineffective in mitigating this trend. In Mexico, the share of waged workers not receiving legal benefits increased during the 1990s, a finding that concurs with the trend of increased employment in micro enterprises.[19] Between 1990 and 2003, employment in micro enterprises as a share of total employment increased from 14.8 percent in 1990 to 17.9 percent in 2003.

Nonregistration of the employment relationship is but one of the transgressions to labor laws. It has been a characteristic feature of the Argentinean labor administration to have few inspectors and a negligible activity of control of compliance, as well as low penalties. Figures for 2000 are revealing of the low number of inspectors relative to the number of waged workers: 1 inspector for each 14,000 workers (including both federal and provincial inspectors)—a rate comparable to that found in Brazil (Beccaria and Galin, 2002). In Brazil, there were over 2,000 inspectors from the Ministry of Labor in 2002, and over 300,000 firms were inspected, reaching almost 20 million wage earners; there were almost 93,000 transgressions detected, and the proportion of items not complying with labor laws that were regularized thanks to the intervention of labor inspectors rose during 1996–2002, from 65 percent to above 80 percent (data from Ministério do Trabalho e Emprego [MTE; Ministry of Work and Employment]). The number of labor inspectors is also appallingly low in Mexico, and is decreasing. In 2000, there were 500 federal labor inspectors, falling to 273 in 2004 (Piore, 2004).[20] Between January and September 2003, federal inspectors surveyed nearly 6,000 firms, covering 865,000 workers, or approximately 2 percent of the working population.[21] The low number of inspectors may reflect the government's new focus on voluntary compliance of labor legislation, as well as preventative programs to ensure health and safety at the workplace.[22]

Summary of Labor Market Regulations and Employment

By the early 2000s, regulations on contracts and dismissals were the most restrictive in Mexico (see Tables 6.A and 6.B). It is difficult, however, to assess how Brazil and Argentina are ranked as compared with the prereform period, in terms of how lenient regulations are, since most of the temporary contracts promoted during the 1990s in Argentina have disappeared, while in Brazil possibilities have been expanded. Regulations on temporary contracts in Argentina remained permissive in comparative terms, in particular considering the trial period, even if "promoted" contracts no longer exist; in Brazil, some of the preexisting restrictions have been relaxed. It could be said that both countries have lax regulations on the employment contract. Regulations on dismissal have been made less costly in Argentina, perhaps changing its relative score, from intermediate to permissive, while in Brazil it was changed with the 1988 constitution, from permissive to intermediate. On balance, one could venture that regulations in the two countries now resemble each other much more than in the prereform period, not necessarily in their specific contents, but in the degree of protection granted.

The structure of formal employment did not change significantly in any one of the three countries in terms of flexible versus indefinite contracts, but all three showed increasing shares of nonprotected waged workers in the 1990s. Clearly, in Argentina, government promotion of temporary contracts, while it lasted, contributed to shape employer practices, as apparently did the substantial rise of dismissal compensation in 2002, which seems to have moderated the rate of layoffs during the crisis. But while the latter could be considered to have checked unemployment growth, the creation of flexible contracts had no visible impacts on improving employment. In Argentina, Brazil, and Mexico, the share of nonprotected employment increased, irrespective of changes (or lack thereof) in legal regulations and nonwage labor costs, and irrespective of the evolution of the level of economic activity.[23] The impact of labor reforms and nonwage labor cost reductions on employment creation is thus at best ambiguous.

Labor Market Policies

Labor market policies comprise both passive policies (concerned with providing replacement income during periods of joblessness or job search) and active policies (focused on labor market integration either through demand or supply measures). Both passive and active labor market policies provide insurance against the increased risks that labor markets face because of globalization. Even if their main aim is to combat unemployment and poverty, the security granted to workers through these policies also gives employers—from both the private and the public sector—the ability to adjust their labor force. In addition, labor market policies provide an important fiscal stimulus during economic downturns and can thus be legitimized on macroeconomic grounds (Auer, Efendioğlu, and Leschke, 2004).

Before the mid-1990s, labor market policies in Argentina, Brazil, and Mexico were sparse and sometimes existed only on paper. In the middle and late 1990s, the governments expanded and diversified programs to respond to the continuous increase of unemployment and poverty within the region. The policies include a wide range of government intervention, from programs to reduce unemployment, to training programs of a general scope. This section discusses five important labor market policies and their use in Argentina, Brazil, and Mexico: unemployment insurance programs, employment creation programs, self-employment and microenterprise creation programs, training programs, and public employment services. The extent of coverage and their impact on the labor market are analyzed in the successive section.

Unemployment Insurance Programs

Unemployment insurance is the typical example of a passive labor market policy based on cash transfers. In some cases, however, receipt of benefits is subject to training or work schemes, or an obligation that the beneficiary be actively engaged in job search. In Argentina, the unemployment insurance system was established in 1991 and in Brazil in 1986. Mexico does not have an unemployment insurance system, although it has developed a pilot program, Apoyo a Buscadores de Empleo Formal (Support to Formal Job Seekers).[24] Argentina's program is funded from a payroll tax collected by the national employment fund. Wage earners dismissed without fair cause, as a result of collective layoffs, who quit due to just cause, or whose temporary contract has ended, are eligible. Employees in construction, agriculture, household services, and public administration are not eligible. Requirements include contributions of at least twelve months in the three years preceding termination of employment, or ninety days in the preceding year in the case of temporary agency workers. Benefits (with a minimum level and a ceiling) are linked to the latest wage, and the amount decreases with the duration of compensation, which in turn varies according to the length of contributions to social security in the three years prior to employment termination, with a minimum of four and a maximum of twelve months (Conte-Grand, 1997). Even though the coverage rose from 13,000 beneficiaries per month on average in 1992, to over 200,000 by 2002, the program is still quite limited (Márquez, 1999). Indeed, only 8 percent of the unemployed in 2002 received benefits (see Table 6.3).

In Brazil, the unemployment insurance scheme is financed by a tax on enterprises collected by the Fundo de Amparo ao Trabalhador (FAT; Workers Protection Fund).[25] The unemployment benefit is a variable proportion of the latest wage, but it cannot be lower than the minimum wage.[26] Its duration depends on the employment record, with a minimum of three and a maximum of five months. To be eligible, workers must have been dismissed without fair cause or have terminated the employment relationship themselves due to employer noncompliance with the contract. They need to have been employed for six months immediately prior to dismissal and must be without alternative income sufficient to support the household.[27] Brazil has the largest unemployment system in the region, with coverage of almost 40 percent of all formal workers fired without just cause (Ramos, 2002). In 1990, 2.8 million workers benefited from the system; by 2001 the number had risen to 4.7 million.

Employment Creation Programs

Direct employment creation. Direct employment creation programs provide work when there is a lack of labor demand and, in the process, furnish a cash transfer to the unemployed who do not have access to unemployment insurance. During the 1990s, many of the Argentine employment creation programs, in practice, were cash transfer schemes for the unemployed, even if on paper they required participation of the unemployed in community or state projects. Such was the case of the Programa Intensivo de Trabajo (Intensive Work Program), targeted at the long-term unemployed, which ran from 1993 to 1995, as well as six other short-lived programs created between 1993 and 1996.[28] The Trabajar (Work) program (including its second and third iterations), which started in 1996 and was discontinued in 2002, was also based on having beneficiaries work in community or other projects.[29]

Similarly, the Programa de Jefes y Jefas de Hogar Desocupados (Program for the Unemployed Heads of Households), established in 2002 in response to the economic crisis, is also a cash transfer program with a mandatory work

Table 6.3 Unemployment and Unemployment Insurance, Argentina and Brazil, 1995–2002

Argentina, 1995–2002

	Unemployed (thousands)[a]	Unemployment Rate (%)	% UI Expenditure per GDP	UI Expenditure (US$ millions)	UI Beneficiaries, Average per Month (thousands)	% UI Beneficiaries per Unemployed
1995	2,033	17.5	0.14	375	122.3	6.0
1996	2,077	17.2	0.15	398	128.7	6.2
1997	1,739	14.9	0.11	314	95.4	5.5
1998	1,585	12.9	0.10	293	90.7	5.7
1999	1,809	14.3	0.13	361	114.2	6.3
2000	2,019	15.1	0.14	387	124.5	6.2
2001	2,510	17.4	0.16	444	144.7	5.8
2002	2,509	21.0	0.19	602	200.4	8.0

Brazil, 1995–2001

	Unemployment Rate (%)	% UI Expenditure per GDP	% Total FAT Expenditure per GDP
1995	4.6	0.73	0.88
1996	5.4	0.65	0.82
1997	5.7	0.56	0.73
1998	7.6	0.61	0.78
1999	7.6	0.51	0.66
2000	7.1	0.41	0.55
2001	6.2	0.43	0.59

Source: Marshall, 2004.
Notes: a. Data are for October.
UI = unemployment insurance.
FAT = Workers Protection Fund.

component. The Jefes program is financed by general funds and taxes on exports; in 2003, funding from a World Bank loan was added (Pautassi, Rossi, and Campos, 2003). The plan provides a benefit of 150 pesos per month, less than half the minimum wage, to unemployed heads-of-household with children, who in exchange must participate in training or community activities at least four hours daily. A subscheme was devised to furnish them with working materials to develop micro projects. Data on the proportion of participants effectively working or in training are sparse, though some estimates show that, in practice, 26 percent are not participating in work or training programs (cited in Pautassi, Rossi, and Campos, 2003). In 2002, there were 1.3 million participants per month on average, though participation has since fallen because of the economic recovery and because the registration of new applicants was officially closed in early 2003. Additionally, the Programa de Emergencia Laboral (Emergency Labor Program) of 2002 granted a similar monthly benefit to some 300,000 unemployed who had no access to the Jefes program, and who had to work in community projects (Pautassi, Rossi, and Campos, 2003). However, the emergency program was discontinued in 2003.[30]

In Brazil, there are no national-level programs of direct employment creation. Although a number of federal emergency jobs programs for the urban poor were designed in the late 1990s, these programs were never implemented. There are, however, several small-scale state and municipal programs, though with minor labor market impact. One example is the emergency unemployment assistance program in the state of São Paulo, which included work in state agencies six hours daily, four days a week, and one-day training or literacy courses, with a benefit set above the minimum wage (Rocha, 2001).[31]

In Mexico, the Programa de Empleo Temporal (PET; Temporary Employment Program) was created in the wake of the 1995 economic crisis and involves work on community projects with intensive use of unskilled labor. Its focus is on marginalized rural areas with up to 2,500 inhabitants, and is geared toward improving social and productive infrastructure, with a benefit equivalent to 90 percent of the local minimum wage (Samaniego, 2002). PET, which is run by the Ministry of Social Development rather than the Ministry of Labor, is very large, with over 1 million jobs created annually since 1998.

Indirect employment creation. Another type of employment creation program involves employment subsidies to the private sector, in exchange for hiring an unemployed worker, or a specifically targeted group of vulnerable workers. By reducing the cost of employment creation for private employers, it is believed that these programs contribute to creating jobs, though critics contend that they simply replace one set of workers who would have been hired with another.

In Argentina, the most salient example of an indirect employment creation program was the "promoted employment contracts" discussed previously, which reduced the cost of labor by eliminating the requirement to pay social security benefits and severance. Notwithstanding the elimination of the contracts in 1998, Argentina has other wage subsidy programs. For instance, the Jefes program includes a subsidy to private sector firms to hire unemployed workers. Employers receiving the subsidy pay the worker the difference between the state's subsidy and the wage corresponding to the job. Nevertheless, the proportion of unemployed workers placed in private firms has been very small, about 15,000 each month (according to data from MTSS; Pautassi, Rossi, and Campos, 2003). Another subsidy program, announced in 2003, is Más y Mejor Trabajo (More and Better Jobs), which aims to promote employment in the private sector in Argentina, with the multiple objectives of recovering lost jobs in firms with sufficient installed capacity, maintaining employment in firms affected by the crisis, and encouraging firms through training and technical assistance to adopt new production processes. The program also intends to strengthen productive sectors on the basis of knowledge and innovation. It offers several incentives: (1) 150 pesos per month toward the employee's wage as long as there is a commitment to not lay off or suspend workers; (2) 150 pesos per month per employee, for maintaining employment in economically viable firms in crisis; (3) improved labor market intermediation, through a network of 200 placement offices, including public and nonprofit agencies (trade unions, universities, employer organizations); and (4) various training programs.

Subsidized employment programs do not seem to have existed in Brazil prior to late 2003, when Primeiro Emprego (PPE; First Employment) was launched. The program is expected to generate decent jobs for young workers without previous work experience who did not complete secondary education and come from families with a per capita income of up to half of the minimum wage. The program thus gives priority to the age group sixteen to twenty-four, which represents 44 percent of the unemployed. The aim is to assist 250,000 young workers per year (Cella Dal Chiavon, 2003). One of its initiatives is to offer employers financial incentives (varying inversely with size of sales) in exchange for maintaining or increasing the average total number of employees they had at the time of joining the program, for at least twelve months.[32] In Mexico, programs in this category were created after the 1995 crisis and consisted of tax incentives (credits to be applied to tax payments; tax exemptions) from the federal government or state governments to formal sector firms that generated additional employment, and state subsidies to new firms with up to 100 workers (Samaniego, 2002). However, these programs were short-lived.

Self-Employment and Microenterprise Creation Programs

Government support for self-employment and microenterprise creation typically involves assisting with financing, which is the greatest obstacle for entrepreneurs, though sometimes other services, such as training and technical assistance, are provided. In Argentina there were some programs within the Ministry of Labor to help micro and small firms (Golbert and Giacometti, 1998), but these were discontinued. In 2003–2004, some schemes to help producers existed within the Ministry of Social Development.[33]

Brazil, on the other hand, has a very large and important program, the Programa de Genação de Emprego e Renda (PROGER; Program for the Generation of Employment and Income), established in 1994. The program grants special credits to sectors with no or little access to the main financial system, such as micro and small firms, as well as cooperatives, in both rural and urban areas. Credit is accompanied by technical, managerial, or professional training, technical assistance, and monitoring of beneficiary businesses. In 2001 there were contracts with 743,000 firms (Ramos, 2002). Estimates of the impact of PROGER on job creation varied; one estimate was that it contributed to create, in 1996, almost 40,000 jobs directly and another 67,000 indirectly (Andraus Troyano, 1998).[34] Another important program is Programa Nacional de Fortalecimento da Agricultura Familiar (PRONAF; National Program for the Strengthening of Family Agriculture), founded in 1995, which provides credit for family farming, as well as for nonfarming activities undertaken by the rural family. The program also includes training components, and provides funding to rural municipalities for improvements in infrastructure. Of the 3.8 million agricultural families in Brazil, 26 percent have benefited from the program, which in 1999 alone amounted to R$1.9 billion in funding (Coutinho García, 2003). Also, Primeiro Emprego includes a component to stimulate, via credit and assistance, entrepreneurship and self-employment among young workers.

In Mexico there are at least three programs targeted at developing micro and small firms and self-employment. Apart from the Fondo para la Micro, Pequeña y Mediana Empresa (Fund for Micro, Small, and Medium-Sized Enterprises)[35] there is the Programa Nacional de Financiamiento al Microempresario (National Program for the Financing of Microentrepreneurship, starting in 2001), which gives credit, through intermediary institutions, to low-income micro firms and self-employed workers without access to financial services. There is also the Programa Nacional de Apoyo para las Empresas de Solidaridad (National Support Program for Solidarity Enterprises, 1993), created to provide financing and entrepreneurial capabilities to poor sectors with productive and organizational capacity but without sufficient access to formal credit (Samaniego, 2002).

Training Programs

Training programs seek to help workers adapt to changing labor markets. Current trends in training include a greater involvement of the social partners, modernization of delivery, as well as an emphasis on private training providers. The

Argentine Jefes program includes a training component that allows beneficiaries to fulfill the work requirement by either completing their studies or by participating in a professional training program. During the year spanning winter 2003 to winter 2004, there were 32,000 beneficiaries of the training program. In 2003 the Ministry of Labor developed several new training programs for working and unemployed persons, including the Programa de Formación y Certificación de Competencias (Training and Skills Accreditation Program), which focuses on four manufacturing industries and was developed in collaboration with employers' organizations and trade unions; the Talleres Ocupacionales (Occupational Workshops), which provides short training courses in specific localities to unemployed and employed workers and to small and medium-sized firms; the Formujer (roughly translated as "Training for Women"), intended to improve the employability of low-income women; the Transferencia Solidaria de Saberes Productivos (Solidarity Transfer of Productive Knowledge), designed to provide training to nongovernmental organizations that promote self-employment and the development of micro firms; and a program to assist persons with disabilities in developing economic activities, known as the Talleres Protegidos de Producción (Sheltered Workshops). There is no information on their implementation.[36]

The principal training program in Brazil is the Plano Nacional de Qualificação do Trabalhador (PLANFOR; National Professional Training Program), initiated in 1996 to improve the skills of the Brazilian labor force. The program is addressed at the unemployed, workers with a high risk of becoming unemployed, micro and small producers, and self-employed workers. It is financed mainly out of the FAT (the unemployment insurance fund), accounting for 7 percent of the FAT's total expenditure in 2001 (data in Ramos, 2002). Between 1996 and 2001, 11 million workers were trained under this program, 68 percent of whom had at most two years of schooling. Despite these large numbers, the program has fallen short of its stated goal of training 15 million workers, or 20 percent of the labor force, each year (Ramos, 2002).[37]

The Mexican unemployed-worker training program, Sistema de Capacitación para el Trabajo (SICAT; Vocational Training System), started in response to the 1982 crisis, has the objective of providing short-term training to workers with job access problems and to those affected by suspensions or facing high risk of losing their jobs. The program provides a benefit equivalent to the regional minimum wage plus medical expenditures, some materials, and help for transportation expenses. The program has expanded dramatically in size, from 12,700 beneficiaries in 1987 to 552,000 by 1999 (Samaniego, 2002).[38]

Public Employment Services

Public employment services facilitate job matching, register the unemployed and manage benefits if they exist, and refer job seekers to reintegration programs. They can also be important in facilitating the coherence of different policies, thus improving workers' prospects for labor market integration. Although state employment services have existed in Argentina for many decades, their activities in practice were minimal, as the services were chronically understaffed and did not keep records on job vacancies or job seekers. In response, during the mid-1990s, the government created the Argentine Employment Service Network to bring together public employment offices, public placement agencies, and similar institutions (Marshall, 1997). These institutions were charged with registering vacancies and workers looking for jobs, providing counseling and intermediation, undertaking local labor market studies, administering unemployment benefits, selecting personnel for employers, helping in worker relocation, and assisting the self-employed and micro employers (Montoya, 1996). Since the late 1990s, the labor ministry's activities in this area have concentrated on providing technical assistance and training to a variety of public and private agencies (such as municipalities, nonprofit private organizations, and trade unions) that intermediate in the labor market. State placement agencies at the national level have practically been discontinued. Of the agencies that replied to a survey of the Ministry of Labor in 1999, municipalities represented some 30 percent, and the largest proportion of applicant workers placed by those agencies, both public and private, had been allocated to the employment programs they were administering.[39] In 1998, 44 percent of the more than 200,000 applicants had been placed, but only one-third of them in vacant jobs registered by employers.[40]

Brazil's Sistema Nacional de Emprego (SINE; National Employment System) and the institutions of the Public Employment System aim to help place workers searching for jobs (Conte-Grand, 1997). Intermediation is funded from the FAT, but its expenditure represents only 2 percent of FAT's total spending (Ramos, 2002). Between 1990 and 2001 the numbers of registered workers, of registered vacancies, and of placements increased drastically (from 477,000 to 4.7 million, from 284,000 to 1.4 million, and from 118,000 to 747,000, respectively). In 2001 the SINE offered potential job opportunities to almost 30 percent of the registered workers, but only 16 percent of the workers registered were effectively placed (Ramos, 2002). Nonetheless, in Brazil the role of public employment services is much more developed than in Argentina, as from 1998 nonprofit organizations such as trade unions have been allowed to participate in intermediation (Ramos, 2002).

In Mexico, the Servicio Nacional de Empleo, Capacitación y Adiestramiento (SNE; National Service for Employment, Skills, and Training) was established in 1978 to place workers, promote training of the unemployed, and conduct regional labor market studies, under the coordination of the secretary of labor, who in turn coordinates with state authorities and local committees, with the participation of productive sectors (Samaniego, 1998). The service registers vacancies as well as workers seeking jobs. In 1995, the equivalent of

32 percent of the unemployed applied to the SNE, and some 23 percent of those who applied were placed (as reported by the National Employment Survey). In 1996, with the economic recovery, the number of applicants declined, stabilizing at around 400,000. During 1995 and 2001, on average, 32 percent of applicants were placed (Samaniego, 2002). Intermediation takes places mainly via *ferias de empleo* (job markets), training workshops to guide the unemployed, and employment exchanges.[41] In addition, the Ministry of Labor initiated in 2001 a job-matching program composed of an online intermediation service (Chambanet), a telephone service (Chambatel), and a free publication for the Federal District called *Mi Chamba* (*My Job*). The three services, which have the organizational support of the SNE, provide listings of jobs and possible candidates. In 2002, Chambanet and Chambatel served approximately 215,000 job seekers and placed roughly 17 percent.[42] The government has also established six job-matching centers, the Centros de Intermediación Laboral (Job-Matching Centers), which give job-placement assistance.

Expenditure, Coverage, and Impact of the Labor Market Policies

Though numerous labor market policies exist in Argentina, Brazil, and Mexico, their impact on the labor market depends on the financial support given to the programs and, consequently, the number of labor market participants covered. Program design, implementation, and management are also important determinants of the policies' effectiveness.

Expenditure

In Argentina, total government spending (national, provincial, and municipal levels) on employment programs plus unemployment insurance reached 0.99 percent of GDP in 2002, the highest level ever, in response to the profound economic crisis (see Tables 6.3 and Table 6.4). Until 2000 it had been around 0.30 percent or less; it was 0.36 percent in 2001.[43] The increase was absorbed by the Jefes program, which constituted 92 percent of national government spending on employment programs. Expenditure on unemployment insurance also increased in relation to GDP, from about 0.15 percent in 1996 to 0.19 percent in 2002, in tandem with movements in the unemployment rate (see Table 6.4).[44]

In Brazil, total expenditures on the FAT as a proportion of GDP (including training programs, intermediation, and unemployment insurance, with unemployment insurance representing 0.41 percent of GDP and the former two 0.04 percent and 0.01 percent, respectively; Ramos, 2002) decreased from 0.88 percent in 1995 to 0.59 percent in 2001. Increasing unemployment rates were not matched by increased expenditures on unemployment insurance and

Table 6.4   Unemployment Rates and Labor Market Policy Spending as Percentage of GDP, 2001/2002

	Argentina (2002)[a]	Brazil (2001)	Mexico (2001)
Unemployment rate (2002)	21.0[b]	7.3[c]	2.8[d]
Labor market policy spending, total	0.99	0.59[e]	(0.13)[f]
Employment programs	0.80	0.08[e]	(0.13)[f]
Unemployment insurance	0.19	0.43[e]	—

Source: Marshall, 2004.
Notes: a. Preliminary.
b. Urban areas.
c. Six metropolitan areas.
d. Urban areas.
e. Only FAT (Workers Protection Fund).
f. Only PET (Temporary Employment Program), support to low-income producers, and fund for assisting micro, small, and medium-sized firms.

other FAT spending; rather, these met with declines. In fact, from 1995, 20 percent of the FAT's revenues were shifted to the national treasury reducing the funding available for labor market policies (Ramos, 2002). Although no estimates of total expenditure on labor market policies in Mexico are readily available, spending on three important programs (temporary employment, assistance for low-income producers, and assistance for small firms) represented about 0.13 percent of GDP in 2001. Estimates on expenditure in training, probably substantial, are not available.[45]

Comparing across the three countries, the level of spending on labor market policies as a percentage of GDP mirrors the differing rates of unemployment; thus Argentina, with the highest level of unemployment, spends the most, and Mexico, with the lowest rate of unemployment, spends the least. Nevertheless, spending on unemployment insurance is substantially higher in Brazil—0.43 percent of GDP in 2001 compared with 0.19 percent in Argentina in 2002—despite a level of unemployment in Brazil that was equivalent to about one-third the rate in Argentina. Expenditure on unemployment insurance in Argentina or Brazil compares unfavorably to the level reached in some OECD countries, which exceeds 3 percent in Denmark, 2 percent in Belgium and the Netherlands, and 1 percent in France, Germany, and Spain. But spending is closer to, and even higher than in the case of Brazil, levels in the United States (0.25 percent) and the United Kingdom (0.32 percent).[46] In Argentina, the proportion of expenditure on "active" policies in relation to GDP, about 0.8 percent, is close to that found in Spain (0.9 percent in 2000; OECD data cited in Mato Díaz, 2003), and to the OECD average in 1998 (0.87 percent), but below the average for the European Union (1.07 percent) (OECD, 2001).[47] In

Brazil and Mexico it is much lower, but in Mexico, spending on certain programs is not included is some studies, thus making comparisons difficult.

Coverage

Despite increased spending on unemployment insurance in Argentina, coverage has been extremely low (about 6 percent of the unemployed, increasing to 8 percent in 2002; see Table 6.3), due primarily to the combination of stringent legal requirements and widespread nonregistered employment. A study based on data from the 1995 household survey (the EPH) showed that coverage was small even in relation to the segment of the unemployed entitled to compensation. In Buenos Aires, only 17 percent of the unemployed were entitled to receive the unemployment benefit, and less than half of this much smaller segment received it (Marshall, 1996a). Young workers, women, persons with higher educational levels, employees from the real estate and financial sectors, as well as employees from small firms, were among those who, despite being entitled to unemployment compensation, were typically not receiving it. This suggests that certain individual characteristics, such as higher education or a secondary position in relation to household income, often combined with a less formalized employment relationship, made workers less prone to request the unemployment benefit (Marshall, 1996a).

Nevertheless, the monthly average number of beneficiaries of national government employment programs increased from a mere 62,000 in 1996 to 1.3 million in 2002, 98 percent of whom were in the Jefes program. According to data from the household survey, beneficiaries of employment programs rose drastically in 2002, increasing their proportion in relation to wage earners, exclusive of household services, from 1.9 percent in 2000 to 3.9 percent in early 2002, and to some 12 percent in late 2002 and early 2003 (data from EPH and INDEC, urban areas). Indeed, it is estimated that one-third of Argentine households have at least one Jefes program beneficiary and that, in October 2002, 45 percent of the unemployed were employment program beneficiaries.[48] Nevertheless, total unemployment is overestimated in the sense that some of the Jefes recipients might have been out of the labor force had the subsidy not been available.

Unemployment insurance in Brazil was estimated to have covered some 40 percent of those dismissed without fair cause (Ramos, 2002), with an average benefit exceeding the minimum wage (1.4 times the minimum wage in 2003). On average, some 400,000 individuals per month received the unemployment benefit in 2002 (data from MTE). Estimates of the monthly average number of beneficiaries of labor market programs in Brazil and Mexico that could be contrasted with the number of unemployed workers do not seem to be available.

Impact

In general, labor market policies in Argentina, Brazil, and Mexico were not subject to evaluation, though this began to change beginning in the mid-1990s. As in other countries, however, evaluations are difficult to carry out in practice, as they are subject to bias and measurement error, and the findings are often contradictory. Nevertheless, they are an important policy tool for the future design of programs.

Since the creation in 2002 of the sizable Jefes program, several assessments of the targeting and labor market impacts of the program have been made. Studies by E. Galasso and M. Ravallion (2003), P. López Zadicoff and J. Paz (2003), and R. Cortés, F. Groisman, and A. Hosowszki (2003) indicate that beneficiaries are from the eligible population in terms of household income and number of children, but that often the unemployment and the household-head requirements have not been met. For example, it appears that many beneficiaries are female spouses who were out of the labor force before entering the program. The program's small benefit and the work requirement, however, have been effective tools for self-selecting the poorest households (Galasso and Ravallion, 2003). Galasso and Ravallion (2003) conclude that the program has reduced unemployment, but as the plan induced labor force participation of previously nonparticipating women, the reduction of the unemployment rate between May and October 2002 was only 2.5 percentage points.

The level of unemployment and its structure depend on institutional and economic factors, of which the existence or absence of unemployment compensation schemes and employment programs is but one. The very limited coverage of unemployment insurance in both Argentina and Brazil makes analysis of the employment effects of unemployment compensation difficult in these particular cases, although it could be more relevant locally if coverage in particular regions or sectors were found to be wider. C. Ramos (2002), studying the Brazilian system of worker protection (including unemployment insurance, the severance pay system, and dismissal compensation) holds that, although it has been usual to assert that the system increased turnover, discouraged investment in skills, and exacerbated informality, these claims have not been grounded on conclusive evidence. In particular, Ramos criticizes studies (such as Paes de Barros, Corseuil, and Bahia, 1999) that, on the basis of only very few surveys, contend that unemployment insurance has negative effects (for example, that it subsidizes persons who are in fact employed and earning almost three times the unemployment insurance benefit).[49] Still, R. Paes de Barros, C. Corseuil, and M. Foguel (2000) found that only 50 percent of unemployment compensation recipients were actually unemployed, casting some doubts on the adequacy of coverage. In relation to other forms of labor market intervention, a study by the Foundation for Economic Research and the University of São Paulo (cited in

Ramos, 2002), analyzing data for six metropolitan areas, found that labor inter-mediation had no statistically significant impact on the likelihood of finding employment. The labor market impacts of other programs in Brazil were found to be mixed.[50]

Evaluations of the impacts of different programs in Mexico showed mixed results, but on the whole reported positive effects either on employment (in the case of the SICAT, the training scheme for the unemployed) or as anti-poverty measures (PET, the temporary employment program; support to micro employers and self-employed workers), although in some cases there were shortcomings in efficiency (Samaniego, 2002).[51]

Comparing the three countries, even if the absence of unemployment in-surance schemes in Mexico is consistent with unemployment being lower in Mexico than in Argentina and Brazil, the relative levels of unemployment are the result of a combination of factors, of which the substantial labor emigra-tion from Mexico to the United States is one of the most important (Hernán-dez Laos, 2000). Moreover, the differential "sensitivity" of low-productivity, informal activities to the pressure of excess labor, resulting from historical, economic, social, and cultural processes, may help explain not only Mexico's lower unemployment rate, but also Brazil's in relation to Argentina's (Mar-shall, 2002). Yet consistent with the absence of unemployment insurance in Mexico is the higher proportion of short-term unemployment in Mexico, 75 percent in 2002, compared with 42 percent in Argentina and 38 percent in Brazil (see Table 6.5).

Clearly, analyses of the labor market effects of unemployment and em-ployment schemes are only at the initial stage in Argentina and Mexico, and although they have been more frequent in Brazil, the findings in the latter have been highly debated. Among the many issues requiring further investigation are the impacts of cash transfer programs—the level and duration of cash sub-

Table 6.5   **Proportion of Unemployed Who Have Been Out of Work for Three or Fewer Months, as Percentage of Total Unemployed, 1991–2002**

Year	Argentina[a]	Brazil[b]	Mexico[c]
1991	65.6	55.5	69.5
1994	61.4	48.2	68.9
1997	48.6	45.0	72.3
2000	53.8	43.7	77.4
2002	42.4	37.5	74.8

Source: Marshall, 2004.
Notes: a. Unemployed up to three months, Buenos Aires.
b. Unemployed up to three months, metropolitan areas.
c. Unemployed up to eight weeks, forty-eight cities.

sidies (relative to the minimum wage, for instance)—on labor force participation, the informal sector, unemployment, labor market competition, and wages and the wage structure, as well as the impacts of financial and other assistance for the self-employed and micro employers on informal activities.

Another neglected research area concerns the macroeconomic effects of labor market policies. Most OECD countries have labor market policies that serve both to increase the level of social protection in the country and to enhance macroeconomic stability. In the United States, for example, it is estimated that the unemployment insurance program mitigated the loss in real GDP by approximately 15 percent during the five recessions that occurred between 1969 and the early 1990s. The program exhibited a substantial and significant countercyclical effect on changes in real GDP over the three decades, resulting in an average peak saving of 131,000 jobs (Chimerine, Black, and Coffey, 1999). Similarly, a household-level analysis of the effect of unemployment insurance on consumption found that in the absence of unemployment insurance, becoming unemployed would be associated with a fall in consumption of 22 percent, compared with the 6.8 percent drop for unemployment insurance recipients in the United States (Gruber, 1997). By comparison with other incentive measures, such as income tax cuts, P. Orszag (2001) calculates that the US unemployment insurance system is at least eight times as effective as the tax system as a whole in offsetting the impact of a recession.

The macroeconomic benefit of labor market policies, in this case unemployment insurance, also aids firms' adjustment during economic downturns. If social protection is provided at the firm level via severance pay, and a firm wishes to lay off workers during an economic downturn, then that firm would be forced to bear the cost of paying severance during an economic slowdown, which may not be feasible or which may have the perverse effect of worsening the firm's adjustment to the economic situation, thereby putting its survival at risk. Similarly, without any social protection, a dismissed worker would bear all of the costs of an economic downturn, which can have a detrimental effect on that person's livelihood. In the case of dismissals, in a given locality, the community in which the workers live would probably also be severely affected, as a result of the income loss and subsequent reduction in consumption. If, on the other hand, a system of social protection is developed whereby the burden of dismissal is shared among the firms, workers, and the state, the negative effect of an economic downturn can be mitigated. Labor market policies can thus play an important role in providing security for workers while giving firms room to respond to market demand.

Summary of Labor Market Policies and Employment

Labor market policies in Argentina emerged in the early 1990s, but were confined to fragmented, small-scale, continually redesigned programs, with no long-term government commitment in terms of funding. They were repeatedly used spuriously to benefit the political clientele, and often announced to avoid the emergence of conflict, or at electoral times, but then not implemented or rapidly discontinued. Moreover, the fiscal restrictions in the convertibility program did not support funding employment policies and unemployment insurance (Cortés and Marshall, 1999). It was only at the end of the 1990s, with the latest phases of the Trabajar scheme supported and monitored by the World Bank, and particularly after the profound recession of the early 2000s and the creation of the Jefes program in 2002, that labor market policies were widened and the government became committed in terms of financial support, viewing them as an important instrument for providing income to the jobless and controlling social conflict. The 2001 policy change also relaxed the fiscal constraint, permitting funding of the more massive employment program demanded by the extremely critical social situation. Nonetheless, the goals of this program were more to reduce poverty than to facilitate labor market integration.

In Brazil, although funding relative to GDP has also been of limited scale and coverage has indeed been small, there has been a longer-term, steadier effort at labor market intervention, through the implementation of unemployment insurance, intermediation and training schemes, and assistance to small-scale employers and self-employed workers, even without considering the contribution of antipoverty programs. Brazil's unemployment insurance fund is far more developed than Argentina's (or Mexico's), and its innovative design allows funding of training and investment programs, serving to reduce dependence on unemployment insurance.

Labor market policies have also been sparse in Mexico, but nevertheless have gained importance, both institutionally and financially. Labor market programs moved from the experimental, transitory, small schemes in the 1980s, which emerged to face the economic crisis of 1982, to programs that in the 1990s were extended to encompass nonformal sector workers, had a wider geographic reach, involved different levels of government, and no longer were of a transitory nature but attempted to respond to structural problems (Samaniego, 2002).

Conclusion

Though the regional labor market initiatives of Mercosur, and to a lesser extent NAFTA, point to the increased importance of labor market standards and policies in addressing the social dimensions of regional integration, the trend in national labor market regulation and policy during the 1990s in Argentina, Brazil, and Mexico was toward less regulation—particularly of employment contracts and dismissal protection—and a reduction in nonwage labor costs.

Yet the analysis of the changes in national labor regulation demonstrated that although they shape employer practices, they do not seem to influence employment generation. This is in agreement with findings of previous studies on Latin America that show that, contrary to the simplistic argument stating that relaxation of constraints on contracts and dismissals would suffice to create employment, supply-side measures such as these are insufficient. Multiple causes intervene in the process of job creation, among which labor regulations are but one.

It could still be argued that the reforms implemented were not the most adequate to stimulate employment generation, or that reforms were not deep enough to stimulate employment growth—hypotheses difficult to confront empirically. Changes in labor regulations and nonwage labor cost reductions might have been favorable to job creation in certain sectors, but they do not seem to be neither necessary nor sufficient conditions. At the same time, the analysis suggests that regardless of the labor regulations and the partial dismantling of these regulations, precarious employment contracts—employment forms not complying with labor and social security regulations—increased in the three countries. Indeed, greater flexibility has principally resulted from labor cost-reducing strategies adopted mainly by the smaller firms to survive in increasingly problematic economic contexts, facilitated by the laxity of control and enforcement.

An important and positive trend in labor market governance, however, has been the increased prominence given to labor market policies, both passive and active, in Argentina, Brazil, and Mexico. A wide array of policies emerged to confront the challenge of increased unemployment, informality, and poverty, including unemployment insurance, direct employment creation, subsidies to the private sector for hiring additional workers, assistance to micro and small enterprises, public employment services, and training programs (see also Appendix Tables 6.C and 6.D). Although the programs are still incipient, piecemeal, and in need of additional and sustained funding, the policies have the potential to improve the operation of the labor market. By providing security to workers to respond to employment shocks, the policies permit employers the flexibility that they need to operate in a global economy. Active labor market policies are thus a necessary component of an encompassing employment policy in contexts where the process of job generation is too slow to absorb all available workers, and when it is foreseeable that it will continue to be so. Indeed, labor market policies contribute much more concretely to alleviating the problems of the unemployed than do "indirect incentives" via the dismantling of labor protection or through generalized rebates on nonwage labor costs that might reduce state revenues without guaranteeing employment generation. Thus, labor market policies provide a potentially powerful tool for the increased risks that workers face because of globalization.

Appendix Table 6.A   Regulations on Unfair Dismissal, Early 2000s: Selected Aspects

Aspect	Argentina	Brazil	Mexico
Compensation	Yes, after three months in a firm, one-twelfth of highest monthly remuneration in latest year of employment, or during employment if shorter than one year, per month of employment. Maximum: three times average remuneration in corresponding collective agreement. Minimum: one-sixth of remuneration as defined above.	Yes, individual capitalization account (severance pay) that replaced one month per year of service compensation, plus 40 percent of accumulated severance fund penalty on employer.	Yes, three months' wages if reinstatement not requested, plus wages due between day of dismissal and application of court sentence. Special compensation for those not entitled to request reinstatement.
Reinstatement	No.	No.	Yes, after one year in firm, option available to workers, with exceptions.
Advance notice	Yes, replaceable by compensation. Between fifteen days and two months, depending on length of employment (no notice if employed up to thirty days).	Yes, after one year in the firm, replaceable by compensation (eight days in advance if wages paid per week or day; one month if wages paid per fortnight or month).	No (written notice only).

Source: Marshall, 2004.

Appendix Table 6.B   Regulations on Fixed-Term Contracts, Early 2000s: Selected Aspects

Aspect	Argentina	Brazil	Mexico
Situations and tasks in which they are permitted	If agreed voluntarily for tasks that "reasonably" demand them.	As long as authorized via collective bargaining.	For temporary tasks. To substitute workers.
Duration	Five years maximum.	Two years maximum.	One year maximum.[a]
Renewals	Renewable, but not "excessively."	One renewal maximum.	Renewable for one year at most.[a]

continues

Appendix Table 6.B Continued

Aspect	Argentina	Brazil	Mexico
Compensation at end of contract, dismissal, or both	One-half of dismissal compensation at end of contract. After one year in firm, compensation for unfair dismissal as in contracts for indefinite period, plus compensation for damages according to ordinary law.	If unfair dismissal, one-half of wages due until end of contract.	If unfair dismissal, one-half of wages received if employment less than one year; otherwise, six months' wages for first year and twenty days' wages per year of service afterward.

Source: Marshall, 2004.

Note: a. Article 39 of the Federal Labor Law stipulates that if, when the term ends, the need for temporary work persists, the contract may be prolonged as long as it continues to be necessary, and Article 40 states that workers with fixed-term contracts are not obliged to continue under this contract for more than one year. This could be interpreted as establishing a maximum of one year for the duration of each contract, but also a maximum to renewals.

Appendix Table 6.C Unemployment Compensation: Selected Aspects

Aspect	Argentina	Brazil	Mexico
Unemployment insurance	Yes, from 1991.	Yes, from 1986.	No.
Eligibility	Unfair or collective dismissal. Voluntary termination with just cause. End of temporary contract. No retirement benefit.	Unfair dismissal. Voluntary termination with just cause. Six months' consecutive wage employment immediately prior to dismissal. No retirement benefit. No alternative own income sufficient to support family.	—
Contributory record required (social security contributions)	At least twelve months in three preceding years. For agency workers, at least ninety days in preceding year.	—	—

continues

Appendix Table 6.C   Continued

Aspect	Argentina	Brazil	Mexico
Unemployment amount	Linked to latest wage, decreasing with the duration of the benefit, with a minimum equivalent to 75 percent and a maximum to 150 percent of minimum wage at inception of the scheme.	Linked to latest wage, with a threshold of one minimum wage.	—
Unemployment duration	Depends on contributory record: minimum four months, maximum twelve months.	Depends on employment record: minimum three months, maximum five months.	—

Source: Marshall, 2004.

Appendix Table 6.D   Labor Market Programs of National/Federal Governments, Early 2000s: Selected Aspects

Aspect	Argentina	Brazil	Mexico
Direct employment creation	Jefes program, with participation in training or community work, benefit below minimum wage. Help for micro projects.	—	PET, community work, in marginal rural areas.
Subsidized employment in private sector	Jefes program, MMT, partial wage subsidy.	PPE, subsidy to employers who hire young workers.	Eliminated.
Self-employment and micro-enterprise creation programs	Small programs for specific producers.	PROGER, credit and assistance to micro and small firms and cooperatives. PRONAF, credit to family agriculturalists and rural, nonagricultural producers.	PRONAFIM, credit to low-income micro firms and self-employed. PNAES, financing and assistance to poor sectors.

continues

Appendix Table 6.D   Continued

Aspect	Argentina	Brazil	Mexico
Training for unemployed	Several small programs announced.	PLANFOR, large-scale program to provide skills to unemployed or in high risk of unemployment. PPE, training young workers.	SICAT, short-term training to unemployed or at high risk of losing job, benefit equal to minimum wage, materials, etc.
Public employment services	National services confined mainly to technical assistance and training of public and private intermediating agencies.	SINE, with increasing but still limited registration of unemployed (29 percent in 2001), vacancies, and placements.	SNE, registered 32 percent of unemployed (1995).

Source: Based on program descriptions given in this chapter.
Note: For acronym definitions, see list at the back of the book.

Notes

1. For more information on the 1980s, see Marshall, 2004.

2. Reforms to work injury protection undertaken in 1992 and 1995 also served to reduce nonwage labor costs, from an average of 12 percent of the wage bill to less than 3 percent (Ministerio de Trabajo, Empleo y Seguridad Social [MTSS], 1996). Some cost reductions were also made to the family allowance scheme.

3. The proportion of workers that could be employed under special temporary contracts was limited according to firm size: 100 percent in firms with up to five employees, 50 percent in firms with six to twenty-five employees, and 10 percent in firms with more than twenty-five employees. The proportions, however, could be increased by collective agreement.

4. Data calculated directly from the RAIS (Annual Report of Social Information), a file of administrative records of the Ministry of Labor.

5. For more details see de la Garza, 2002, and Cook, 1998.

6. F. Zapata (1998) examines some of these changes since the 1980s.

7. H. Szretter (1999) presents data on incidence of nonwage labor costs also for other types of contracts; "promoted" temporary contracts and the trial contract show distinctly lower incidences; at that time these contracts accounted for 3.7 percent and 1.5 percent, respectively, of registered employment in manufacturing and services.

8. The reform of the Mexican Social Security Institute included a new option for employers, who are now allowed to reclaim 40 percent of their contributions to the healthcare and maternity system if they show that they are able to provide an adequate, alternative service to their workers (Moreno, Tamez, and Ortiz, 2003; no information about actual implementation or impacts).

9. Cacciamali is citing J. Pastore, "A batalha dos encargos sociais," *Folha de São Paulo,* February 28, 1996. See also Pochmann, 1999, on the incidence of nonwage

labor costs in contracts for an indefinite period, including the cost of dismissal (thirteenth wage, holiday pay, severance, employment termination, insurances, social security, etc.). R. Paes de Barros, C. Corseuil, and M. Foguel (2000) present data that show a higher incidence of nonwage labor costs in Brazil, having increased from almost 47 percent in 1982–1988 to 56.6 percent in 1990–1998, mainly as a result of increases in compulsory social security contributions and the vacation bonus.

10. Data from MTSS for Buenos Aires, firms with ten or more wage earners; data include fixed-term and trial contracts as well as persons employed through labor agencies (Marshall, 2001; Perelman, 2001).

11. Estimates based on data for wage earners, exclusive of domestic servants, from Encuesta Permanente de Hogares (EPH; Permanent Household Survey) and Instituto Nacional de Estadística y Censos (INDEC; National Institute for Statistics and Census).

12. During 1999, data on trial contracts ceased to be shown separately, and workers with trial contracts were subsumed in the category of workers with indefinite contracts (MTSS).

13. M. Cacciamali and J. Pires (1995) noted that studies on temporary employment are almost nonexistent in Brazil.

14. Cacciamali and Britto are citing J. P. Chahad, "Trabalho flexível e modalidades especiais de contrato de trabalho: Evidências empíricas no caso brasileiro," Ministério do Trabalho e Emprego e Fundação Instituto de Pesquisas Econômicas, Saõ Paulo, 2001.

15. E. Hernández Laos (2000) finds a similar level of temporary contracts in 1996, based on data from the National Employment Survey.

16. Estimates based on EPH and INDEC (Buenos Aires-Cordoba-Rosario; proportion of workers not receiving any of the legally stipulated social benefits and not contributing to social security).

17. These data do not include household services (usually nonprotected) and beneficiaries of government employment programs (Marshall, 2003).

18. Typical examples are found in telephones and electricity. Expansion of subcontracting within manufacturing industries has been analyzed in case studies (see, e.g., Giosa, 2000, and references cited therein, in relation to subcontracting of production of parts and of services in the automobile industry and other oligopolistic sectors).

19. In Table 6.2 we present two alternative series for Mexico, one with a wider urban coverage, showing much higher rates of nonprotected wage employment than the other. The two series of annual data do not describe coincident annual variations.

20. Because Mexico is a federal state, there are both state and federal labor inspectors. State coverage of labor inspection is unequal, with DF, Guadalajara, and Monterrey having the most extensive coverage and some states having no coverage at all (Piore, 2004).

21. Data from http://www.stps.gob.mx.

22. STPS, "Nuevo rumbo de la inspección federal del trabajo."

23. Although some regulations may have contributed at certain times to its expansion—for example, the 2002 increase of dismissal compensation in Argentina.

24. The program, created in 2002, provides a benefit of $1,900 pesos (approximately US$175 dollars) to displaced formal sector workers who have contributed to the social security system, are eighteen to forty years of age, and have dependents. The program is intended to provide support to unemployed formal sector workers so that they can finance their search for a formal sector job, thus dissuading them from entering the informal sector. Its goal is to cover 50,000 unemployed workers and to offer training and job search services (Samaniego, 2002).

25. The FAT was created in 1988 with the constitutional reform, absorbing other previous existing funds. In 2001 its expenditure in relation to GDP was 0.59 percent, including unemployment insurance (0.43 percent of GDP), the *abono salarial* (a wage supplement of one minimum wage to be paid to all workers employed in the formal sector who earn up to two minimum wages, with an expenditure equivalent to 0.08 percent of GDP), training schemes (0.04 percent), intermediation (0.01 percent), and support to micro and small firms.

26. On how the amount is to be calculated in relation to national treasury bonds, see Conte-Grand, 1997.

27. More information can be found in Conte-Grand, 1997; Andraus Troyano, 1998; and Ramos, 2002.

28. Details are in Marshall, 1997.

29. Argentina also has numerous provincial cash transfer programs. A detailed account of the provincial programs existing in 2001 can be found in Facelli et al., 2002. In that year, total average monthly beneficiaries of provincial employment programs, considering those provinces for which data were available, amounted to 203,000. Some 64 percent of funding for these programs, implemented in the provinces, was funded by provincial government revenues, 4 percent from national revenues, and 32 percent from both.

30. Data from MTSS on beneficiaries of employment programs. By 2002–2003 there were practically no beneficiaries of other national employment programs, as most had been discontinued, except for Recuperación Productiva (Production Recovery), with some 9,000 beneficiaries per month on average. For details on the many Argentine national temporary employment programs of the 1990s no longer existing in 2003, see Marshall, 1997; and Golbert and Giacometti, 1998.

31. All these emergency programs are analyzed in Rocha, 2001.

32. Information from the website of Brazil's Ministry of Labor and Employment (http://www.mte.gov.br).

33. One example is the Fondo de Capital Social (Fund for Social Capital), a public-private enterprise established by the ministry in 2000 that funds and advises institutions providing credit to micro firms, mainly small producers of agricultural and other primary sector exports. Loans have reached over 15,000 micro employers (Economic Supplement of *Página 12,* January 11, 2004).

34. Other programs targeted at sectors with potential for employment generation include PROEMPREGO (I created in 1996, II in 1999), a more traditional credit program targeted at transportation, manufacturing restructuring in areas with unemployment problems, and tourism. PROTRABALHO I and II, started in 1999, finances strategic projects in the poorest regions. Programa de Crédito Popular (Popular Credit Program) is a microcredit program with fewer financial resources than the others. See Ramos, 2002.

35. This program was started in 2001, subsuming previous schemes with similar targets; its purpose is to help micro, small, and medium-sized firms that are competing successfully in national and external markets. It is addressed to a sector concentrating a large segment of employment, as, according to Samaniego, 2002, these three categories of firms represent 95 percent of Mexican enterprises.

36. For information on the many training programs created in the 1990s that did not survive in 2003, see Marshall, 1997; and Golbert and Giacometti, 1998.

37. On a much smaller scale is the Voluntary Civil Service, which plans to train 5,000 young workers and place at least 20 percent of them in jobs. Within the context of PROGER's "young entrepreneur" component, the service provides skills to 16,000 youth, with financing from the FAT (Cella Dal Chiavon, 2003).

38. Another important, though more general, training program in Mexico is the Programa de Apoyo a la Capacitación de Trabajadores en Activo (Support Program for the Training of Workers in the Labor Market), created in 1987. It is geared at employed workers with the objective of promoting training in micro, small, and medium-sized firms, to motivate the introduction of higher productivity and quality work practices. It grew from 365 training events and technical assistance actions in 1988 to almost 73,000 in 1999 (Samaniego, 2002).

39. The distribution of agencies was: 29.4 percent, municipal offices; 18.6 percent, civil associations; 13.4 percent, religious institutions; 12.4 percent, trade unions; 11.9 percent, educational institutions; the rest, national and provincial offices and employer associations (data from MTSS).

40. In 1999, 35 percent of applicants were placed, 15 percent in job vacancies, the other 20 percent in employment programs (data from MTSS).

41. More details in Samaniego, 2002.

42. Data estimated based on statistics given for the Mexican government's *Anexo del segundo informe de gobierno 2002,* January–August, p. 91.

43. Data from the Ministry of Economy (http://www.mecon.gov.ar) and MTSS. Expenditure on assistance to small and micro firms is not included, as data on such are not readily available.

44. Based on data from MTSS.

45. Verdera, 1998, presents data showing that expenditure on active labor market policies in 1995 was equivalent to 2.09 percent of GDP in Brazil, and to 0.61 percent in Mexico, but these estimates include programs that cannot be considered to be labor market policies, strictly speaking; in the case of Brazil, for instance, if PROEMPREGO (as we have seen, not strictly an employment program) is excluded, the GDP share drops to 0.28 percent.

46. Data are for 1998 (http://www.oecd.org).

47. The UK spends only 0.4 percent of GDP in active policies, but the Netherlands spends 1.6 percent. More data are available in OECD, 2001.

48. Data on the number of households with beneficiaries, from MTSS. Data on the percentage of unemployed who are beneficiaries, calculated from employment program beneficiaries in October 2002 (MTSS) and estimated total urban unemployed population in the same month (Ministry of Economy), with the number of unemployed being the sum of the unemployed and employment program beneficiaries.

49. Paes de Barros, Corseuil, and Foguel (2000) also found that unemployment insurance did not contribute to reducing poverty. However, unemployment insurance systems are not necessarily conceived as antipoverty measures, but rather as labor protection schemes.

50. See Ramos, 2002, for details on evaluations of PROGER, PLANFOR, and the like.

51. For full details, see Samaniego, 2002.

7

Social Dialogue
and Employment

During times of economic change or uncertainty, social dialogue can be instrumental in ensuring that job creation is an economic as well as a social priority. Social dialogue is based on tripartite political consultation and bargaining: the willingness of worker and employer organizations and the state to cooperate in addressing a wide range of issues, from wages and working conditions to other social and economic challenges. Effective social dialogue requires that each party be autonomous and well prepared; consequently, a weakening of one of the parties can affect the nature and outcome of dialogue, or impede its use altogether.

Like the other policy areas discussed in this book, social dialogue in Argentina, Brazil, and Mexico was affected by the sweeping economic reforms of the 1980s and 1990s. The replacement of a state-led industrialization development model with a market-led approach and the consequent economic restructuring had a dramatic effect on the power of the state, as well as the worker and employer organizations linked to national industries. Labor regulations, union structures, collective action, patterns of dialogue between capital and labor, as well as the patterns of state intervention, have all changed in the three countries, though at varying degrees. This chapter analyzes these changes with a view to assessing the role of the social partners and social dialogue in reshaping the labor market and contributing to the creation of quality employment.

Origins of the Industrial Relations Systems

The industrial relations systems of Argentina, Brazil, and Mexico have many similarities, but the differences cannot be overstated. The differences stem

This chapter is based on a background paper by Adalberto Moreira Cardoso, *Industrial relations, social dialogue, and employment in Argentina, Brazil, and Mexico,* Employment strategy paper, no. 2004/7 (Geneva, ILO, 2004), http://www.ilo.org.

from the process of consolidation of the relations between state and society and with the scope and timing of the political and economic changes of recent years. The systems of the three countries evolved in tandem with the process of economic development based on state-led, import-substitution industrialization (ISI). The governments strengthened and controlled labor at the same time as they expanded state bureaucracies, subsidized industries and agriculture, created state enterprises in strategic branches, controlled foreign investment, and closed internal markets to foreign competition.

If the industrial relations systems of the three countries are very stable over time, that of Mexico has been by far the most stable. The still operative labor legislation that governs Mexican labor relations is the Ley Federal del Trabajo (LFT; Federal Labor Law), passed in 1931 (Bensusán, 2000; Bizberg, 1999). This far-reaching labor legislation covered collective bargaining procedures, working conditions, health standards, and remuneration, and recognized the weaker position of labor in capitalist economies. Although the LFT was revised over the years, including a new law decreed in 1970 under the same name, the main features of the original legislation remain in force, most importantly the quid pro quo between government and labor. Essentially, in exchange for legal protection, worker organizations would acquiesce to state policies, while state control over employer and worker associations' internal affairs would halt labor-capital conflicts (Bensusán, 1992).

The passage of the labor law coincided with the institutionalization of the Partido Revolucionario Institucional (PRI; Revolutionary Institutional Party), the political party that would govern the country for more than seventy years. In 1938, the Central de los Trabajadores Mexicanos (CTM; Confederation of Mexican Workers) was legally incorporated in the structure of the PRI, becoming a main source of the party's political legitimacy and support. The process of social and political incorporation of workers in Mexico implied strict control over labor actions via administrative and repressive measures, including the possibility of control of union elections, deposition of leaders, ratification of strikes, as well as the ousting of unions. It also meant that only one union could represent the workers of a particular firm and that all workers were obligated to join this union (closed shop). Employers were also formally integrated into the system through mandatory chambers (the chamber of commerce, the chamber of industry, and the chamber of small and medium-sized enterprises). Industrial and economic policies in the ISI period were almost always designed in close connection with employer representatives.

Although the political and legislative agreements established formal rigidity in Mexican labor relations, there is a consensus among specialists that the regulations have always been flexible in practice. G. Bensusán (1992) has named this system "corporatist flexibility," as the system was allowed to adapt to the different social and economic environments of the century (ISI, the crisis of the 1980s, and the new model of development based on exports).[1] As E. de la Garza (1998) points out, the system allowed management discretion within the firms to establish nonwritten flexible practices. In sum, the Mexican system of labor relations has been based on a clear exchange of labor acquiescence for legal protection and social policies, with labor rights enshrined in the constitution.

As in Mexico, the consolidation of the labor law in Brazil and the industrial relations system occurred hand-in-hand with the process of national and economic development. The enactment of labor law in Brazil occurred from 1930 to 1943, and was finally consolidated in a labor code, known as the Consolidação das Leis do Trabalho (CLT; Consolidation of Labor Laws). The CLT, like the Mexican LFT, would regulate both the labor market and the institutions representing labor and capital. It offered populist and authoritarian regimes control over the organizations of the urban masses and, at the same time, protected workers with minimum social policies and provisions. Also, as in Mexico and Argentina years later, labor courts were created to process labor demands and workers' grievances (Cardoso, 2003).

In Brazil, as in Mexico and Argentina, state regulation granted unions the monopoly of representation in a given jurisdiction (the firm in Mexico, the economic sector or activity in Argentina, the municipality in Brazil), and unions were financed by a tax charged on all workers of that jurisdiction. Union affiliation was not necessary, as unions would represent all workers irrespective of affiliation. During his dictatorial years (1937–1945), Getúlio Vargas forbade strikes, and for the following decades the legislation, if applied, would have made strikes virtually impossible.[2] But as in Argentina, state control over unions' actions varied throughout history. In general, authoritarian regimes (Vargas from 1937 to 1945, and the military from 1964 to 1981) would apply the restrictive laws, and democratic regimes would treat them as nonexistent. Another distinctive feature of labor relations in Brazil is that trade unions would never establish strong ties with political parties, at least until the 1980s.

By the 1930s, Argentina already had one of the strongest labor movements in Latin America. The first major central federation of Argentina, the Confederación General del Trabajo (CGT; General Labor Confederation), was founded in 1930, and in 1932 it delivered to the parliament a series of demands, including fewer working hours, severance pay, retirement benefits, and other welfare measures (Bergquist, 1986). From the mid-1930s onward, the labor movement in Argentina would gain strength, though it was still a secondary force in the political arena, mostly because of the restrictions to union action and to collective bargaining. The creation of the Labor Secretariat in 1943, however, formalized the channels of consultation with worker representatives, bringing them into the policymaking process, and providing state assistance to unions recognized by the state. Employers were forced to negotiate with recognized unions, and faced important defeats in labor disputes.

The government also began to enforce the existing legislation and to increase its scope and coverage by approving new regulations, including establishing a minimum wage, providing accident insurance, and most important, restricting the dismissals of workers. A labor court was also established to process workers' grievances. In 1945, the Professional Associations Law was passed; it ended many antilabor provisions, but it also legitimized state control over unions, by giving the state the ability to recognize or not recognize unions, thereby granting them the right to strike and bargain collectively. A centralized union structure was established and union finances were improved through automatic payroll deductions of union dues.

After Juan Perón's election to the presidency in 1946, the pattern of control and recognition of unions was deepened. The right to strike was limited and interventions in recalcitrant unions increased. The CGT, which was under the complete control of Perón in 1950, was used to take over non-Peronist unions, and by 1954 virtually all of Argentina's largest unions had suffered intervention and had their leadership removed. At the same time, as a counterpart to the control over unions, in 1947 the "Rights of the Worker" were enacted and then included in the 1949 constitution. By 1948 more than 1.5 million workers were unionized and in some sectors the density rate was as high as 70 percent (Torre and de Riz, 1991).

These main characteristics of the industrial relations system in Argentina would not suffer major changes until the beginning of the 1990s, despite the harsh antilabor actions of the military regime in the 1970s. The Mexican model would begin to change only in the 2000s. In Brazil, the constitution of 1988 would introduce some changes in the union structure, freeing them from state control, but, by focusing on specific labor rights, would make it harder to change the regulation of labor relations. Yet only in Mexico did the industrial relations system consolidate stable, tripartite institutions to accommodate labor/capital conflicts, but with the clear intent of control over labor unions and their leaders. Compared to Mexico, corporatism was never as strong in Argentina or Brazil, notwithstanding the measures taken during Perón's first term and the strong stake of Peronism in Argentine politics.

Union Responses to Economic Restructuring

Though the industrial relations systems in Argentina, Brazil, and Mexico have changed little, economic restructuring in the late 1980s and 1990s has affected unions, collective bargaining, and social dialogue. As discussed in Chapters 3 and 4, economic restructuring was centered on introducing market mechanisms and opening the economies to external competition. The Washington Consensus view that geared these policies also held that labor markets needed to be flexible in order to allow labor to move easily into sectors that would benefit from trade liberalization. As a result, there was a strong motivation for the countries that were reforming their goods and financial markets to also reform their labor markets. As discussed in Chapter 6, Argentina was the most far-reaching in adopting legislative changes to its labor code. Labor flexibilization was also achieved in Brazil and Mexico, though the changes, particularly in Mexico, were de facto as opposed to de jure. The relationship between the social partners, which we address in this section, partly explains why the countries reformed their labor markets at varying degrees.

In Argentina, the economic and labor reforms of the early 1990s were passed without substantial resistance from the labor movement.[3] The support of the reforms is attributed to four main reasons. First, the CGT was divided in two main factions in the beginning of the 1990s, but both of them were Peronists, with the predominant group supporting Peronist president Carlos Menem. As a result, the political affiliation of most union leaders restricted their willingness to act against public policies. Second, the public supported the reforms. A 1991 survey found that 68 percent of Argentines supported the privatization of public enterprises, 77 percent favored a more open economy, and 82 percent favored the reduction of public spending. A third important reason was that the Convertibility Plan, adopted by Menem, succeeded in taming hyperinflation, which had lowered workers' incomes in the 1980s and disorganized the economy. The Convertibility Plan stabilized the currency and, in the initial years, fostered economic growth, explaining its broad support, including from labor. A fourth reason was that many important CGT leaders saw in the privatization process the opportunity to spread CGT's leadership in constituencies normally averse to its representation, such as the metalworker unions of the public enterprises (Murillo, 2001). M. Murillo also notes that many unionists benefited directly from privatization, as the Menem administration sold shares to workers at subsidized prices. The support of the Peronist trade unions to the reforms of the 1990s is evident when comparing strike activity. During Menem's first term (1989–1995) there was only one (frustrated) strike attempt, in comparison with the term of Radical Party president Raúl Alfonsín (1983–1989), when the CGT coordinated thirteen general strikes (Munck, 1997).

In Brazil, on the contrary, the main central federation, the Central Única dos Trabalhadores (CUT; Central Workers Union), opposed President Fernando Cardoso's economic plan, yet the union was unsuccessful in fighting the reforms, partly as a result of the government's strategy to delegitimize unions. Perhaps the most significant event was the confrontation with petroleum workers in 1995, whereby the Brazilian state-owned petroleum company, Petrobras, refused to honor a collective agreement that indexed wage growth to past inflation and, in doing so, signaled to all other workers that the government would not longer "tolerate" indexing. After weeks of frustrated negotiations, a thirty-day violent strike took place, yet the CUT failed to obtain its demands. Public opinion turned against the strikers, with 60 percent of São Paulo's population disapproving the strike and more than half attributing it to political motives against President Cardoso, rather than wage demands.[4]

Other attempts by unions to block Cardoso's neoliberal programs, including the privatization of state-owned enterprises, failed. What is striking is that, unlike Argentina, privatization was undertaken without widespread support among the public. In 1990, the Datafolha Institute found that only 30 percent of Brazilians were in favor of privatization, while 30 percent were against it and 36 percent had no clear opinion.[5] By 1998, the rate of rejection had grown to 52 percent, with only 34 percent supporting the selling of public enterprises.[6] In November 2000 the institute found that 65 percent of the voters in São Paulo were against "privatization in general."[7] Nevertheless, opposition forces were not able to channel the public's sentiment in order to stop the selling of former bastions of the Brazilian labor movement, particularly those public enterprises dominated by the CUT. This was a heavy blow to the leftist strategy of confrontation based on nationalist reasoning. Yet as in Argentina, competing union leaders benefited from the sale of subsidized stocks, giving them a personal stake in privatization.

As discussed in Chapter 6, in Brazil the changes in the labor legislation were not as deep as in Argentina, and would only take place in the second half of the 1990s. Yet the legislation did not have to change much for the flexibility measures to be implemented in the day-to-day running of businesses. As R. Barros and R. Mendonça (1996) and Barros and colleagues (1997) have demonstrated persuasively, the Brazilian labor market is among the most flexible in the world in response to economic shocks, both in terms of reallocation of the labor force and in terms of wage flexibility. For this reason, the pressure for legislative change has not been strong from either government agencies or the employer organizations. Nonetheless, the National Confederation of Industry, the National Confederation of Transport, and the Brazilian Federation of Banks all submitted projects to the legislature, attempting to change items such as severance pay or the regulation of working hours. The labor reform that did finally pass in Congress concerned the so-called bank of hours, a flexibility measure that permits the adjustment of the working time in accordance with variations in demand during the year.

In Mexico, because of its corporatist labor-capital relations, the economic reforms only suffered some opposition from the traditional social dialogue partners, and only after the crisis of 1994. Presidents Miguel de la Madrid, Carlos Salinas, and Ernesto Zedillo were able to restructure the economy, including the inclusion of Mexico in the North American Free Trade Agreement (NAFTA), without opposition from labor. G. Bensusán (1993 and 2000) shows very convincingly that although the labor movement was represented in negotiations for the Pacto de Solidaridad Económica (PSE; Pact of Economic Solidarity) in 1987, NAFTA in the 1990s, and other tripartite agreements concerning Mexican restructuring, their influence was always marginal. During the NAFTA process, while more than 500 employers were represented in the working groups, only six union leaders took part in the negotiations. Despite this, social resistance or protests against the economic policies would only appear in the mid-1990s.

Yet the process of restructuring represented the destruction of the painfully constructed affinity between protectionist regulation of the labor market, industrialization centered on the internal market, and an authoritarian, corporatist political system (Bensusán, 2000; Bizberg, 1999). As discussed previously, the traditional Mexican compromise included the recognition by the state that workers were the weaker party in labor relations, hence the multidimensional legislation of protection and its enforcement by state officials and union leaders. Yet under the new economic and political environment, though the laws were unchanged, economic restructuring shifted the bargaining power against workers. Labor was unable to halt the impoverishment of their constituency, but instead complied with the policies in order to maintain control over their union structure.

The depth and scope of restructuring in Argentina, Brazil, and Mexico have been remarkable. The financial markets, the manufacturing sector, and basic services have all been reconfigured, often shifting from national to international ownership. The labor market also changed considerably, with employment migrating from manufacturing to services and also to unemployment. Considering the depth of the changes—affecting the welfare of both workers and employers—one would have expected major resistance, but this did not happen, partly because of the organizational ties of the social partners with the state.

The Structure of Worker and Employer Organizations

The structure of worker and employer organizations in Argentina, Brazil, and Mexico bears the weight of the past administrative and political control of state officials and political parties. Despite the democratization process in Brazil and Argentina in the 1980s, and more recently in Mexico, these organizations shoulder the legacy of corporatist relations with the state.

In Mexico the legacy of corporatism is apparent in the dual and pyramidal structure of its unions (Bensusán and Alcalde, 2000). Within the union structure are the institutions affiliated with the Congreso del Trabajo (CT; Workers Congress) as well as independent unions. The summit of the official pyramid is the CT itself and the leaders of the central federations affiliated to it. At the base are the myriad of unions of various kinds, size, and scope: unions of professionals, company unions, unions of industry, and national industry federations. The CT is still the prevailing organization, not only for its large membership, but mainly for its special relationship with the state and its institutional resources. For instance, the unions affiliated to it still have precedence in collective bargaining. They also hold seats on the tripartite boards that administer labor and the labor courts, a situation still prevailing after the democratization at the beginning of the 2000s.

The CT was created in the mid-1960s and organizes unions of both the private and public sectors in local and federal jurisdictions.[8] In 1978, 84 percent of all union members—74 percent of the private sector's and 99.8 percent of the public sector's affiliated workers—were represented by the CT (Zazueta and de la Peña, 1984). In recent years some important unions have left the CT, reducing its representation in the private sector to 67 percent; its affiliation of public sector workers remains intact (Bensusán and Alcalde, 2000).[9] The most important departure from the CT occurred in 1997, when the telephone union and different teacher unions formed the Unión Nacional de Trabajadores (UNT; National Workers Union). Since then, it has gained the adhesion of 160 peasant and worker organizations and is estimated to represent 1.5 million workers (Vadi, 2001).[10] The UNT has a dual political approach, combining the public denunciation of policies contrary to the interest of workers, such as the independent labor movement used to do, and negotiating with high-level state officials, as the corporatist unionism does (de la Garza, 2003c).

Another important type of union in Mexico are the *sindicatos blancos* (white unions, also referred to as *sindicatos de protección*), which are unions under the control of the individual firms, and found mainly in the northern states of the country (Bouzas Ortiz, 2003). These unions vary from paternalistic unions that work closely with management, to unions entirely under management control, to the extent that workers may not be aware of their existence (de la Garza, 2003b). Because of exclusion clauses, workers in some cases automatically become a member of the union upon signing a work contract. The union can thus sign a contract with management that workers are not privy to, which is then deposited in the registry of the Conciliation and Arbitration Boards, which are tripartite committees comprised of representatives of the government, employers, and workers, and who often represent white unions (Fair Labor Association, 2004). Because the contracts look like any other contract, it is difficult to know how many white unions exist in Mexico. Still, analysts agree that these unions have grown strongly over the past decade, particularly in the northern border states and in dynamic sectors such as telecommunications and the glass sector (Bensusán and Alcalde, 2000).

There are twelve employer organizations in Mexico, seven of which are permanent members of the Consejo Coordinador Empresarial (CCE; Business Coordination Council), including CONCAMIN and COPARMEX, arguably the two strongest employer organizations. Another important organization is CANACINTRA, which represents small and medium-sized employers, mainly from the manufacturing sector. Like unions, employer organizations were an important component of Mexico's corporatist political structure, with businesses required by law to be affiliated to a chamber. In 1997, however, the law was revised and now membership is voluntary. As a result, the associations have lost some representation and financing, as well as power.

The Brazilian "soft" corporatism has also created a structure that is officially pyramidal, but in practice local unions concentrate the collective bargaining power. The law permits only one union per economic sector or occupation in a given municipality or region, and this union has monopoly of representation over its members, whether affiliated or not. This practice is known as "unicity" *(unicidade sindical),* and it applies to both unions of workers and unions of employers. The law does not allow for firm-based unions. Although the union structure may seem as if it restricts competition, the system is highly fragmented and competitive. For example, even though there cannot exist two unions of metalworkers in the same city, there can be unions of drillers, of spinning-drillers, of hammerers, of car-assemblers, none of which is necessarily affiliated. Because the worker has the ability to choose being represented by the sector union or the union representing the worker's occupational category, there is segmentation within the union structure. As a consequence, unions have become increasingly fragmented, resulting in a 43 percent growth in the number of employer, employee, self-employed, and professional unions between 1991 and 2001 (see Table 7.1).

Within Brazil's union structure there are unions of a municipality, federations of at least two unions of the same economic branch or occupation in different municipalities, and confederations of at least two federations in different provinces. Formally, federations and confederations can perform collective bargaining when, for instance, the employers involved have various plants in different municipalities or states. But in practice the collective bargaining process is headed by local unions, with important exceptions. Since its creation in 1983, the CUT has been trying to consolidate a parallel structure of federations (first outlawed by the labor code, the CLT, and later permitted by the constitution of

Table 7.1   Number and Type of Unions, Brazil, 1991 and 2001

Type of Union	1991	2001
Urban	6,695	10,258
Employers	1,751	2,767
Employees	3,838	6,101
Self-employed	727	927
Professionals	379	463
Rural	4,498	5,705
Employers	1,522	1,782
Employees	2,976	3,923
Total	11,193	15,963

Source: IBGE, 2002.

1988), through which the CUT would negotiate national or multiprovince collective agreements in specific worker categories. Bank workers, for instance, have national employers, and metalworkers (from the auto industry) sometimes have the same employer across municipalities and provinces. The CUT has managed to strengthen these three federations in the 1990s, and they coordinate the collective bargaining processes of local unions. They are also entitled to formally endorse the agreements, something that the CLT does not address but that the federations have managed to include in collective agreements.

There are two major central federations in Brazil, the CUT and Força Sindical (Trade Union Force).[11] The CUT is by far the largest, with almost 3,000 affiliated unions in 2001, representing 66 percent of the total; 20 percent of unions belonging to a confederation were part of Força Sindical, mostly from the manufacturing sector. Employer unions are also pyramidal in structure, with confederations, federations, and unions represented. The leading confederations are the National Industrial Confederation, the National Comercial Confederation, and the National Agriculture Confederation.

The structure of employer and worker associations in Argentina is also pyramidal. The Unión Industrial Argentina (UIA; Argentine Industrial Union) encompasses a range of business chambers from all sectors of the economy, and represents industry in tripartite negotiations. Similarly, workers are represented by unions, federations, and confederations. Unions can be of company, sector, or profession, with sector unions prevailing. The CGT is the principal confederation in Argentina. At the beginning of the 1990s, the CGT had about 1,400 unions affiliated to it, of which 75 were organized as national federations. Two-thirds of these (50 federations) cover the provinces. But the majority of the unions are small. Almost half of them have less than 1,000 members, and only one in seven extends its jurisdiction beyond one province, department, district, or city. Argentine law guarantees freedom of association. Unions have the right to represent workers and to collectively bargain. As in Brazil and Mexico, in Argentina the state grants unions the "personeria gremial," or official recognition that allows unions to automatically collect union dues from workers, regardless of whether or not the worker is affiliated.

Union Density

Although the formal union structures in Argentina, Brazil, and Mexico have changed little over time, economic restructuring has had a major effect on the power of unions in the three countries. In fact, most labor movements in Latin America have lost economic resources, affiliates, political power, and broader social influence, leaving new social actors to occupy center stage of the social movements. Falling union density is probably the most powerful evidence of this trend. Table 7.2 gives union density rates for Argentina, Brazil, and Mexico

Table 7.2 Union Density, Various Years

Argentina

	Economically Active Population (a)	Employed Population (b)	Wage Earners (c)	Union Members (d)	(d)/(a)	(d)/(b)	(d)/(c)
1975	8,500,000	8,245,000	6,000,000	5,000,000	58.8	60.6	83.3
1985	11,000,000	10,340,000	7,500,000	4,000,000	36.3	38.7	53.3
1998	14,000,000	12,040,000	8,200,000	3,600,000	25.7	29.9	43.9
2002	15,840,000	13,340,000	8,804,000	3,850,000	24.3	28.9	43.7

Mexico

	Economically Active Population (a)	Unionizable Population of Manufacturing (b)	Union Members in Manufacturing (c)	Union Members (d)	(d)/(a)	(c)/(b)
1992	30,200,000	6,500,000	1,400,000	4,100,000	13.6	22.1
1994	35,000,000	6,800,000	1,000,000	3,600,000	10.4	14.9
1998	40,100,000	7,400,000	1,100,000	3,700,000	9.3	15.5
2000	41,000,000	8,000,000	1,200,000	4,000,000	9.8	15.0

Brazil

	Economically Active Population (a)	Employed Population (b)	Wage Earners (c)	Union Members (d)	(d)/(a)	(d)/(b)	Membership Among Wage Earners
1988	53,595,963	51,732,445	34,279,202	9,092,685	17.0	17.6	21.9
1995	65,413,222	63,909,393	37,060,634	11,319,065	17.3	17.7	21.6
1999	71,853,858	68,341,333	39,528,703	11,616,738	16.2	17.0	19.7
2002	76,950,394	73,364,193	44,085,216	13,309,123	17.3	18.1	20.1

Source: Cardoso, 2004.

based on national household surveys that ask workers directly whether they are affiliated to unions.

In the three countries, the different time spans covered notwithstanding, the trend toward union decline is strong. In Argentina, union density fell from more than 60 percent in 1975 to 36 percent in 1985 and to 24 percent in 2002, a loss of more than 60 percent in the affiliation rate of the economically active population. In Mexico the fall has also been quite dramatic, with more than 30 percent density lost in less than ten years. In Brazil, on the contrary, the figures are fairly stable.

The differences between countries concern the process of economic restructuring, as well as political factors. In Argentina, the loss in union density began in the 1970s, when the military government opened the country to external trade, which led to job losses in the highly unionized manufacturing sector. Union density also declined as a result of the persecution of union leaders during this era. Overall, unions lost 40 percent of their density between 1975 and 1985. During the 1990s, deindustrialization and privatization, and the resulting upsurge in unemployment, furthered the loss of union density. In Brazil, the stability of union density results from the ability of the labor movement to cope with the structural changes within the labor market. Manufacturing lost more than 2 million jobs and 500,000 affiliates between 1988 and 1998 (Cardoso, 2003), but the service sector grew almost at the same pace, mainly in education and food and catering. Yet even though union density has held its ground, the job and union losses in the politically powerful sectors of manufacturing, banking, and public services have resulted in their overall weakening. In Mexico, the loss in affiliation has similar causes: privatization, the deindustrialization of the central areas of the country, the growth of the services and informal sectors, the growth of micro and small companies (unions are permitted in companies with at least twenty employees only), and the failure of the union leaders to attract affiliates in new, emerging industries, particularly in the maquiladoras (de la Garza, 2003b). Nevertheless, union density rates have remained fairly constant in Argentina and Mexico since 1998, and the number of union members has actually increased.

Collective Bargaining

Collective bargaining has also faced important changes in recent years. In Mexico, as in Brazil, the issues collectively negotiated are narrowing in scope. In Argentina, on the contrary, collective bargaining has enlarged its scope to include functional flexibility measures and industrial restructuring. But the formal labor market, where collective bargaining takes place, has shrunk dramatically.

Collective bargaining in Argentina has never been a steady process, halted by the economic policies to curtail inflation in the 1970s and 1980s, and in the

1990s by the convertibility program, which required that wage increases be tied to productivity growth. As a result, many unions chose not to bargain during this period, leaving untouched earlier agreements, based on the "ultra-activity" principle that if an agreement is not reached in a negotiation, previous clauses will hold. (Ultra-activity was removed in 2001.) Still, in response to changes in the economic environment and labor market regulations, many other unions did bargain during the 1990s. Yet the new environment altered negotiations, which became increasingly decentralized and considered a broader range of issues, including functional flexibility and firm productivity. The increased decentralization of collective bargaining is apparent when comparing collective agreements signed in 1991 with those signed in 2002. In 1991, negotiations at the firm level represented only 19 percent of agreements, while in 2002 they accounted for 82 percent of agreements signed. Between 2000 and 2002, not a single sector-level collective agreement was signed (Cardoso, 2004).

By shifting negotiations from the sector level to the firm level, the focus of agreements changed as well. In 1991, 40 percent of agreements contained only salary provisions; by 1999 this figure had fallen to just 12 percent (Novick, 2001). Flexibility measures, concerning temporary employment contracts, distribution of working hours, and organization of work, became an important subject of agreements. From 1991 to the first semester of 1999, employers and unions reached 1,598 agreements, of which 58 percent had at least one clause related to flexibility. After 1996, most contracts had at least three flexibility clauses. Working hours constituted the most important clause (appearing in 571 agreements), followed by flexible contracts (484 agreements) and flexible organization of work (478 agreements). Flexible pay appeared only in 252 agreements (Novick, 2001). M. Novick (2001) finds that it was those sectors most exposed to competition in the 1990s—manufacturing, particularly autos, and recently privatized basic services—that had the greatest number of flexibility clauses in their collective agreements.

In sum, the general trend in collective bargaining has been decentralization, an increase in the number of clauses, and the diversification of the resulting agreements to encompass issues far beyond wages, the major theme at the beginning of the 1990s. Decentralized collective bargaining is associated with more focused agreements that address issues specific to a firm and its workers' interests; the agreements are also more flexible. Nevertheless, the number of workers covered by collective agreements fell in tandem with the reduction of the formal labor market and the increase in unemployment, but also with the shift to decentralized bargaining.

In Mexico, unlike Argentina, there has been a clear reduction of the areas in which collective bargaining could influence the organization of work. Based on two rounds of a manufacturing survey, we can assess which work issues are regulated, whether regulated by formal collective agreements, firm-specific regulations, or accords of any kind.[12] In general, the existence of collective bargaining on issues such as job design, functional mobility, dismissals, and use of subcontracted labor is low. The issue most bargained was "job design and assignment of tasks," yet only 18 percent of firms in 1995 considered this issue, falling to just 7.2 percent by 1999 (see Table 7.3, "All Firms" column). "Use of subcontracted labor" was considered by just 4.3 percent of firms in 1995, falling to 1.6 percent in 1999. Of the eleven issues given in Table 7.3, not one gained influence between 1995 and 1999; instead the bargaining incidence fell by nearly 60 percent in the five-year period.

Disaggregating the analysis by firm size is quite revealing and shows that the low overall rate of bargained work issues is mainly due to the large number of micro-sized firms, which account for approximately 92 percent of the survey sample. Nevertheless, within big firms, there was an almost 30 percent decline in bargained work issues in five years. Of particular note is the decline in the regulation of job promotion from 77 to 62 percent, signaling the dissolution of the job classification system, known as *el scalafón*, whereby workers had clear career expectations related to job assignment and where transfers could not be conceded without approval from unions or worker representatives.

Thus, contrary to Argentina, Mexico has fewer firms bargaining on a comprehensive set of issues. If the incidence of bargaining items can be taken as a good proxy of what is actually negotiated, firms have managed to make agreements less complex and more flexible than before. The reduction in the number of stances of regulation means that firms are gaining bargaining power vis-à-vis the individual worker and also the unions. Moreover, there has not been any trade-off between measures, say flexibilization of the promotion system in exchange for greater job security, nor has there been more union authority over quality-control programs or power within the firms (see de la Garza, 2003c).

In Brazil, there have been three main trends in collective bargaining since 1990.[13] First, employment has came to the fore as the main issue, replacing wages, which were the focus of union concerns during the 1980s as a result of the high levels of inflation. Yet despite unions' concerns, the number of clauses negotiated on this issue has been small. Only in a few cases did clauses address the maintenance or increase of jobs, such as guarantees on employment during a particular period, often in exchange for reductions in pay. For example, in exchange for some job security the metalworkers union of the São Paulo ABC Region conceded through collective bargaining, fringe benefits and other important gains obtained in the 1980s in exchange for keeping open an automobile plant in São Bernardo do Campo (Cardoso, 2003). Second, even though reskilling and training related to restructuring started to appear in some collective conventions, most were blanket clauses, not specific to the needs of the firm. Agreements that would compromise firms by establishing amounts of investments or that retained workers in case of economic restructuring or technological change were rare, and when they did exist, the clauses were generic and ineffective.

Table 7.3 Existence of Labor Regulations by Large, Micro, and All Firms in Manufacturing, Mexico, 1995 and 1999 (percentages)

Labor Regulation	Large Firms		Micro Firms		All Firms	
	1995	1999	1995	1999	1995	1999
Job design and assignment of tasks	78.1	74.1	14.3	4.0	18.0	7.2
Promotion	76.8	61.5	7.1	5.6	10.5	5.2
Hiring of part-time labor	74.8	64.6	9.8	4.9	13.1	7.2
Selection of personnel	69.1	55.8	9.7	3.3	12.8	6.0
Quality and productivity programs	68.6	53.7	16.8	6.0	19.4	8.6
Functional mobility	51.6	28.2	8.3	2.8	10.1	4.2
Dismissals	46.0	28.4	9.3	1.3	11.3	2.3
Changes in the organization of work	45.7	27.1	6.9	2.6	8.6	3.7
Creation of advisory jobs	41.1	26.2	9.8	5.0	6.8	3.2
Introduction of new technologies	38.7	24.3	5.0	2.0	6.5	3.0
Use of subcontracted labor	25.0	16.8	3.5	1.2	4.3	1.6
Mean variation (1995 = 100)		71.8		39.9		42.9

Source: Cardoso, 2004; adapted from Hererra and Melgoza, 2003, pp. 342–344.

Third, and much as in Argentina and Mexico, in Brazil "essential guarantees for the creation of an environment allowing for the equilibrium between the parties in collective bargaining—like plant level organization of workers and access to information about firms—are still absent" (Departamento Intersindical de Estadística e Estudos Socio-Econômicos [DIEESE], 1997, p. 62). The absence of clauses related to union power at the firm level is an important issue in all three countries. Without access to information concerning the economic performance of the firm, unions must restrict their demands to what the employer states to be the "possible" concessions in the new, competitive economic environment. Many negotiations in the 1990s were performed under the threat of firm closure. Moreover, much like in Argentina, collective bargaining in Brazil was strongly decentralized, with collective accords between one union and one firm prevailing over collective conventions that covered all the firms of a municipality (see Oliveira, 2003).

As a general trend, it can be said that the loss of power and capacity for collective action reduced unions' ability to interfere via collective bargaining in the two measures of flexibility: internal, functional flexibility, and external flexibility. In all three countries, unions would either not negotiate employment issues, or do so in ineffective ways. In many cases, concession bargaining served to reduce workers' rights and the scope of the working conditions that were regulated either by the law or by previous collective agreements. As a result, the collective bargaining process would neither halt labor market flexibility nor reduce its pace.

Collective Action

Collective action in Argentina, Brazil, and Mexico, according to strike statistics,[14] has fallen sharply since 1990. In Argentina, between 1980 and 2002, there were close to 10,000 labor conflicts, according to the Centro de Estudios Nueva Mayoria (see Figure 7.1).[15] During the beginning of the 1980s, strike activity was under 400 cases per year. Yet beginning in 1986, there was a burst of collective action, reaching a peak of 949 strikes in 1988, as a result of the democratization process, the consolidation of trade unions and central federations, as well as the deteriorating economic environment. High inflation in Argentina, as in Brazil, made it rational for union leaders to develop a contentious social strategy based on large, branch-level strikes demanding the indexing of salaries to past inflation. The stabilization of the Argentine economy in the 1990s brought labor's conflictive strategies to a halt. After 1991, strikes decreased to a rate equivalent to that in the early 1980s, falling to a minimum of 125 conflicts, only to start to escalate again after 1997, peaking at 358 strikes in the crisis year of 2001. Nevertheless, strike activity did not

Figure 7.1   Number of Strikes, Argentina, 1980–2002

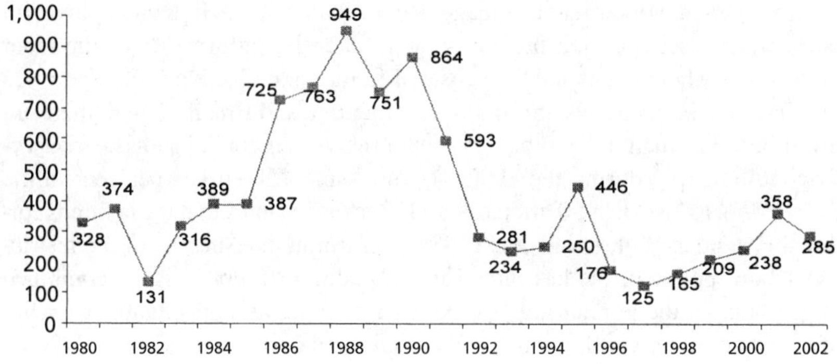

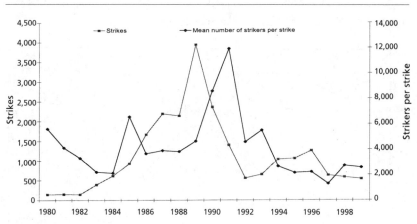

Source: Cardoso, 2004, based on data from the Centro de Estudios Nueva Mayoria.

reach the levels of the late 1980s. In an environment of high and rising unemployment, workers were less inclined to demand wage increases.

In Brazil, strikes, though less frequent since 1992, are still important. Figure 7.2 depicts strike evolution and the mean number of strikers per strike between 1980 and 1999. As in Argentina, the number of strikes escalated from 1982 to 1989, the period of democratization and also of high inflation, and then dropped to more stable levels in the 1990s, varying from 500 to 1,500 per year. The number of participants followed suit. Like Argentina, Brazil saw its apex

Figure 7.2   Number of Strikes and Strikers, Brazil, 1980–1999

Source: Cardoso, 2004.

of labor unrest in the 1980s, a period of rebirth and reorganization of the labor movement. Nevertheless, the strong fall from the 1980s to the 1990s likely reflects increased worker fear to engage in collective action. High unemployment rates, wage insecurity, job insecurity, and increasing informality of the labor market as a whole augmented the costs of failure of collective action.

In Mexico, the trends are similar to Argentina and Brazil, though there are fewer conflicts than in the other two countries. As Figure 7.3 shows, strike activity fell sharply during the 1990s, from around 150 strikes per year in the early 1990s to less than 50 after 1995. G. Bensusán states that these trends follow the "tendency observed since 1984, confirming the success of the restrictive labour policy of the last three [federal] administrations, which combined huge losses in the purchasing power of wages with an undisputable capacity of control of labor conflict through the traditional corporatist channels" (2003, p. 55).

The figures for Argentina, Brazil, and Mexico highlight the decline of the labor movement in the 1990s. Unions lost affiliates, money, capacity for collective action, and strength in collective bargaining. Thus it is not surprising that by the turn of the twenty-first century, they had also lost legitimacy. In Brazil in 1990, more than 60 percent of the adult population trusted unions, rating them just below the Catholic Church; in 2001 the figured had dropped to 27 percent (Cardoso, 2003). In Argentina in 1996, a mere 8 percent of the adult population trusted unions (Valdovinos, 1998). The history of the economic restructuring process in Latin America is also the history of the delegitimization of unions as parties in their own right in social relations at large, and more specifically, in economic and labor relations.

Figure 7.3   Number of Strikes, Mexico, 1990s

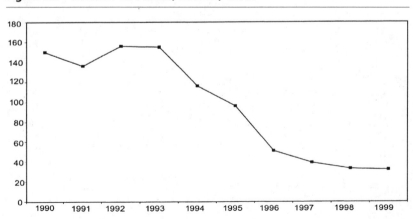

Source: Cardoso, 2004, adapted from Bensusán, 2003, p. 60.

Social Dialogue

Social dialogue concerns formal, state-led, or state-mediated forms of social and political consultation between the state and employer and worker organizations regarding major economic issues, such as development, investment, and employment.[16] Because social dialogue is based on political consultation, a weakening of the state or the social partners can affect the nature and outcome of the dialogue. The use of social dialogue historically, and in recent times in Argentina, Brazil, and Mexico, is quite varied. Mexico has a strong tradition of social dialogue, as labor and capital are deeply embedded in the state. In Argentina, social dialogue was the very base of Perón's power, but then ceased to exist during the military regime; since then, social dialogue has been reinstated, but without clear results. Similarly, in Brazil, successive attempts have been made at social dialogue since the transition to democracy in the 1980s, yet most of the successful experiences have been local or restricted in scope. The Lula government has initiated a more systematic social dialogue process, but its results are still to be seen.

In Mexico, the best-known experiences with social dialogue were the series of socioeconomic pacts between the government and employer and worker organizations undertaken beginning in 1987, first to tackle inflation, but afterward to regulate growth and related issues, including employment creation, labor relations, and working culture.[17] The Economic Solidarity Pact was the first attempt, followed in 1988 by the Stability and Economic Growth Pact, which would be revised many times until 1994 and then renamed the Pact for Well-Being, Stability, and Growth. The Economic Solidarity Pact joined employer, worker, and peasant organizations inside the PRI to design income, fiscal, and monetary policies to control the rampant inflation that was plaguing the country. The pacts were quite effective in controlling inflation, reducing it from 160 percent to 19 percent a year between 1987 and 1991.[18] Yet employment creation and working conditions were never explicitly considered or targeted within the pacts. Rather, the main issues were productivity, inflation, and growth. During the first pacts, an explicit policy of wage contraction was adopted to fight inflation, which caused a fall in real contractual wages of 29 percent and a fall in real minimum wages of 42 percent between 1989 and 1999 (Bensusán, 2003). The reduction in real wages was promoted as being beneficial to employment creation.

A further agreement aimed at controlling inflation and restructuring the economy was the National Agreement for the Raising of Productivity and Quality, signed in 1992 by the CTM, COPARMEX (National Employers Confederation of the Mexican Republic), and the state. However, the pact offered little but general guidelines for organizational restructuring and technological and educational advancement, and though it allowed for the revision of collective agreements to tie wages to productivity gains, CTM unions were unable to secure these revisions, in part because they lacked effective power to negotiate better conditions. In 1995 only 13.7 percent of revisions of contractual wages resulted in increases linked to productivity, and the figure fell to less than 7 percent in 1997 (de la Garza, 2000).

Another important social dialogue experience in Mexico was the Nueva Cultura Laboral (New Labor Culture) pact, signed in July 1995 by the CTM and COPARMEX in response to a legislative initiative of the Partido de Acción Nacional (PAN; Party of National Action) to reform the corporative union structure and improve social benefits. In ten statements, employers and workers affirm the ethical and transcendental value of work, recognize it as a source of rights and obligations, and state that ensuring better benefits to workers must take the economic situation of firms and the country into account. The ninth principle says that the new labor culture must be based on social consultation and dialogue, and on a combined effort from employers and workers' organizations.[19] Nevertheless, the pact did not result in any institutional change that would favor modernization, cooperation, or dialogue between the parties in labor relations, though it is possible that it may have contributed to reducing strike activity in the 1990s. Also, an agreement was made to give more transparency to the information about unions and union density processed by the secretary of labor (Bensusán, 2000).

Since entering office in January 2000, the government of Vicente Fox has engaged two consultations, the Mesa Central de Decisión (Central Decision Board), which brought together representatives from the Workers Congress and the National Workers Union, as well as the Business Coordination Council, to discuss possible reforms to the labor law. The National Workers Union, however, abandoned negotiations at an early stage when it realized that the table would approve reforms without unanimity.[20] The proposal that emerged from the board includes provisions for allowing part-time work as well as instituting a trial period for new hires. The proposal was introduced in 2002 to the Mexican congress, but has not been approved. Another social dialogue effort of the Fox government is the Consejo para el Diálogo con los Sectores Productivos (Council for Dialogue with the Productive Sectors), created in February 2001, which brings together representatives from worker and employer organizations along with different branches of government. The council is a permanent, consultative board that discusses ways to improve the country's competitiveness, attract investment, and generate well-paying jobs.[21]

Following redemocratization in Argentina in 1983, the government of Raúl Alfonsín promoted social dialogue, initiating the Conferencia Económico y Social (CES; Social and Economic Conference), which grouped representatives of employers and unions (the UIA and the CGT) as well as representatives of the Ministries of Economy and Labor, to address a broad range of macroeconomic and social issues. Concurrently, the National Minimum Wage Council was established as a tripartite committee to formulate wage policies. Despite these initiatives, employer and worker organizations withdrew at times over concerns that the process was not a genuine attempt at dialogue, but rather a mechanism to legitimate public policies unilaterally designed by state bureaucracies (Gaudio and Thompson, 1990). After a series of government-ordered salary readjustments, the CGT formally abandoned the tripartite dialogue in June 1986.

In the 1990s, the idea of a broader social dialogue was set aside due to the hegemony of the state-led Convertibility Plan. As already mentioned, the majority of the CGT and of most employer organizations supported Menem and his economic policies without formal consultation. The first attempt at social dialogue would only occur in 1994, with the Acuerdo Marco para el Empleo, la Productividad y la Equidad Social (Framework Agreement for Employment, Productivity, and Social Equity). The agreement was an initiative of the Menem government to negotiate issues such as employment creation, granting unions access to information, solutions for individual labor conflicts, health and safety at work, professional training, revision of the bankruptcy legislation, and reform of labor relations. The agreement brought together the CGT and all major employer organizations, with the Ministry of Labor in charge of the organization and follow-up. In most cases, the consensus issues were never put into practice. In other cases—such as the various sectoral agreements on productivity and training, the local councils of professional training, as well as the efforts of some tripartite tables under Working Subgroup No. 10 of Mercado Común del Sur (Mercosur; Southern Cone Common Market) to set common rules for the region—results were experimental and never gained a systemic character, in part because the Menem administration failed to support the agreements (Margheritis, 1999). In 1997 the CGT signed another agreement with the government, the Acta de Coincidencias (Coincidences Act), but the employers abandoned discussions, allegedly when they learned that the contractual system would not be touched.

The crisis of December 2001 brought social dialogue to the forefront once again. The Diálogo Argentino (Argentine Dialogue) of 2002 provoked a cascade effect which fertilized many local attempts at consultation. The dialogue was initiated by the federal government, this time with the support of the Catholic Church and technical assistance from the United Nations Development Programme (UNDP), and joined labor and capital associations as well as nongovernmental organizations (NGOs), social movements, political parties, and other social actors. Sectoral roundtables were created, and the actors in the "sociolabor productive" table agreed on the urgent creation of the Social and Economic Council to advise the central government. The council's goal was the elaboration of social policies to soften the impacts of the economic crisis. Consensus was reached on important issues such as the necessity of social policy reforms based on principles of universality, transparency, and social control. At the same time, the Programa de Jefes y Jefas de Hogar Desocupados (Program for the Unemployed Heads of Households) expressly incorporated the reasoning of the dialogue tables in the elaboration of the minimum incomes policy for the families of the unemployed. Also, the Mesa de Diálogo para el Trabajo Decente (Dialogue Table for Decent Work), created by the Ministry of Labor and joined by representatives from employer and worker organizations, including the Federal Council of Labor, is discussing issues such as income, working hours, nonregistered employment, and job security, beyond the distributive issues that led to its institution. Social dialogue has certainly helped to reconstruct the social fabric of the country and to legitimize the transition process to a Peronist, but anti-Menem, government.[22]

In Brazil, the transition to democracy in the 1980s would favor some experiments of social consultation, but as in Argentina, all the pacts attempted by the government of the New Republic (1985–1989) were organized either before the implementation of unilaterally designed economic adjustment plans or after their demise. Moreover, the attempts at social consultation would fail to address the main issue of the decade, inflation. The first attempt occurred at the beginning of 1986, inspired by the experience of the successful Moncloa Pacts, which ensured democratic transition in Spain. Organizations of employers and workers joined the federal government and started negotiations to adopt wage and price controls aimed at reducing inflation, and also began discussing reform of the state and of the economy. But the attempt was derailed by the Cruzado Plan before its third meeting. The Cruzado Plan was based on the Argentine experience (the Austral Plan) of heterodox economic shock that froze wages and prices. Labor left the negotiations, calling a (frustrated) general strike against the plan.

In this and in the other pacts to come, the main problem was the representativeness of the actors involved. The CUT, the central federation founded in 1983, had in its statutes an explicit clause against social dialogue. It would take part in one first meeting, present its list of demands (against the International Monetary Fund, for agrarian reform, for direct elections for the presidency of the republic, and for other broader political demands) and then withdraw from the dialogue. As the CUT was the most important and representative federation, without them no social pact could be possible. Although the CGT would always participate in the attempts at social dialogue, its representation was not clear.[23] It claimed to represent 10 million workers, but in 1989 had only 300 affiliated unions (Cardoso, 1999a). This was also true of the employer organizations. The Federação das Indústrias do Estado de São Paulo (FIESP; Federation of the Industries of the State of São Paulo) had substantial capacity to intervene in the public debate via the mass media, but limited ability to force its constituency to assume the burdens of the social pacts, when negotiating economic restraint or price freezing. During the New Republic (1985–1989), three social pacts were called for by the federal government, and all three would fail.

At the beginning of the 1990s, President Fernando Collor attempted another social pact when his plan of economic adjustment failed to tame inflation. However, disputes within the labor movement, coupled with the refusal of some employer organizations to take part in negotiations, jeopardized the endeavor. In 1992 the metalworker union of the ABC Region, in the metropolitan area of São Paulo, proposed the creation of a sectoral chamber, joining employer and worker representatives and the state to discuss and formulate sectoral policies for the auto industry. The then-president of the worker union had visited Detroit and seen the social disaster that the crisis of the 1980s had provoked in that city. To avoid the same fate for his region, he proposed the formation of the chamber, reluctantly accepted by employers at first, but later joined by all the associations of car assemblers and auto-parts producers when the government promised to reduce taxes on automobiles and parts. The chamber met until the end of 1994 and was able to stop the crisis in the sector, to increase the internal market by more than 60 percent via price cuts, and to save the jobs of more than 100,000 workers in the field. Job security was a central issue negotiated with workers, and although negotiations assured security in the sector as a whole, it could not be assured for each particular firm (Cardoso and Comin, 1995). Other chambers were formed in the same period in sectors such as textiles, shipbuilding, and chemicals, but with modest results (Guimarães, 1995). The chambers succeeded where trade unions were strong, and the state had strong intervening power via tax reductions, thus attracting employer organizations.

The most important social dialogue experience involving employment creation in Brazil has probably been the Regional Chamber of the Greater ABC Region. An initiative of the government of the state of São Paulo, the chamber would join the mayors of the four major industrial cities in the metropolitan area of São Paulo—Santo André, São Bernardo do Campo, São Caetano do Sul, and Diadema—at a time of crisis after the neoliberal policies and the "competitive shock" of the economic adjustment plan. The local community joined in a program of regional development involving infrastructure renewal, redefinition of the commodity chains including more attention to small and medium-sized firms, training of dismissed workers, attraction of new investments, and other issues (de Leite, 2003). These policies were important and timely, as unemployment had reached heights of 25 percent in the 1990s. Until 2001, four annual meetings had taken place, resulting in the diagnosis of the problems and definition of public policies in strategic areas. Organized as working groups dedicated to different production chains (auto industry, petrochemicals, energy, etc.), the chamber enrolled employer and worker organizations as well as NGOs and politicians at different levels of government. Although it is difficult to assess the specific impact of the chamber in employment creation, the symbolic and economic impact of the chamber in the redefinition of the ABC Region in favor of small businesses, services, and high-technology firms, is undeniable.

In 1995 the Cardoso government discontinued the sectoral chambers and other tripartite agencies within the state bureaucracies, such as the surveillance of social security fund commissions. Only the commission of the Fundo de Amparo ao Trabalhador (FAT; Workers Protection Fund)[24] has remained tripartite, with representatives of central worker and employer federations joining officials of the Ministry of Labor. Within the FAT committee, employment policies have been designed and implemented based on the view that attention should be redirected toward small and medium-sized firms and the reskilling of workers. As a result, funds have been dispersed to support reskilling and entrepreneurial projects.

The Lula government brought social dialogue to the center of the political arena again with the institution of various councils, the most important being the Conselho de Desenvolvimento Econômico e Social (Council of Economic and Social Development), which included a wide spectrum of representatives from civil society as well as representatives of employer and worker organizations. The council was intended to be responsible for the discussion of development strategies, but it spent its first year consumed by the reforms of the social security and of the tax systems. Although the council discussed the labor reform, a new tripartite forum, the Forum Nacional do Trabalho (FNT; National Labor Forum), has been created solely for that purpose because of the priority given to labor reform by the Lula administration. Though the role of the council is to create "a modern union structure,"[25] it is difficult to discern the outcome, as the worker federations intend to strengthen centralized collective bargaining as opposed to firm-level bargaining, which is favored by employers. As a result, the suggestions for reform may be minimum-consensus only, which will likely transfer the burden of reform to the government.

As can be seen, in Argentina and Brazil, social dialogue has only been a marginal policymaking mechanism during economic restructuring, despite the history of state corporatism in Brazil and of strong relations between Peronism and worker and employer organizations in Argentina. During the 1980s, the role of the social partners was limited. The 1990s ushered in neoliberal and unilateral policymaking, most of which was supported by civil society, and opposed by unions in Brazil from the beginning and in Argentina after the creation of the Congreso de los Trabajadores Argentinos (CTA; Congress of Argentine Workers). However, the experiences of the ABC Region, the recent dialogue in Argentina, and the various councils convened by the Lula government show that social consultation has changed its character from conflict to consensus-seeking and including other emergent actors of civil society, beyond the traditional representatives of employers and workers. On the other hand, the Mexican experience shows that social dialogue is no panacea, especially when the partners are not autonomous from the state. The economic restructuring plans of the 1980s and 1990s were discussed with employers and unions, but union influence in the substance of the policies was limited. As a result, the social pacts emerging from the dialogue centered on arresting inflation, through the use of explicit targets to control prices and wages. Economic restructuring was permitted without major changes in labor legislation and without addressing the problem of decent employment creation.

At the regional level, social dialogue is still limited, though it has gained importance, particularly in Mercosur. Mercosur has established the Foro Consultative Econômico y Social (Consultative Social and Economic Forum), to increase and improve the involvement of employer and worker organizations in the integration process. The forum, composed of employer and worker representatives, discusses social and labor issues and gives recommendations to the Grupo Mercado Común (Common Market Group), the executive organ of Mercosur. Also within Mercosur is the tripartite Socio-labor Commission. Its main role is the promotion of fundamental rights as stipulated in the tripartite Socio-labor Declaration, the improvement of monitoring and control mechanisms and tools, as well as the broadening of labor rights. The commission, which is supported by national social and labor commissions, is also expected to propose recommendations and concrete action plans and programs. NAFTA has a labor commission, the Commission for Cooperation on Labor Issues, but it is not tripartite—only governments are represented—and its duties are limited to supervising the implementation of the North American Agreement on Labor Cooperation (NAALC), NAFTA's side agreement on labor standards (International Labor Organization [ILO], 2003a).

New Social Agents and Social Movements

Although labor movements and union power have weakened in Argentina, Brazil, and Mexico, the countries have witnessed a strong revival of civil society, protest against neoliberal policies, raising of awareness of social issues, and demand for remedies. In Argentina in March 1997, the country exploded "in a bout of social conflict and popular upheaval" (Pozzi, 2000, p. 63), a new form of social protest known as the *cortes de rutas* (road blockages) in protest of the worsening economic environment, particularly the sharp rise in unemployment. Though initially the movement comprised the unemployed, more and more sympathizers joined as the economy deteriorated, resulting in 2,334 road blockages during 2002.[26] Another new and important form of organization is the Congress of Argentine Workers. Initially bringing together state employees and the teacher union, the congress has extended its affiliation to other social actors, trying to encompass, in its collective action and organization process, demands from broader sectors of the population, such as NGOs, the unemployed, as well as neighborhood associations. In a way, the congress is more properly a "social movement unionism," as it tries to organize interests far beyond that of the employed workers (Rauber, 2000). Its form of organization is innovative; it accepts the affiliation of individual workers as well as the unemployed. In August 1997 it organized its first general strike in association with dissident CGT unions and the Corriente Clasista y Combativa (Militant and Class Movement). With the stoppage of 40 percent of the wage earners in the country and strong adhesion from the provinces, the congress established itself as a viable alternative to the official (pro-Peronist) CGT.

Mexican civil society was also revitalized in the second half of the 1990s, amid the new climate of democratic transition and spurred as well by armed social movements, most importantly the influential Frente Zapatista de Liberación Nacional (FZLN; Zapatista National Liberation Front). But there have also been important civil moments, for example, the Barzón, a middle-class debtors' movement, which was formed by small and medium-sized business owners and mortgage holders who faced mounting interest rates and debts following the 1995 devaluation of the Mexican currency.[27] More than 200,000 lost their businesses in the first eighteen months following the devaluation, and many of them feared poverty. The group, which has collaborated with the Partido Revolucionario Democrático (PRD; Revolutionary Democratic Party) as well as the FZLN, managed to force the government to absorb one-third of their debt, helping to reduce the costs of the crisis, in terms of poverty and unemployment (Ross, 1998).

In Brazil, the most dynamic and influential political movement is the Movimento dos Trabalhadores Rurais Sem Terra (MST; Movement of the Landless Farmworkers), which occupies and farms vacant land to pressure for agrarian reform. The MST is highly organized in rural areas, with representation in twenty-five of Brazil's twenty-seven states; it has also captured the attention of the urban unemployed. The MST's strategy centers on the effective use of the existing legal system and the appeal to commonsense economic goals, by bringing unoccupied farmland into production, reducing unemployment, and increasing the food supply. With a strong media presence, acknowledged efficacy, and widespread support, the MST has reached the forefront of the social movement arena in Brazil.

Restructuring the Labor Movement to Promote Social Dialogue

The future of the labor movement in the three countries is not clear. Each faces a transitory junction, but each differs in nature. Since Argentina's political and economic crisis of December 2001, the country has been in the process of reconstructing the social fabric, the political regime, and the economy. In Brazil, the government of the Workers' Party is promoting significant changes in the labor legislation, and may change the union structure anew, thus redefining the very character of labor relations. In Mexico, the political regime has changed, though not dramatically, and democracy is at the fore of the debates and action of most social actors. Relations among the state, capital, and labor may also change dramatically. Yet it is still unclear how these changes will occur and whether they will serve to improve social dialogue in the countries, so that it can be used to promote decent employment.

In Brazil, the National Labor Forum, a tripartite forum created by the Lula government to reform the labor and union laws, has advanced a proposition that would profoundly change the structure of Brazilian unionism. The proposition involves ending the compulsory union tax as well as ratifying the ILO's Freedom of Association and Protection of the Right to Organize Convention of 1948 (No. 87). Ratifying the convention would end "unicity," by forcibly eliminating the provision that grants monopoly union representation in a given economic sector or occupation. The CUT and Força Sindical favor this proposition, though it is opposed by the other trade unions and also by employer organizations represented in the forum. Yet because the federal government is determined to reform the union structure, the reform will likely occur. If so, two parallel movements may take place. First, large firms may force their employees to form company unions, a move that would be opposed by different worker organizations, but that would probably thrive in the long run. Second, there would be a longer process to centralize representation of labor and capital, because thousands of small unions would disappear along with the compulsory taxes. The CUT wants to legalize individual workers' affiliation to the federations and to centralize the collective bargaining process, which may completely change the role of federations in labor relations. Today, the right to endorse contracts is exclusive to the many individual unions.

Because of the enormous risks involved in deeply changing the union structure (employer organizations fear the strengthening of the CUT, the CUT and other labor federations fear losing power, local unions fear extinction), it may be the case that changes will be minor—for instance, allowing the central federations to participate in collective bargaining. In that case, the system will remain intact and unions weak. The union structure has proved to be quite flexible in the process of restructuring, and with the exception of the larger unions in selected economic sectors, collective agreements are poor in regulating internal labor markets. Most labor regulations are inscribed in the federal constitution and in the CLT, including health and safety, minimum wages, regulation of dismissals, protection of certain groups, as well as the duration of employment contracts. An important benefit of the proposed union reforms is that they will likely reduce the role of the courts in labor relations, which receive roughly 2 million demands per year (Camargo, 1997). Because unions have lost power and state officials have been less willing to enforce the labor code, the courts have evolved as the main instrument to ensure rights denied to workers.

During the 1990s in Mexico, numerous proposals were submitted to the congress to reform the labor code and the union structure, by COPARMEX (the national employer association) as well as by the political parties, the PAN and the PRD. None has been accepted (Bizberg, 1999). Despite this, the new, autonomous unions that emerged during the recent process of democratic transition are capable of introducing pressure to change union legislation. There have been some advances. For example, the Fox government has legitimized the National Workers Union, making it the first autonomous federation to ever appear without the sponsorship of the Mexican state. The union has been included in the social dialogue process, and it is now an official member of the table that discusses changes to the federal labor law (Bizberg, 2003).

The dilemmas in the Mexican case are very similar to those in the Brazilian case, though tension for democratic change may be stronger. The association between Mexico's ruling party, the PRI, and the labor movement is under severe stress. Nevertheless, the Confederation of Mexican Workers, by far the largest union, seems resistant to change, often opposing measures that would free unions from state control. Thus, it is hard to forecast what will result from the efforts of reform, but as in Brazil, one should expect minor changes in Mexico, simply because the traditional unions are still powerful and benefit from the status quo. Decentralized bargaining will likely prevail, as well as closed-shop guarantees and monopoly of representation by the largest union.

In Argentina, changes to the labor law are probably consolidated, and the trend toward decentralized, firm-level collective bargaining continues, eroding the very pillars of the traditional pattern of relations among the state, labor, and capital. Though Peronism is still strong within the labor movement, "unicity" no longer exists, nor is there exclusive representation by economic sector. But new social actors have emerged, within and outside the labor movement. The most important is clearly the Congress of Argentine Workers, proposing autonomous union action vis-à-vis the state, the political parties, and the employers, as well as other social forces beyond workers.

In all three countries, affiliation has fallen since 1990, due to structural as well as political reasons. The share of the work force that can potentially be unionized is decreasing sharply because of the fragmentation of the labor market, the increase in micro and small firms, the growth of the informal sector, and the increase in unemployment. As a result, one cannot forecast a single, convergent pattern of union structure in the three countries; even within each country the enormous structural differences between manufacturing and services, agriculture and commerce, recommend parsimony in fortune-telling. In any event, three scenarios for the future of the labor movements in the countries are likely. The first is one of the persistence of the corporatist or quasi-corporatist (depending on the country) union structure. The second scenario would be a hybrid, more or less transitory structure, wherein the corporatist and quasi-corporatist structures and leaderships are given time to adapt to a new situation in which freedom of association prevails. The third scenario would be one of freedom of association according to ILO conventions and recommendations. This last scenario is less probable, however, as it would signify a complete change in labor relations, neglecting sixty or seventy years of industrial relations history. It is important to note as well that none of the scenarios ensures the representation of informal wage earners and the self-employed, who constitute large segments of the working population in these countries. Nevertheless, how these trends evolve will affect social dialogue in the countries, which until now has largely occurred through traditional corporatist channels. If social dialogue would entail representative and autonomous parties of worker and employer organizations, whether at the firm, industry, or national level, it is more likely that employment concerns would receive greater attention, and more likely that the agreements to come out of the social dialogue would be abided by.

Conclusion

The principal historical feature of the industrial relations systems in Argentina, Brazil, and Mexico is that the law, rather than collective bargaining, regulated state, labor, and capital relations. Essentially, the state-led development model dominant until the 1980s was based on a quid pro quo between unions and government in which unions acquiesced to the government their potential for collective action, in exchange for political recognition and autonomy in gaining control of their constituencies. This agreement was bound by federal laws that, in turn, regulated collective labor relations and bargaining.

Because of the historical tradition of regulating state, labor, and capital relations via the legal system, social dialogue—defined as formal, state-led, or state-mediated forms of social and political consultation—has not traditionally played an important role in policy reforms, despite the existence of tripartite mechanisms for consultation, particularly in Mexico. Because well-defined regulations guided actions during import-substitution industrialization, the weakness of social dialogue was not a major concern. Yet with the opening of the economies in the 1980s and 1990s and the concomitant economic restructuring, the lack of a "strong and autonomous" labor movement meant that workers' interests—particularly employment—did not get the attention they deserved. As a result, social dialogue did not stop the decline of quality employment. Moreover, because restructuring led to widespread job loss in the highly unionized sectors of traditional manufacturing and the newly privatized state enterprises, unions found themselves severely weakened at a time when workers most needed them. Falling unionization rates, coupled with the initial acceptance of the reforms by the principal unions in Argentina and Mexico, led to a certain delegitimization.

Nevertheless, there have been some positive outcomes amid the turmoil. First, the vacuum left by unions during economic restructuring has led to the emergence of "new social movements," including new, more independent unions in Argentina and Mexico, advocating for greater freedom of association. Second, there have been recent examples of successful social dialogue leading to employment creation, such as the agreements concluded by the social partners of the ABC Region of São Paulo, Brazil, which led to improvements in the efficiency of production and job retention despite contrary employment trends in the industry. At the national level, the National Labor Forum convened by the Lula government has been successful in reaching consensus on a number of difficult issues concerning the proposed reform of labor law. Similarly in Mexico, the Fox government has taken important steps in convening social dialogue forums to respond to the challenges of competing in a globalized economy. In Argentina, the response to the economic and social crisis of the 2000s has been of a shared awareness of vulnerability from the social partners, which may be important for the reinvigoration of social consultation.

Still, employment concerns have been of secondary importance in tripartite consultation. Depending on whether and how proposed reforms in Brazil and Mexico are adopted, as well as the political evolution in Argentina, this could change, as more representative and autonomous worker and employer organizations would be more likely to tackle employment concerns, including pressing issues such as labor market flexibility, worker security, and informality (see also Appendix Table 7.A).

Appendix Table 7.A Summary of Collective Bargaining Systems

Country	General Features	State Intervention	Level of Centralization/Decentralization
Argentina	High and centralized state intervention. There have been efforts to decentralize.	The state affords official recognition to unions, determining the representatives of collective bargaining. The agreements must be approved by the administrative authority. Agreements are judged according to their impact on the economy or consumers. The constitution of 1994 authorizes the federal government to suspend agreements for reasons of economic emergency. The legality of strikes is also a prerogative of the state. As well, the state presides at conciliation processes and can impose arbitrage.	Until 1993, legislation centralized the system. Unions could only get official recognition at company level if no union existed at the sector level. Unions with official recognition had monopoly of representation of both affiliated and nonaffiliated workers. Seven percent of all unions represented seventy-five percent of the workers. Seventy percent of the agreements were by sector of activity. Since 1993 the system has been decentralized. From 1995 to 1999, seventy-six percent of all agreements were at the firm level.
Brazil	Centralized, high state intervention, attenuated by the constitution of 1988. Still considered corporatist, but mostly because of the judicial intervention of labor courts. Monopoly of representation in transition, but there can be only one union by sector or profession in a municipality. Unions have administrative autonomy, but are still financed by mandatory taxes imposed on all workers of the municipality. Central federations recognized since 1988.	The constitution of 1988 protects union autonomy; state is no longer able to confer union status or intervene in union administration. However, intervention still exists, but is enforced through labor courts. The bargaining process not regulated, though outcome is. The state continues to invoke the old labor code, declaring invalid any clause of a collective agreement that directly or indirectly goes against government economic policy, but only in case of the unions of state enterprises. The Ministry of Labor can initiate mandatory	The constitution of 1988 maintained corporatist structure. Only one officially recognized union can represent a profession by industry in geographic territory. The law doesn't allow for firm-based unions. Unions can bargain at the firm or the sector level, and often pursue a bi-level strategy to avoid the salary limits imposed by government policy. There is a trend toward decentralization. The constitution of 1988 provides that workers in firms of more than 200 employees have right to one elected representative to promote direct negotiations with employer. In 2000,

continues

Appendix Table 7.A   Continued

Country	General Features	State Intervention	Level of Centralization/Decentralization
		arbitration through the judicial arbitration process in cases of essential services. The judicial arbitration process triggers mandatory conciliation and arbitration courts, which ceased to be tripartite in 1999. Collective bargaining opportunities are now enforced by the state, and this is the preferred form of conflict composition. Judicial arbitration can only be called for in cases of frustration of collective bargaining. Labor courts are valuing conventional clauses.	mandatory conciliation commissions were instituted at the company or municipality level. Individual conflicts of right must be processed in these bipartite stances before reaching labor courts.
Mexico	Centralization is achieved through a corporatist structure and union discipline. High state intervention, but negotiations are highly decentralized and uncoordinated.	The most important form of intervention is the recognition of unions by the state and the intervention in case of strikes. Most often, unions outside the corporatist structure are not recognized and don't have the right to strike. Unions hardly negotiate autonomously and fill the obligation to negotiate at a minimum level. The state intervenes in conflict resolution through councils of conciliation and arbitrage or by declaring strikes nonexistent. The negotiation process is not strongly regulated, but it is integrated in the process of conflict resolution (normally through conciliation), in which state intervention is very strong.	Different kinds of unions are allowed; most are at the firm level. The union with a majority of affiliates represents all workers. Agreements at the industry level must be approved by the Ministry of Labor, but these are few, and many are being repealed. Tripartite negotiations and the social pacts had an integral role in the process of economic recovery and adjustment, as they helped maintain wage increases below inflation.

Source: Cardoso, 2004.

Notes

1. See also de la Garza, 1990, 2003c; Bizberg, 1998; and Dombois and Pries, 2000.

2. As in Mexico, to be declared legal, a strike had to obey strict procedures, such as informing the employer forty-eight hours prior to the strike, winning the approval of the majority of the workers via secret ballots, as well as receiving assurance by state officials that the rules were followed.

3. The following is based on McGuire, 1997; Ranis, 1997; Geddes, 1994; and Nelson, 1992.

4. Datafolha poll of a sample (1,079 interviews) of São Paulo's population over fourteen years of age, held on May 23, 1995, archived at the Center of Public Opinion Studies, University of Campinas.

5. Poll of a representative sample of Brazilian voters (3,643 interviews) in August 1990, undertaken by the Brazilian Institute for Public Opinion and Statistics, archived at the Center of Public Opinion Studies, University of Campinas.

6. Datafolha poll of a representative sample (4,380) of the Brazilian adult population aged eighteen and older, July 1998, archived at the Center of Public Opinion Studies, University of Campinas.

7. *Folha de S. Paulo,* November 13, 2000, p. B-1.

8. The CT's affiliated federations are the Revolutionary Confederation of Peasant Workers, the Regional Confederation of Mexican Workers, and the Confederation of Mexican Workers, the latter being the largest and most important.

9. Nevertheless, there are fewer public sector unions as a result of privatization.

10. Another important dissident union was the First of May Intertrade Union Coordination, formed in 1995, the result of a movement to organize the May Day march that year when the official unions decided not to organize it for fear of losing control over the workers. Its origin, then, was the coordination of dissident unions, community organizations, and various leftist organizations. However, it has since dissolved.

11. The other confederations are the General Workers Confederation, the Social Democratic Trade Union, and the Autonomous Workers Trade Union.

12. Data are from the National Employment, Wages, Technology, and Training Survey. They are not strictly comparable to the findings of Argentina and Brazil.

13. The DIEESE, the Interunion Department of Socioeconomic Studies and Statistics, is the only source of regular information on collective bargaining results in Brazil.

14. Strike statistics are often unreliable, as few countries have an official system of data collection, forcing analysts to rely on secondary sources of all kinds, such as newspapers or interviews with union leaders. Mexico is an exception, and because of the connections that structurally linked unions to the Ministry of Labor, more accurate administrative registers of their collective bargaining actions are available. But corruption and mishandling of official data also make them unreliable. In Brazil and in Argentina, the data are precarious and, more importantly, vary from one year to another due to different reasons: a researcher who stops collecting the data, a labor regulation that changes the definition of a strike, or a fall in the salience of (and public interest in) labor conflicts in democratized societies, which reduces their media coverage and attention. As a result, comparative analyses based on these data are limited.

15. Half of the labor conflicts involved state-enterprise workers and public servants; manufacturing workers contributed to 25 percent of the conflicts, with service workers accounting for 23 percent.

16. This definition of social dialogue is slightly narrower than the official ILO definition, which includes "all types of negotiation, consultation or simply exchange of information between or among representatives of governments, employers and workers on issues of common interest relating to economic and social policy" (http://www.ilo.org/public/english/dialogue/ifpdial/sd/index.htm).

17. This discussion is based on Bensusán, 2003.

18. See Clavijo and Valdivieso, 2000, tab. A35.

19. The principles can be found at http://www.stps.gob.mx/cultura_laboral/cult_lab.html.

20. Interview with Francisco Hernández Juárez, Sindicato de Telefonistas de la República de México (the national telephone union), which is part of the UNT, in April 2003.

21. For more information, see http://www.presidencia.gob.mx/actividades/index.php?contenido=9054.

22. Most of the information on recent social dialogue experiments in Argentina was taken from the preliminary Argentine report to the twelfth Encuentro de Ex-Becarios de Bolonia–Castilla La Mancha–Turin (Twelfth Meeting of Former Scholarship Holders of Bologna–Castilla La Mancha–Turin).

23. The CUT was founded in 1983 as a "new unionist" central federation, combating the union structure and the labor code. The leaders of the old union structure founded the Conselho Nacional da Classe Trabalhadora (CONCLAT; National Council of the Working Class) (later renamed Confederação [Confederation]), which would become the CGT in 1987. For an in-depth analysis of unionism in the 1980s, see Cardoso, 1999b.

24. The FAT was instituted by the constitution of 1988 and is composed of contributions from employers. It finances unemployment insurance and also special programs for the interest of workers, such as reskilling.

25. *Jornal do Comércio,* August 9, 2003, p. A-17.

26. Data from Centro de Estudios Nueva Mayoria.

27. For more information, see the Barzón website (http://www.elbarzon.org).

8

Strategies for Meeting the Employment Challenge

The employment challenges in Argentina, Brazil, and Mexico are many. New job growth since 1990 has been insufficient to cope with the increase in labor supply. Compared with 1990, employment rates in 2004 were lower in Argentina and Brazil; the share of workers employed in the informal sector was higher in Brazil and Mexico; and average real manufacturing wages increased only marginally in Brazil and Mexico, and declined in Argentina. Social security covers less than half the working population in Argentina, 63 percent in Mexico, and 69 percent in Brazil. The traditional skewed distribution of income and wages, evident in high Gini coefficients, is partially the result of these labor market patterns and remains a major source of concern. Yet amid these challenges are important policy lessons for the future. Well-designed and well-executed policies at the macro, meso, and micro levels are essential for creating decent employment. This volume has shown that when it comes to employment creation, a laissez-faire approach is insufficient. Effectively considering employment as an economic and social goal requires a concerted effort by governments and social partners to strategically orient policies to achieve this goal. To the contrary of the 1990s, when it was believed that employment creation would simply result from the reorientation of policies toward trade and financial liberalization, price stability, and small government, the countries under review—though to different degrees—now seem to recognize the limits to laissez-faire and the importance of an institutional framework to steer market forces.

Even though the evolution of employment during the period of analysis was disappointing, all three countries provide a number of useful lessons for creating decent work. Argentina's recent experience is no exception. Though Argentina was the country hardest hit by the fallout from ill-conceived economic reforms, its economy has performed well since 2002 under a new, much more interventionist government, with unemployment cut by 40 percent between January 2003 and March 2005. The devalued and competitive exchange rate has boosted export growth, put the import-competing sector on a more level playing field, and, as a result, has led to job growth in the tradable sector. But the government has not just been a witness to the recovery; it has played an active role in lessening the social costs of the crisis and improving the economy's performance. To begin, the government responded quickly to the grave social situation by levying an export tax to fund an emergency employment program that at its peak had 2.2 million beneficiaries. From the experience in the 1990s, the government has learned that cheapening labor will not necessarily create employment, but will certainly deteriorate working conditions. It thus responded by revising labor regulations that had diminished social security coverage and by improving labor inspection and enforcement. Recognizing as well that workers' earnings are the main source of consumption and thus economic growth, the government has raised the minimum wage. Most recently, Argentina successfully negotiated a restructuring of its debt that will allow it to once again access external credit markets.

Brazil took a more tempered approach to its economic reforms, which curtailed possible negative effects on the labor market. Though the government liberalized trade in 1991, it managed to maintain a positive trade balance until 1994. And in early 1999, when the government floated its currency—to the contrary of Argentina, which maintained parity between the peso and the dollar—unemployment that year increased negligibly. Moreover, many of Brazil's leading industries of the import-substitution industrialization era—autos, aircraft, chemicals—adapted well to economic opening based on their accumulated knowledge and the facilities that existed in concentrated, local areas. This industrial clustering was also beneficial for facing challenges that confronted the sector, as was the case in the auto industry of the ABC Region, which brought together government, workers, and employers to construct solutions to maintain production and employment. Brazil also provides a number of useful lessons and insights into the design of social protection policies. It has the most developed social protection system of the three countries and the highest coverage rate, but more interesting is the innovativeness of its programs. The funds that provide severance pay and unemployment benefits upon job loss are also used for such varied purposes as large-scale investment projects and union-run training programs.

Mexico was the only one of the three countries where job growth benefited directly from the new economic model, as investment was centered on the labor-intensive maquiladora sector. In particular, following devaluation in December 1994 and until 2000, the sector had strong annual employment growth. The government has also been successful at the macroeconomic level, replacing much of its short-term, dollar-denominated debt following the 1995 bailout with long-term, peso-denominated instruments. The debt level has been brought down dramatically giving the government much more fiscal space. It has also created some important active labor market policies, such as the training program Sistema de Capacitación para el Trabajo (SICAT; Vocational Training System) and the rural, infrastructure-building program Programa de Empleo Temporal (PET; Temporary Employment Program), that have been beneficial in providing income to displaced workers while teaching valuable skills that promote labor market integration. Moreover, social security coverage of formal sector workers has improved. The government has also taken important steps to promote dialogue among the social partners.

In sum, this book highlights the beneficial effects on employment of different policy areas but also shows that though all policies are important, one alone cannot ensure decent work. Therefore it is the combination of policies rather than any single policy that will be best for creating employment.

But the book also shows that a strong and willing government that puts employment high on its political agenda is essential for employment creation. The 1990s were not good for employment, as employment was considered a derivative of economic activity and economic growth, and the drivers of growth were assumed to lie in the unleashing of market forces. A disbelief in the role of institutions and governments as well as the social partners prevailed. The new millennium is a better era for employment growth: the international financial institutions have changed their view somewhat regarding the supremacy of market forces after reckoning some failures in their former policy advice and acknowledging the positive effects that government policy can have on development, as well as the contributions that institutions and social policy can make (World Bank, 2005). The countries have also understood that too much dependence on external advice and financing restricts their room to maneuver on national policy. They have engaged in more active dialogue with their neighbors and expanded their power of negotiation by agreeing on similar policies in a regional framework, facilitated by similar political views.

Thus, although the room to maneuver in an open and globalized economy is small, it can nevertheless be used: macroeconomic policies, trade policies, investment policies, industrial policies, labor market and social protection policies, including training policies, all play a role and all have to be coordinated to be successful. But this is not to imply that policy alone can do all. Policies must rely on market forces; they should accompany these forces, rather than go against them. Indeed, it is a "frame" that the market needs, not a straightjacket. And such a frame consists of well-designed institutions and policies.

Employment Creation Strategies

Creating employment depends on good policies at the macro, meso, and micro levels. Because of deeper integration in the global economy, international and regional policies can also have important effects on employment. The following are recommendations for employment creation at these three policy levels as well as concerning regional agreements. Though they may appear ambitious, some of the countries have already achieved success in the policy areas mentioned and others are taking steps in this direction.

Macroeconomic Policies

The central macroeconomic recommendation is that job creation should be at the center of macroeconomic policy, as there has been little consideration about the importance of generating jobs when deciding on macroeconomic policy. As a result, the tools of macroeconomic policy—monetary, fiscal, and exchange rate policy—have not been best used to promote job creation. Instead, price stability has been the overarching goal since liberalization in the late 1980s and early 1990s. While controlling inflation is important, it should not come at the expense of unemployment and underemployment. Rather, it should be considered along with policies that boost economic welfare.

The boldest and most direct way of having employment creation regain its importance as an objective of macroeconomic policy is by setting employment targets, subject to an inflation constraint, that the government and the central bank should try to achieve. Making employment creation a mandate of the central bank would ensure that employment gains its prominence at the center of economic policy. Though there are policy options that government and central banks could adopt to achieve their employment targets, it is likely that these policies will require a more interventionist approach, for example by controlling the money supply through credit allocation mechanisms. We recommend three complementary policies that could be part of a macroeconomic, employment-targeting objective: (1) ensuring a stable and competitive exchange rate, (2) improving the financial environment for domestic investment, and (3) maintaining a countercyclical fiscal policy. Functioning well, these policies would lessen volatility and promote economic growth, which would boost employment.

1. Ensure a stable and competitive exchange rate. As shown clearly in the experiences of Argentina, Brazil, and Mexico, maintaining a competitive exchange rate is essential for job creation. An overappreciated exchange rate cheapens the cost of imports relative to domestically produced goods, hurting demand for domestic goods and thus lessening the demand for labor. Unfortunately, Argentina, Brazil, and Mexico suffered from overappreciated exchange rates during the 1990s as a result of their fixed exchange rate policies and the decision to open their goods and financial markets. The countries received a strong inflow of foreign capital that caused real exchange rate appreciation. The appreciation hurt the competitiveness of the export sector and led to an import boom and subsequently to deterioration in the balance of payments.

Consequently, there were negative repercussions on employment. Firms, which had to adjust to fiercer competition, did so by rationalizing and modernizing production using less labor.

Ensuring a stable exchange rate would improve the competitiveness of the tradable sector, and thus encourage firms to expand production and employment in this sector. This policy would not only help stimulate exports, but also develop the internal market, as domestic firms would be more competitive with imports, both of consumer goods as well as of intermediary products, as the relative prices of local goods would improve. This in turn would favor the evolution of the balance of payments, lessening reliance on capital inflows. Yet for macroeconomic policy to be centered on having a competitive and stable real exchange rate, the central banks must be willing to control expansions and contractions in the money supply through the use of credit allocation mechanisms such as quantitative credit controls, interest rate ceilings, and reserve requirements on bank deposits. The countries must also be willing to impose capital requirements if needed when flows reach levels that prevent the central bank from properly conducting its operations. Regional coordination of exchange rate policy would also help to ensure the growth of a healthy and sustainable trade relationship between neighboring countries.

2. Improve the financial environment for domestic investment. Argentina, Brazil, and Mexico now have floating exchange rates, yet macroeconomic policy, both fiscal and monetary, remains restrictive because of the policy of inflation targeting pursued by their central banks as well as the need to control and reduce the large debt burden. Thus, monetary policy has centered on using the interest rate to rein in economic growth and keep inflation low. Fiscal policy has centered on controlling government spending and using the primary surplus to service the debt. The countries have experienced success in maintaining low inflation, and Mexico and Brazil, and most recently Argentina, have been managing to control their debt burden. Yet the current structure of debt repayments imposes vulnerabilities on the economies since the countries must run a fiscal surplus to finance debt repayments, as well as entice foreign investors with high interest rates in order to roll over existing liabilities. With interest rates high because of inflation-fighting policies and the need to attract foreign investment to roll over liabilities, credit for domestic investment is not only squeezed, but also too expensive. As a result, domestic investment is tempered, resulting in less economic growth and fewer new jobs.

Yet a strong financial system for domestic investment is essential for development. An advantage of considering employment goals in macroeconomic policy is that the interest rate would be viewed in a new light—as an essential instrument for allowing investments and job creation, whose longer-term effects would also be beneficial for inflation. Thus, interest rates could be lowered, which would help stimulate domestic investment, aiding domestic production and employment. The current high–interest rate policy of Brazil, for example, is aggravating a credit crunch already felt sharply by small and medium-sized enterprises. But high interest rates are just one of the barriers faced in stimulating domestic investment; another important factor is lack of access to credit. Currently, credit markets are skewed toward the largest firms, with small enterprises, particularly micro enterprises, sidelined. For example, in Mexico, only 13 percent of micro enterprises receive any credit, despite employing significant portions of the labor force. Moreover, consumption is hampered by an inefficient financial system: an estimated 57 percent of Brazilians and 74 percent of Mexico City residents have no bank accounts. The development of the financial system through the creation of complementary capital market institutions and products to reach new clients would help alleviate the credit crunch. Remittances, which are already an important source of financing, particularly in Mexico, could be better integrated into the financial system, which could also aid formalization of the informal sector. Policies such as these to stimulate domestic investment and consumption would ultimately enhance the development of the internal market, which is a vital source of job growth.

3. Maintain a countercyclical fiscal policy. Fiscal policy in Argentina, Brazil, and Mexico has tended to be procyclical, with government spending booming during an upturn and then shrinking considerably when the economic environment sours. This tendency has been further aggravated by increases in the ratio of debt to gross domestic product (GDP) when the economies crashed, since substantial portions of the debt were in dollars but the local currency was depreciated. Consequently, a higher share of government outlays has then been dedicated to debt repayment as opposed to jump-starting the economy. Developing a fiscal policy that is countercyclical requires policy initiatives such as restructuring debt so that it does not aggravate procyclicality, as well as developing stabilization funds to smooth public spending across the economic cycle.

One solution that has been gaining attention, and that was discussed in the International Monetary Fund's April 2004 *World Economic Outlook,* would be to index debt repayment to the growth of GDP. Countries could issue GDP-indexed bonds, in which yearly coupon payments would be reduced or increased depending on deviations from historical trends in the country's economic growth. If GDP growth turns out to be lower than usual, debt payments due would be lower than without indexation, helping maintain debt-to-GDP levels at sustainable levels as well as allowing greater space for fiscal policy to pursue countercyclical objectives. Another option would be to restructure debt so that it is valued in national currency, but set at a fixed rate that is indexed to inflation. Debt issued in national currency, rather than the US dollar, would protect against currency depreciations that are responsible for the sharp increases in the real cost of the debt following devaluation. Thus this proposal will also reduce the procyclicality of the debt burden, giving the government more room to increase spending during downturns.

An important policy instrument for ensuring countercyclicality is stabilization funds. Stabilization funds smooth public spending across the economic cycle by saving excess revenues during good times to compensate shortfalls in government revenue in bad times. They have increasingly been implemented in the region. For example, in its 2000 Budget Law, Mexico created an oil-revenue stabilization fund, whereby unexpected revenue—from oil or other sources—in excess of 0.9 percent of initial projections would be divided between amortizing debt obligations (60 percent) and creating a stabilization fund (40 percent) (OECD, 2002). Though this policy centers on controlling swings in the price of export commodities, the principle of budget smoothing can just as easily be applied to general government revenues, particularly since many taxes are highly sensitive to economic growth.

Still, in order for stabilization funds to have an anticyclical effect, they must be sufficiently large. In Mexico, where oil revenues are a critical source of government spending, the stabilization funds are not likely to be of great importance unless the government can increase tax revenues. Increased tax revenues can occur by expanding the tax base, raising taxes, as well as improving administration and enforcement. All three countries could improve enforcement, and Mexico could consider both broadening the tax base as well as raising taxes. Argentina and Brazil could consider expanding the personal and corporate income tax, as income taxes account for just 16 percent of revenues in Argentina and 21 percent of revenues in Brazil, compared with roughly 38 percent in Mexico. Though more cyclical than the value-added tax (VAT), the income tax has the benefit of improving equity in taxation.

A fundamental component of countercyclical fiscal policy is labor market policies. A well-designed social safety net to protect vulnerable groups during crises not only helps groups in need, but improves economic performance by propping up consumption. In the United States, for example, the unemployment insurance program has been estimated to have mitigated the loss in real GDP by approximately 15 percent during the five recessions that occurred between 1969 and the early 1990s (Chimerine, Black, and Coffey, 1999). Effective labor market policies can therefore operate as a stabilizing mechanism for the economy. Active labor market policies, in particular, can be combined with public investment programs, such as infrastructure building, to provide employment and income to displaced workers, while building much-needed public infrastructure. Particularly important is designing labor market policies that are institutionalized and thus stable over political cycles, but adapt flexibly to economic cycles, and whose design can contribute to macroeconomic stability. Besides their beneficial effect of providing social protection to vulnerable groups, the policies can play an important role in mitigating the effects of structural change and economic downturns.

Mesoeconomic Policies

The importance of macroeconomic policies for growth and employment is undeniable, but the success of an employment strategy depends as well on the sectoral, or mesoeconomic, level of an economy. The challenge for countries is to find an appropriate export specialization not just in primary products but also in higher value-added goods to improve their position in the world market, while at the same time the large internal and regional markets of these countries should not be neglected as they offer development opportunities for domestic producers. In a more liberal and globalized setting, market forces play an increasingly important role in the shaping of those sectors, but here as well these forces should be complemented by policies that can improve the competitiveness of an economy and create quality employment.

1. Promote an export specialization in higher value-added goods. Trade liberalization in Argentina and Brazil had the unintended consequence of increasing the countries' specialization in goods that are stagnant on the world market, mainly low-processed goods in capital-intensive sectors that do not create significant employment. Mexico increased its exports of high value-added goods, which also created significant employment because of the labor intensity of the production process, but the import content of these goods is high and as a result, there are few backward and forward linkages with the rest of the economy. Though there have been some successes, for example in the automobile and aircraft industries, there is potential in the countries to enhance specialization in higher value-added goods, particularly of those products in which backward and forward linkages with domestic producers can be developed to create a multiplier effect on production and employment. An active industrial policy that facilitates the integration of domestic firms into the world market can help to improve the quality of a country's specialization. The government, in consultation with the social partners, can play a beneficial role by supporting the creation of local research and development centers, education and training programs, as well as improving physical infrastructure (e.g., transport and communication) through public investment. In addition, firm clustering and third-generation maquiladoras should be further supported:

- *Firm clustering.* Since 1990, successful industrial clusters in high-technology sectors have emerged, such as the software industry in Blumenau (Brazil), aeronautics in São Paulo, electronics in Jalisco (Mexico), or the agricultural mango-grape cluster in Petrolina (Brazil). These clusters have succeeded in value chain upgrading as well as in building backward and forward linkages in their regional area, with important multiplier effects on production and employment. These clusters are a successful industrial development experience that the countries can learn from and build upon.

- *Develop third-generation maquiladoras.* Though the maquiladora industry is one of the most dynamic sectors in terms of the technological content of the products, inflows of foreign direct investment (FDI), as well as employment and wage growth, the sector is vulnerable, as the recent decline in FDI and job losses have demonstrated. But one encouraging prospect has been the creation of third-generation maquiladoras, based on technology-intensive production activities carried out by high-skilled workers. Through quality rather than price competition, the firms are in a better position to fight off low-wage competitors. The development of third-generation maquilas could be facilitated by public support; in particular, efforts could be made to link these maquilas with other sectors of the economy, through the promotion of joint ventures or strategic alliances with domestic suppliers.

2. Rebalance policies toward boosting domestic production. Because governments have been focused on attracting FDI since 1990, domestic producers have been somewhat neglected, and worse, policies have sometimes been slanted in favor of foreign over domestic investment. For example, imports were facilitated by the reduction of tariffs, exchange rate appreciation, and specific privileges like the value-added tax exemption for maquiladoras in Mexico. While this can be justified for specific sectors that create products with many foreign in-sourced intermediary products, it punishes those that use more local content. Yet domestic producers using local content in their products and services are essential for building the internal market and for providing jobs. Thus, governments should ensure that a level playing field exists between domestic and foreign firms, for example by maintaining a competitive exchange rate and by reassessing import privileges.

FDI is an important source of financing; it can help modernize production and better integrate the domestic economy into the world market. The 1990s saw a strong rise in FDI in all three countries, but the employment impact was rather disappointing, aside from positive results for the maquiladora industry in the second half of the 1990s. Moreover, the inflows of FDI had a slight crowding-out effect on domestic investment in the three countries and, because the flows were often volatile, they contributed to raising the countries' external vulnerability. Another negative macroeconomic effect was that the inflows contributed to the appreciation of the exchange rate and caused high real interest rates. Because not all foreign investment is helpful for development, the countries should take a more proactive stance toward foreign investment; in particular, they should encourage investment in those sectors that are promising for sustainable economic and employment growth. Governments can also create rules or provide incentives to encourage foreign investors to work with domestic firms, both small and big, to promote value-chain upgrading and to invest in human capital development. Additionally, governments should try to stimulate domestic investment through measures that increase the liquidity of the domestic financial market as well as through specific support for micro and small and medium-sized enterprises, as these firms are important employers in all three countries. Greater domestic investment will strengthen internal demand with important concomitant employment effects. Moreover, a more balanced share between foreign and domestic investment—as envisaged by Argentina and Brazil—would reduce external vulnerability.

3. Support the creation of quality employment in the service sector. The share of services in employment has increased significantly since 1990 in Argentina, Brazil, and Mexico, and it is likely that this trend will continue in the future. Though this sector has some very promising areas of good-quality job growth, it is quite heterogeneous, spanning high-skilled work in the financial and business services sectors to semi- and unskilled work in construction and domestic services. Policies in support of the service sector could range from developing trade in services through a "service policy," in analogy to an "industrial policy," to improving working conditions in less-skilled, nontradable service activities.

Trade in services has become increasingly important as a result of technological advances in communication and the globalization process. Outsourcing of specific services to developing countries that require high-skilled workers has been a trend among multinationals that will likely expand in the future. The state could build upon these trends and boost employment in the service sector by designing a service policy. A service policy could promote a conducive environment for service investment, through the adaptation of business regulations to the specific needs of service activities, by improving information on the industry through market research, by promoting training for skill-upgrading, by supporting the clustering of service firms, as well as by developing local research and development centers. This service policy should steer private initiative and promote promising trends that create employment, in particular quality employment.

But the state is also an important player in the nontradable service sector. The countries have a deficit in human and physical capital compared with the most advanced countries and the reduction of this gap is a key element of their development agenda. The state continues to be a direct and important service employer, particularly in the areas of education and health as well as physical infrastructure. Increased spending on education and health has the potential to create new jobs of good quality for medium- to high-level educated workers in the public sector, but there is also a potential for employment creation in civil society organizations. Retail trade, hotels, restaurants, and domestic serv-ices are also important sectors for employment, but the jobs are typically of low quality and are often informal. Training programs and better enforcement of some key regulations could improve working conditions in these sectors.

Microeconomic Policies

Our focus at the microeconomic level is on the institutions, regulations, and policies that govern labor markets. Labor market policies are essential for helping workers adapt to a less certain labor market as a result of globaliza-tion. Labor market regulations and policies, if well designed, can improve job quality by increasing the income security of workers, while allowing firms to adjust to changes in market demands.

1. Promote efficiency in labor market institutions through an established and enforced set of labor regulations and policies. Although labor regula-tions such as employment protection, minimum wages, and regulations of basic working conditions improve job quality, provide security to workers, and introduce basic stability into the labor market, they are effective only if they are applied. Yet in Argentina, Brazil, and Mexico, there has been an increase since 1990 in the share of nonprotected workers in wage employment, a prob-lem that is particularly widespread among micro and small firms. There are two ways of addressing this problem. First, enforcement of labor regulations must be improved. In all three countries, there are too few labor inspectors and, as a result, enforcement is weak. Yet as shown in Chapter 6, labor inspec-tion is a highly effective tool for regularizing work conditions. Thus the coun-tries would benefit from greater enforcement.

A second issue concerns the current body of labor legislation. For over a decade, there has been an ongoing debate in Latin America as well as the OECD on whether labor laws are too rigid to allow firms to respond rapidly under globalization. The observed low compliance level on many aspects of labor legislation begs the question of whether it would make more sense to have less restrictive rules, but truly enforce them for all workers. While it is not ev-ident that current legislation in Argentina, Brazil, and Mexico impedes the movement of workers across the economy—indeed mobility among the formal sector manufacturing sector was shown to be quite high—there are neverthe-less some guidelines for developing regulations and policies that ensure suffi-cient mobility, without necessarily jeopardizing workers' security. Some of the newer thinking on labor market institutions (e.g., Blanchard and Tirole, 2004) and on how to optimally design unemployment insurance and employment pro-tection (e.g., Blanchard, 2005), can be helpful. For example, it seems to be bet-ter for labor market functioning to finance income replacement in case of job loss via an unemployment insurance fund financed by employers, workers, and the state, rather than having an individual, firm-based severance pay system, which places a large financial burden on firms exactly at the moment when they are suffering from recession and lack of liquidity. European experiences with so-called flexicurity arrangements are also a useful example, as the system protects workers' financial security as they transition between jobs, and in the process encourages mobility on the part of workers and allows firms to respond to the changing economic environment.

Other areas of debate that affect labor market participation and mobility include part-time and temporary contracts. Based on the experience of successful European countries, part-time work that is subject to prorated protections similar to those for full-time work can be beneficial for integrating workers into the labor market, as they can help accommodate the differing labor supply decisions of (female) workers. If used for training purposes, for example apprenticeship schemes, they can also aid the integration of unemployed youths into the labor market. Temporary contracts also give more flexibility to employers if used for temporarily replacing workers or for accommodating short-term increases in demand. Some basic rules on temporary contracts, however, such as a limit on recurrent renewals, and disallowing the direct substitution of temporary contract workers for permanent contract workers, should be applied to these forms of employment.

2. Expand the use of labor market policies (LMPs). The increased exposure to external competition arising from the economic reforms and increased economic integration has meant that the labor markets of Argentina, Brazil, and Mexico are more exposed to external shocks than in earlier decades when the economies were closed. As a result, even if labor market regulations have not changed, employment security has lessened. An important tool for increasing worker security is labor market policies, both passive and active. Well-funded and comprehensive labor market policies help individual workers cope with economic shocks, as they improve labor market integration as well as provide income support to displaced workers in need. As discussed in Chapter 6, since 1990 the countries have recognized the benefits of labor market policies, and have developed new or enhanced existing policies. The level of spending and coverage of these policies, however, remains limited, with Brazil and Mexico dedicating less than 1 percent of GDP to LMPs, and Argentina spending just 1 percent, but only because of the massive emergency employment program, the Programa de Jefes y Jefas de Hogares Desocupados, which was started in response to the economic crisis. The countries would therefore benefit by discussing with the social partners how to expand their labor market policies to make them a more permanent, yet flexible, component of government policies toward what has become a more volatile labor market.

Labor market policies typically include a passive component to give income replacement to displaced workers for a short period while they conduct their job search. Currently, only Argentina and Brazil have unemployment insurance systems, and the Argentine program is quite restricted. Because unemployment insurance is an important form of short-term income support and because it can help deter formal sector workers from entering the informal sector, the countries would benefit from adopting or expanding such a form of insurance against labor market risks. The design of an unemployment benefit system can take many forms, and ILO conventions and technical departments can give advice on replacement rates, duration, and qualifying periods under which such programs are effective. Interesting unemployment programs that Argentina and Mexico could draw lessons from are the Brazilian unemployment insurance system (Fundo de Amparo ao Trabalhador [FAT]), which uses a share of the money in the fund to finance investment projects, thus potentially generating employment, or the Chilean unemployment fund, which is funded by employers, workers, and the government.

Active labor market policies (ALMPs) have the advantage of addressing the needs of both informal and formal sector workers and are therefore a critical component of labor market policies for developing countries. ALMPs also have the added benefit of facilitating integration into the labor market by providing work or training, which bestows economic and social benefits in addition to income replacement. Evaluations of ALMPs have shown that they typically function better if designed at the local level, as communities are better able to identify their needs. Their management, however, must be carried out with appropriate safeguards and proper monitoring. In order to ensure that the work content of the programs is implemented, it is important to carefully select those parties able to organize work for larger groups, whether regions, communities, nongovernmental organizations, or organizations of social partners, including private firms.

Because organizing work requires experience, policymakers cannot expect to institute these programs for a onetime crisis. Rather, the programs should be a permanent feature of economic policy, since even though extreme economic crises may be rare, business cycle fluctuations and partial adjustment shocks are recurrent. Thus LMPs, particularly active policies, should not be considered a short-term solution. They can be designed and used effectively during different stages of the economic cycle (e.g., public works programs in times of job destruction or stagnation, or in response to natural catastrophes; emphasis on employment subsidies and training during recovery periods for those workers finding it difficult to integrate in the expanding labor market). Making LMPs a permanent government policy will not only improve effectiveness at the micro level, but also help stabilize economic cycles. LMPs improve macroeconomic stability, since they mitigate a recession by providing income to displaced workers and thus help sustain aggregate demand in the economy. If LMPs are funded through a "labor market stabilization" fund, the fund could be used to collect revenues during boom times, and then be accessed during recessions to fund passive and active labor market policies. This would make fiscal policy more countercyclical. Increases in taxes, particularly in Mexico but also in Argentina, may be needed to fund employment policies. Though this may seem like an extra burden on the economy, the micro and macro benefits of LMPs outweigh their cost.

Regional-Level Policies

Regional integration has become an important element of the outward-oriented development strategy in Argentina, Brazil, and Mexico. The creation of the North American Free Trade Agreement (NAFTA), the regional agreement between Argentina, Brazil, Paraguay, and Uruguay (Southern Cone Common Market [Mercosur]), and the possible creation of a Free Trade Area of the Americas (FTAA), imply shifts in production that affect the labor markets of these countries. As a result, employment policies at the regional level are needed.

Regional integration is an opportunity to combine economic opening led by market forces with socioeconomic adjustment considerations, allowing for a balance between competition and cooperation among member countries. But because regional integration can cause increased volatility and insecurity in labor markets, it is important that regional agreements include policies to mitigate social adjustment costs, as well as measures that enable the countries to better allocate labor.

To better reallocate workers and jobs, regional integration would benefit from allowing the free movement of workers, through the harmonization of professional qualifications and certification, and by reducing bureaucratic obstacles to professional activities in and between member countries. Regional integration would also be improved if regional structural funds would be made available to promote the development of marginalized regions, as well as regions suffering from production and employment declines. As the European experience has shown, the sustainable development of a region depends on the acceleration of development in its least-favorable areas. Economic progress and social coherence is only realistic if the losers of the integration process are compensated and brought into the integration process. Yet in NAFTA, for example, only the United States has created a specific program for coping with trade-related layoffs (the Trade Adjustment Act), and this program primarily consists of worker-training initiatives; there are no specific provisions or policies to guarantee more even development among member countries. Another set of policies to help avoid unfair competition concerns the setting of clear economic rules, such as rules avoiding tax wars to attract FDI. With regard to labor rules, setting common standards for labor rights and working conditions by upgrading them, where needed, would improve job quality throughout the region by avoiding "social dumping."

In the case of NAFTA, the inclusion of relevant socioeconomic concerns is not foreseen, though the proposed FTAA contains clauses recognizing the different levels of socioeconomic development of the participating countries as well as a commitment to the International Labour Organization's Declaration on the Fundamental Rights of Workers. Nevertheless, labor issues are not prominent. Mercosur, however, appears to be taking steps in addressing common social and labor market issues of its member states by the adoption of the "Declaración Sociolaboral" and through the creation of different social spaces, some of them tripartite. Though Mercosur is still far from having a European Union–type regional integration, local adaptation of some elements of the EU model has been discussed. In particular, the latest Declaration of Mercosur Labour, in Buenos Aires in April 2004, recommended a strategy for employment growth, emphasizing the integration of different policies, in particular macro, industrial, and labor market policies. This strategy should contribute to the overarching objective to increase quality employment in the region. In implementing this declaration, Mercosur could benefit from the experience of the European Employment Strategy, which sets quantitative employment goals and common guidelines, and has a unique system of follow-up, called the "open method of coordination." The method relies on "convergence by comparison" of selected key labor market indicators and implements policies through national action plans and joint employment reports. European Union targets of a 70 percent employment rate overall, and a 60 percent employment rate for women, by 2010, have been set.

How to Implement an Employment Creation Strategy

For an employment strategy to be successfully implemented, there must be a functioning social dialogue and a proactive government that secures coordination between employment policies and programs. The government can be an organizing force, for example in setting up active programs for labor force adjustment and ensuring proper implementation and evaluation. However, governments must cooperate with the rest of the civil society and knit efficient alliances with the social partners and the private sector to both design and deliver on the various policies. For example, it is essential that any revisions to labor legislation or implementation of new policies be done through social dialogue, as this allows employer and worker organizations to express their concerns about existing legislation, giving them the opportunity to commonly agree to a set of labor market regulations and policies that will be effectively applied. An effective consultative process will not only help to avoid unnecessary labor disputes, but also help with enforcement, as regulations would be agreed to rather than imposed. Thus, to be effective, social dialogue among government, worker, and employer organizations—as well as new social actors

representing informal workers and the unemployed—should be institutionalized, through continuous dialogue as well as through the creation of tripartite,
but autonomous, social and economic councils. This discussion, of course, pre-
supposes a functioning dialogue with equal partners who are willing to discuss
and compromise rather than dwell on adversarial positions.

An effective employment strategy also requires policy coherence among
the different areas of government. The goal of quality job creation cannot rest
solely with the labor ministry. Because employment policies must consider
macroeconomic issues such as monetary, exchange rate, and fiscal policy, public investment decisions (e.g., labor-intensive infrastructure programs),
mesoeconomic policies (trade, industrial, and service policies, regional integration, education policies), as well as micro policies (labor regulations, labor
market policies, wage setting), it is essential that other government ministries
adopt employment creation as a policy goal. But for there to be coherence in
policy, it is necessary for the governments to form joint decision and monitoring bodies to coordinate the design and implementation of various policies and
programs.

Another important issue that must be addressed concerns the limited policy space that national governments have. As globalization often moves deci-
sionmaking to the international level, strong institutions are needed not only at
home, but also at the international level to guarantee a fair globalization, to reduce contagious effect of financial crisis, and to avoid a race to the bottom of
employment and working conditions (World Commission on the Social Dimension of Globalization, 2004).

This volume has analyzed for Argentina, Brazil, and Mexico the contribution to employment creation of several policy areas, and has found that the expectations of financial and trade liberalization and the associated laissez-faire
policies of the 1990s did not deliver in terms of growth or employment. There
is now a need to rebalance policies. Without proposing a backlash and a return
to economic planning, we propose the reaffirmation of institutions, which together with market forces should ensure a stronger employment content of
economic growth and greater security for those affected by globalization.

Acronyms

ALADI	Asociación Latinoamericana de Integración/Associação Latinoamericana de Integração (Latin-American Integration Association) (Uruguay)
ALMP	active labor market policy
CCE	Consejo Coordinador Empresarial (Business Coordination Council) (Mexico)
CEMPRE	Cadastro Central de Empresas (Central Company Register) (Brazil)
CES	Conferencia Económica y Social (Social and Economic Conference) (Argentina)
CET	common external tariff
CGT	Confederación General del Trabajo (General Labor Confederation) (Argentina)
CLT	Consolidação das Leis do Trabalho (Consolidation of Labor Laws) (Brazil)
CONCLAT	Conselho Nacional da Classe Trabalhadora (National Council of the Working Class) (later renamed Confederação [Confederation]) (Brazil)
CT	Congreso del Trabajo (Workers Congress) (Mexico)
CTA	Congreso de los Trabajadores Argentinos (Congress of Argentine Workers)
CTM	Central de los Trabajadores Mexicanos (Confederation of Mexican Workers)
CUT	Central Única dos Trabalhadores (Central Workers Union) (Brazil)
DIEESE	Departamento Intersindical de Estadística e Estudos Socio-Econômicos (Interunion Department of Socioeconomic Studies and Statistics) (Brazil)
ECLAC	Economic Commission for Latin America and the Caribbean

217

EIL	Encuesta de Indicadores Laborales (Labor Indicators Survey) (Argentina)
EPH	Encuesta Permanente de Hogares (Permanent Household Survey) (Argentina)
EU	European Union
FAT	Fundo de Amparo ao Trabalhador (Workers Protection Fund) (Brazil)
FDI	foreign direct investment
FIESP	Federação das Indústrias do Estado de São Paulo (Federation of the Industries of the State of São Paulo) (Brazil)
FNT	Forum Nacional do Trabalho (National Labor Forum) (Brazil)
FTAA	Free Trade Agreement of the Americas
FZLN	Frente Zapatista de Liberación Nacional (Zapatista National Liberation Front) (Mexico)
GDP	gross domestic product
GMC	Grupo Mercado Común (Mercosur)
IADB	Inter-American Development Bank
IBGE	Instituto Brasileiro de Geografia e Estatística (Brazilian Geographical and Statistical Institute)
ICLS	International Conference of Labour Statisticians
ILO	International Labour Organization
IMF	International Monetary Fund
INDEC	Instituto Nacional de Estadística y Censos (National Institute for Statistics and Census) (Argentina)
INEGI	Instituto Nacional de Estadística, Geografía e Informática (National Institute for Statistics, Geography and Informatics) (Mexico)
ISI	import-substitution industrialization
ISIC	International Standard Industrial Classification
LFP	labor force participation
LFT	Ley Federal del Trabajo (Federal Labor Law) (Mexico)
LMP	labor market policy
M&As	mergers and acquisitions
Mercosur	Mercado Común del Sur (Southern Cone Common Market)
MMT	Más y Major Trabajo (More and Better Employment) (Argentina)
MST	Movimento dos Trabalhadores Rurais Sem Terra (Movement of the Landless Farmworkers) (Brazil)
MTE	Ministério do Trabalho e Emprego (Ministry of Work and Employment) (Brazil)
MTSS	Ministerio de Trabajo, Empleo y Seguridad Social (Ministry of Work, Employment, and Social Security) (Argentina)
NAALC	North American Agreement on Labor Cooperation

NAFTA	North American Free Trade Agreement
NGO	nongovernmental organization
NTB	nontariff barrier
OECD	Organisation for Economic Co-operation and Development
PAN	Partido de Acción Nacional (Party of National Action) (Mexico)
PET	Programa de Empleo Temporal (Temporary Employment Program) (Mexico)
PISA	Programme for International Student Assessment
PITEX	Programa de Importación Temporal para la Exportación (Temporary Imports for Exports Program) (Mexico)
PLANFOR	Plano Nacional de Qualificação do Trabalhador (National Professional Training Program) (Brazil)
PNAD	Pesquisa Nacional por Amostra de Domicílios (National Household Sample Survey) (Brazil)
PNAES	Programa Nacional de Apoyo a las Empresas de Solidaridad
PPE	Primeiro Emprego (First Employment) (Brazil)
PPP	purchasing power parity
PRD	Partido Revolucionario Democrático (Revolutionary Democratic Party) (Mexico)
PRI	Partido Revolucionario Institucional (Revolutionary Institutional Party) (Mexico)
PROGER	Programa de Genação de Emprego e Renda (Program for the Generation of Employment and Income) (Brazil)
PRONAF	Programa Nacional de Fortalecimento da Agricultura Familiar (National Program for the Strengthening of Family Agriculture) (Brazil)
PRONAFIM	Programa Nacional de Financiamiento al Microempresario
PSE	Pacto de Solidaridad Económica (Pact of Economic Solidarity) (Mexico)
RCA	revealed comparative advantage
SICAT	Sistema de Capacitación para el Trabajo (Vocational Training System) (Mexico)
SINE	Sistema Nacional de Emprego (National Employment System) (Brazil)
SITC	Standard International Trade Classification
SMEs	small and medium-sized enterprises
SNE	Servicio Nacional de Empleo, Capacitación y Adiestramiento (National Service for Employment, Skills, and Training) (Mexico)
SOE	state-owned enterprise
TNC	transnational corporation
TNI	transnationality index

UIA	Unión Industrial Argentina (Argentine Industrial Union)
UK	United Kingdom
UN	United Nations
UNCTAD	United Nations Conference on Trade and Development
UNDP	United Nations Development Programme
UNESCO	United Nations Educational, Scientific, and Cultural Organization
UNIDO	United Nations Industrial Development Organization
UNT	Unión Nacional de Trabajadores (National Workers Union) (Mexico)
VAT	value-added tax
WITS	World Integrated Trade Solutions
WTO	World Trade Organization
YPF	Yacimientos Petrolíferos Fiscales SA (Argentina)

Bibliography

Abramo, L. 2003. *Desigualdades e discriminação de gênero e raça no mercado de trabalho brasileiro,* paper presented at the International Forum for the Eradication of Poverty, Employment Creation, and Gender and Race Equality (Brasilia, ILO), October 13–15.

Agosin, M. R.; Mayer, R. 2000. *Foreign investment and developing countries: Does it crowd in domestic investment?* Discussion paper, no. 146 (Geneva, UNCTAD).

Alarcón, D.; Zepeda, E. 2004. "Economic reform or social development? The challenge of a period of reform in Latin America: Case study of Mexico," in *Oxford Development Studies,* vol. 32, no. 1, March.

Altenburg, T.; Qualman, R.; Weller, J. 2001. *Modernización económica y empleo en América Latina: Propuestas para un desarrollo incluyente,* Serie macroeconomía del desarrollo, no. 2 (Santiago, ECLAC, Division of Economic Development).

Amadeo, E. J.; Melo Filho, P. G. 1999. "Apertura, productividad y empleo en Brasil," in V. E. Tokman and D. Martinez (eds.): *Productividad y empleo en la apertura económica* (Lima, ILO).

Andraus Troyano, A. 1998. "Programas de empleo e ingresos en Brasil," in IADB-ILO: *Programas de empleo e ingresos en América Latina y el Caribe* (Lima, ILO).

Anuatti-Neto, F.; et al. 2003. *Costs and benefits of privatization: Evidence from Brazil,* Research network working paper, no. R-455 (Washington, DC, IADB).

Asociación Latinoamericana de Integración (ALADI). 2000. *El comercio intra-industrial en el intercambio regional* (Montevideo, ALADI), December.

Audley, J.; et al. (eds.). 2003. *NAFTA's promise and reality: Lessons from Mexico for the hemisphere* (Washington, DC, Carnegie Endowment for International Peace).

Auer, P.; Efendioğlu, U.; Leschke, J. 2004. *Active labour market policies around the world: Coping with the consequences of globalisation* (Geneva, ILO).

Ayyagari, M.; et al. 2003. *Small and medium enterprises across the globe: A new database,* Policy research working paper, no. 3127 (Washington, DC, World Bank).

Baer, W.; Borges Rangel, G. 2001. "Foreign investment in the age of globalization: The case of Brazil," in W. Baer and W. R. Miles (eds.): *Foreign direct investment in Latin America: Its changing nature at the turn of the century* (New York, Harworth Press).

Banco de México. 2002. *Informe anual 2001* (Mexico, DF).

Barros, R. de; Mendonça, R. 1996. "Flexibilidade do mercado de trabalho brasileiro: Uma avaliação empírica," in J. M. Camargo (ed.): *Flexibilidade do mercado de trabalho no Brasil* (Rio de Janeiro, FGV Editora).

Barros, R. de; et al. 1997. "Uma avaliação empírica do grau de flexibilidade alocativa do mercado de trabalho brasileiro," in *Texto para discussão*, no. 499 (Rio de Janeiro, Instituto de Pesquisa Econômica Aplicada).

Baumann, R. 1998. *Foreign investment in Brazil and the international financial markets,* paper prepared for presentation at the conference "Brazil in the world context" (London), LC/BRS/DT.014 (Brasilia, ECLAC).

———. 2001. "Mercosul: Origens, ganhos e desencontros e perspectivas," in R. Baumann (ed.): *MERCOSUR: Abanicos e desafios da integração* (Brasilia, Instituto de Pesquisa Econômica Aplicada/ECLAC)

Beccaria, L. 1999. "Modalidades de contratación por tiempo determinado: El caso argentino," in V. E. Tokman and D. Martínez: *Flexibilización en el margen: La reforma del contrato de trabajo* (Lima, ILO).

Beccaria, L.; Galin, P. 2002. *Regulaciones laborales en Argentina: Evaluación y propuestas,* Colección diagnósticos y propuestas no. 3 (Buenos Aires, Fundación OSDE-CIEEP).

Benavente, J.; et al. 1997. *Nuevos problemas y oportunidades para el desarrollo industrial de América Latina,* Working paper, Serie desarrollo productivo, no. 31 (Santiago, ECLAC).

Bensusán, G. 1992. *Institucionalización laboral en México, los años de la definición jurídica,* PhD diss. (Mexico, DF, Universidad Autónoma Metropolitana).

———. 1993. "Trasgresión y discrecionalidad en el mundo del Trabajo," in *Revista Trabajo,* no. 9.

———. 1998. "Los determinantes institucionales de la flexibilidad laboral en México," in F. Zapata (ed.): *¿Flexibles y productivos?* (Mexico, DF, El Colegio de Mexico).

———. 2000. *El modelo mexicano de regulación laboral* (Mexico, DF, FLACSO/Universidad Autónoma Metropolitana/Friedrich Ebert Stiftung/Plaza y Valdés).

———. 2003. *Exclusión social en América Latina: La dimensión institucional* (Mexico, DF, Universidad Autónoma Metropolitana-X), mimeo.

Bensusán, G.; Alcalde, A. 2000. "Estructura sindical y agremiación," in G. Bensusán and T. Rendón (eds.): *Trabajo y trabajadores en el México contemporáneo* (Mexico, DF, Miguel Ángel Porrua).

Bergman, M. 2003. "Tax reforms and tax compliance: The divergent paths of Chile and Argentina," in *Journal of Latin American Studies,* vol. 35.

Bergquist, C. 1986. *Labor in Latin America* (Stanford, Stanford University Press).

Bernardes, R. 2001. *Articulação e especialização produtiva de MPMES: O caso do cluster aeronáutico da região de São José dos Campos* (São Paulo, ECLAC).

Bielschowsky, R. 1999. *Investimentos na indústria brasileira depois da abertura e do Real: O Mini-ciclo de modernizações, 1995–1997,* Serie reformas económicas, no. 44 (Brasilia, ECLAC).

Bienen, D. 2002. *Mindestlohnreformen in Südamerika: Ökonomische Rechtfertigung und praktische Umsetzung,* Discussion paper, no. 90 (Göttingen, Ibero-American Institute for Economic Research).

Bisang, R. 2000. "The responses of national holding companies," in B. Kosacoff (ed.): *Corporate strategies under structural adjustment in Argentina: Responses by industrial firms to a new set of uncertainties* (Basingstoke, Hampshire, Macmillan).

Bizberg, I. 1998. "Las relaciones industriales en México: Cambio y permanencia," in R. Dombois and L. Pries (eds.): *Las relaciones industriales en el proceso de trans-*

formación en América Latina: El caso de México, Documentos de investigación (Bremen, University of Bremen).

————. 1999. "Le syndicalisme mexicain face à la mondialisation et à la décomposition du régime politique," in *La Revue de L'IRES,* no. 29, Winter 1998–1999.

————. 2003. "Estado, organizaciones corporativas y democracia," in A. Asís: *México al inicio del siglo XXI: Democracia, ciudadanía y desarrollo* (Mexico, DF, Porrua-CIESAS).

Blanchard, O. 2005. "Designing labor market institutions," in J. Restrepo and A. Tokman (eds.): *Labor Markets and Institutions* (Santiago, Central Bank of Chile).

Blanchard, O.; Tirole, J. 2004. *The optimal design of labor market institutions* (Cambridge, MA, MIT), mimeo.

Blázquez, J.; Santiso, J. 2004. "Mexico: Is it an ex-emerging economy?" in *Journal of Latin American Studies,* vol. 36.

Blecker, R. 1999. *Taming global finance* (Washington, DC, Economic Policy Institute).

Blomström, M.; Kokko, A. 1997. *Regional integration and foreign direct investment,* Working paper, no. 6019 (Cambridge, MA, National Bureau of Economic Research).

Bonelli, R. 2001. "Fusões e aquisições no Mercosul," in R. Baumann (ed.): *Mercosul: Avanços e desafios da integração* (Brasilia, ECLAC/Instituto de Pesquisa Econômica Aplicada).

Bouzas Ortiz, J.A. 2003. "Contratos colectivos de protección y el proyecto oficial de reformas laborales," in J. A. Bouzas Ortiz (ed.): *Reforma laboral: Análisis crítico del proyecto Abascal de reforma a la Ley Federal del Trabajo* (Mexico, DF, UNAM).

Buitelaar, R. M.; Padilla Ruth Urrutia, R. 1999. "Industria maquiladora y cambio técnico," in *ECLAC Review* (Santiago), no. 67, April.

Cacciamali, M. C. 1999. "Desgaste na legislação laboral e ajustamento do mercado de trabalho brasileiro," in A. C. Posthuma (ed.): *Abertura e ajuste do mercado de trabalho no Brasil: Políticas para conciliar os desafios do emprego e competitividade* (São Paulo, Ed.34/ILO).

————. 2005. *Mercado de trabajo juvenil: Argentina, Brasil y México,* Employment strategy paper, no. 2005/02 (Geneva, ILO).

Cacciamali, M. C.; Britto, A. 2002. "A flexibilização restrita e descentralizada das relações de trabalho no Brasil," in *Revista do ABET,* no. 3.

Cacciamali, M. C.; Pires, J. M. 1995. *Instituções do mercado de trabalho brasileiro e desempenho econômico* (São Paulo, USP), mimeo.

Calcagno, A. 1997. "El régimen de convertibilidad y el sistema bancario en Argentina," in *ECLAC Review* (Santiago), no. 61, April.

Calcagno, A.; Manuelito, S.; Titelman, D. 2003. "From hard-peg to hard landings? Recent experiences of Argentina and Ecuador," in *Financiamiento del Desarrollo,* vol. 15 (Santiago, ECLAC).

Calderon-Madrid, A. 2000. *Job stability and labor mobility in urban Mexico: A study based on duration models and transition analysis* (Washington, DC, IADB).

Camargo, J. M. 1997. "Brazil: Labour market flexibility and productivity, with many poor jobs," in E. J. Amadeo and S. Horton (eds.): *Labour productivity and flexibility* (Basingstoke, Hampshire, Macmillan).

Cardoso, A. M. 1999a. *Sindicatos, trabalhadores e a coqueluche neoliberal* (Rio de Janeiro, FGV).

————. 1999b. *A trama da modernidade: Pragmatismo sindical e democratização no Brasil* (Rio de Janeiro, Revan).

————. 2003. *A década neoliberal e a crise dos sindicatos no Brasil* (São Paulo, Boitempo).

————. 2004. *Industrial relations, social dialogue and employment in Argentina, Brazil, and Mexico,* Employment strategy paper, no. 2004/7 (Geneva, ILO).

Cardoso, A. M.; Comin, A. A. 1995. "Câmaras setoriais, modernização produtiva e democratização nas relações entre capital e trabalho no Brasil," in N. A. Castro (ed.): *A máquina e o equilibrista: tecnologia e trabalho na indústria automobilística brasileira* (São Paulo, Paz e Terra).

Cardoso, J. C. 2001. *Crise e desregulação do trabalho no Brasil,* Discussion paper (Brasilia, Instituto de Pesquisa Econômica Aplicada).

Carillo, J. 2003. "Los retos de las maquiladoras ante la pérdida de competitividad," in *Comercio Exterior,* vol. 53, no. 4, April.

Carneiro, F. G. 2003. *A poverty profile and functional aspects of Brazilian labour markets* (Brasilia, ECLAC).

Cella Dal Chiavon, E. M. 2003. "A geração de emprego, trabalho e renda como motor para o desenvolvimento," in *Boletim de Mercado de Trabalho: Conjuntura e Análise,* vol. 22 (Brasilia, Instituto de Pesquisa Econômica Aplicada).

Chimerine, L.; Black, T.; Coffey, L. 1999. *Unemployment insurance as an automatic stabilizer: Evidence of effectiveness over three decades,* Occasional paper, no. 99-8 (Washington, DC, US Department of Labor).

Christiansen, H.; Oman C.; Charlton, A. 2003. *Incentives-based competition for foreign direct investment: The case of Brazil,* Working paper on international investment, no. 1/2003 (Paris, OECD), March.

Chudnovsky, D.; López, A. 2002. *Integración regional e inversión extranjera directa: El caso del MERCOSUR,* Serie RedInt (Buenos Aires, INTAL).

Clavijo, F.; Valdivieso, S. 2000. "Reformas estructurales y política macroeconómica," in *Reformas económicas en México 1982–1999,* 1st ed. (Mexico, DF, FCE).

Collier, R. B.; Collier, D. 1991. *Shaping the political arena* (Princeton, Princeton University Press).

Conte-Grand, A. H. 1997. *Seguros de desempleo, formación profesional y servicios de empleo,* Working paper, no. 57 (Santiago, ILO).

Cook, M. L. 1998. *The politics of labor law reform: Comparative perspectives on the Mexican case,* presentation at the twenty-first meeting of the Latin American Studies Association (Chicago), mimeo.

————. 2000. *Contrasting rounds: Democratic transitions, neo-liberal economies, and labor law reform in Argentina and Brazil,* paper presented at the twenty-second meeting of the Latin American Studies Association (Miami), mimeo.

Correa, P. 2001. *Merger control in infrastructure industries* (Washington, DC, Inter-American Development Bank), April.

Cortés, R.; Groisman, F.; Hosowszki, A. 2003. *Transiciones ocupacionales: El caso del plan Jefes y Jefas,* 6th Congreso Nacional de Estudios del Trabajo (Buenos Aires, ASET), CD-ROM.

Cortés, R.; Marshall, A. 1999. "Estrategia económica, instituciones y negociación política en la reforma social de los '90," in *Desarrollo Económico,* vol. 39, no. 154.

Coutinho García, R. 2003. *O desenvolvimiento rural e o PPA 2000/2003: Uma tentativa de avaliação,* Texto para discussão, no. 938 (Brasília, Instituto de Pesquisa Econômica Aplicada).

de Abreu Campanario, M.; Muniz da Silva, M. 2003. *Perspectivas e desafios da inserção competitiva e tecnológica brasileira* (São Paulo, University of São Paulo).

de la Garza, E. 1990. "Reconversión industrial y cambio en el patrón de relaciones laborales en México," in A. Anguiano (ed.): *La modernización de México* (Mexico, DF, Universidad Autónoma Metropolitana).

———. 1998. *Estrategia de modernización empresarial en México: Flexibilidad y control sobre el proceso de trabajo* (Mexico, DF, Friedrich Ebert Stiftung).

———. 2000. "La contratación colectiva," in G. Bensusán and T. Rendón: *Trabajo y trabajadores en el México contemporáneo* (Mexico, DF, Porrúa).

———. 2002. "La flexibilidad del trabajo en México (Una nueva síntesis)," in B. García Guzmán (ed.): *Población y sociedad al inicio del siglo XXI* (Mexico, DF, El Colegio de México).

———. 2003a. "Estructura industrial y condiciones de trabajo en la manufactura," in E. de la Garza Toledo and C. Salas (eds.): *La situación del trabajo en México, 2003* (Mexico, DF, Plaza y Valdéz).

———. 2003b. "La crisis de los modelos sindicales en México y sus opciones," in E. de la Garza and C. Salas (eds.): *La situación del trabajo en México, 2003* (Mexico, DF, Universidad Autónoma Metropolitana/Solidarity Center/IET/Plaza y Valdés).

———. 2003c. *Reestructuración productiva, empresas y trabajadores en México al inicio del siglo XXI* (Berkeley, Center for Latin American Studies, University of California), mimeo.

de Leite, M. 2003. *Trabalho e sociedade em transformação* (São Paulo, Perseu Abramo).

Departamento Intersindical de Estadística e Estudos Socio-Econômicos (DIEESE). 1997. *Collective bargaining agreements* (São Paulo).

Diaz-Alejandro, C. 1985. "Goodbye financial repression, hello financial crash," in *Journal of Development Economics,* vol. 18.

Diez de Medina, R. 2001. *Jóvenes y empleo en los noventa* (Buenos Aires, ILO-Cinterfor).

Dombois, R.; Pries, L. 2000. *Relaciones laborales entre mercado y estado* (Caracas, Nueva Sociedad).

Dussel Peters, E. 2000a. *El tratado de libre comercio de Norteamérica y el desempeño de la economía en México,* Working paper, no. LC/Mex/L.431 (Mexico, DF, ECLAC), June.

———. 2000b. *La inversión extranjera en México,* Serie desarrollo productivo, no. 80, (Santiago, ECLAC), October.

———. 2003. "Ser maquila o no ser maquila: ¿Es ésa la pregunta?" in *Comercio Exterior,* vol. 53, no. 4, April.

———. 2004a. *Efectos de la apertura comercial en el empleo y el mercado laboral de México y sus diferencias con Argentina y Brasil (1990–2003),* Employment strategy paper, no. 10/2004 (Geneva, ILO).

———. 2004b. *Oportunidades y retos económicos de China para México y Centroamérica,* Working paper, no. LC/Mex/L.633 (Mexico, DF, ECLAC).

Economic Commission for Latin America and the Caribbean (ECLAC). 2001. *Foreign investment in Latin America and the Caribbean* (Santiago).

———. 2002. *Foreign investment in Latin America and the Caribbean* (Santiago).

———. 2003a. *Balance preliminar de las economías de América Latina y el Caribe* (Santiago).

———. 2003b. *Base de estadísticas e indicadores sociales* (Santiago).

———. 2003c. *Estudio económico, 2002–2003* (Santiago).

———. 2003d. *Panorama social de América Latina, 2002–2003* (Santiago).

————. 2003e. *Statistical yearbook for Latin America and the Caribbean, 2002* (Santiago).

————. 2003f. *TradeCan 2002* (Santiago).

————. 2004a. *Base de estadísticas e indicadores sociales* (Santiago), http://www.eclac.cl/badeinso/badeinso.asp.

————. 2004b. *Desarrollo productivo en economías abiertas* (Santiago).

————. 2004c. *Latin America and the Caribbean in the world economy, 2002–2003* (Santiago).

————. 2004d. *Panorama social de América Latina, 2003–2004* (Santiago).

————. 2004e. *Statistical yearbook for Latin America and the Caribbean, 2003* (Santiago).

Epstein, G. 2005. *Alternatives to inflation targeting monetary policy for stable and egalitarian growth: A brief research summary,* paper presented at the WIDER Jubilee Conference (Helsinki), June 17–18.

Ernst, C. 1996. *Mercosur: The trade and industrial policies of the member countries in the presence of the economic integration process,* Working paper (Vienna, UNIDO), March.

————. 1997. *Le Mercosur et l'Union Européenne: Un rapprochement économique prometteur?* (Regensburg, Transfer Verlag).

————. 2005a. *The FDI–employment link in a globalizing world: The case of Argentina, Brazil, and Mexico,* Employment strategy paper, no. 17/2005 (Geneva, ILO).

————. 2005b. *Trade liberalization, export orientation, and employment in Argentina, Brazil, and Mexico,* Employment strategy paper, no. 15/2005 (Geneva, ILO).

Ernst, C.; Hernández Ferrer, A.; Zult, D. 2005. *The end of the multi-fibre agreement and its implication for trade and employment,* Employment strategy paper, no. 16/2005 (Geneva, ILO).

Estevadeordal, A.; Goto, J.; Saez, R. 2000. *The new regionalism in the Americas: The case of Mercosur* (Buenos Aires, INTAL), April.

Facelli, S.; et al. 2002. *Informe sobre los programas de empleo de ejecución provincial 2001,* Documento de trabajo, no. GP/13, Serie gasto público (Buenos Aires, Ministerio de Economía).

Fair Labor Association. 2004. *Annual public report* (Washington, DC).

Favero, C.; Giavazzi, F. 2002. *Why are Brazil's interest rates so high?* Working paper, no. 224, IGIER (Milan, Bocconi University).

Ferraz, J. C.; Kupfer, D.; Iootty, M. 2004. "Competitividad industrial en Brasil: 10 años después de la liberalización," in *ECLAC Review* (Santiago), no. 82, April.

Food and Agriculture Organization. 2004. *The state of food and agriculture* (Rome).

Frenkel, R. 2004. *Las políticas macroeconómicas, el crecimiento y el empleo,* paper presented on behalf of the ILO for the Mercosur regional employment conference (Buenos Aires).

Frenkel, R.; González Rozada, M. 1999. "Apertura comercial, productividad y empleo en Argentina," in V. Tokman and D. Martínez (eds.): *Productividad y empleo en la apertura económica* (Lima, ILO).

Frenkel, R.; Ros, J. 2003. *Unemployment, macroeconomic policy, and labor market flexibility: Argentina and Mexico in the 1990s,* paper presented at the New School Economic Workshop series (New York).

Frischtak, C. R. 1992. *Learning, technical progress, and competitiveness in the computer aircraft industry: An analysis of Embraer,* Industry series paper, no. 58 (Washington, DC, World Bank).

Galasso, E.; Ravallion, M. 2003. *Social protection in a crisis: Argentina's plan Jefes y Jefas* (Buenos Aires), mimeo.
Galbraith, J. 1999. "The inflation obsession: Flying in the face of the facts," in *Foreign Affairs,* January–February.
Galhardi, R. 2005. *Empleo en México bajo la perspectiva de la OIT: El papel de los actores sociales,* presentation at the seminar "La problemática del empleo en México desde la perspectiva de las organizaciones internacionales" (Guadalajara, Mexico, DF), March.
Garrido, C. 2001. *Fusiones y adquisiciones transfronterizas en México durante los años noventa,* Serie desarrollo productivo, no. 111 (Santiago, ECLAC), October.
Gasparini, L. 2004. "América Latina: Estudio de la protección social y el empleo sobre la base de encuestas de hogares," in F. Bertranou (ed.): *Protección social y mercado laboral* (Santiago, ILO).
Gasparini, L.; Bertranou, F. M. 2004. "Protección social y mercado laboral en América Latina: ¿Qué nos dicen las encuestas de hogares?" in *International Social Security Review,* Special no. 2005 on Latin America (Geneva), August 24.
Gaudio R.; Thompson, A. 1990. *Sindicalismo peronista, gobierno radical* (Buenos Aires, Friedrich Ebert Stiftung).
Geddes, B. 1994. "Challenging the conventional wisdom," in *Journal of Democracy,* vol. 5, no. 4.
Gerchunoff, P.; Greco, E.; Bondorevsky, D. 2003. *Comienzos diversos, distintas trayectorias y final abierto: Más de una década de privatizaciones en Argentina, 1990–2002,* Serie gestión pública, no. 34 (Santiago, ILPES/ECLAC).
Gerchunoff, P.; Llach, L. 2003. *El ciclo de la ilusión y el desencanto: Un siglo de políticas económicas argentinas* (Buenos Aires, Ariel Sociedad Económica).
Ghose, A. K. 2003. *Jobs and incomes in a globalizing world* (Geneva, ILO).
———. 2004. *Capital inflows and investment in developing countries,* Employment strategy paper, no. 11/2004 (Geneva, ILO).
Giambiagi, F.; Ronci, M. 2004. *Fiscal policy and debt sustainability: Cardoso's Brazil, 1995–2002,* Working paper, no. WP/04/156 (Washington, DC, IMF).
Giosa, N. 2000. "Neoliberalismo, reestructuración productiva y empleo en la Argentina de los 90," unpublished master's diss. (Campinas, Universidad Estadual de Campinas, Instituto de Economía).
Golbert, L.; Giacometti, C. 1998. "Programas de empleo e ingresos en Argentina," in IADB-ILO: *Programas de Empleo e Ingresos en América Latina y el Caribe* (Lima, ILO).
Gregory, P. 1986. *Myth of market failure: Employment and the labor market in Mexico* (Baltimore, Johns Hopkins University Press).
Gruber, J. 1997. "The consumption smoothing benefits of unemployment insurance," in *American Economic Review* (Nashville, TN, American Economics Association), vol. 87, no. 1.
Guigale, M.; et al. (eds.). 2001. *Mexico: A comprehensive development agenda for the new era* (Washington, DC, World Bank).
Guillén, A. 2000. "Efectos de la crisis asiática en América Latina," in *Comercio Exterior,* vol. 50, no. 7.
Guimarães, I. G. 1995. *Câmaras setoriais: Notas sobre sua constituição e quadro atual,* Série seminários, no. 22/94 (Rio de Janeiro, Instituto de Pesquisa Econômica Aplicada).
Gutiérrez, H. (2003): *Oportunidades y desafíos de los vínculos económicos de China y América Latina y el Caribe,* Serie comercio internacional, no. 42 (Santiago, ECLAC).

Haar, J.; Leroy-Beltrán, C.; Beltrán, O. 2004. "Efectos del TLCAN en la competitividad de la pequeña empresa en México," in *Comercio Exterior,* vol. 54, no. 6, June.

Heckman, J.; Pagés, C. 2004. *Law and employment: Lessons from Latin America and the Caribbean* (Cambridge, MA, National Bureau of Economic Research).

Hernández Laos, E. 2000. "Productividad y empleo en la apertura económica de México," in *El Trimestre Económico,* vol. 67, issue 1, no. 265.

Herrera, F.; Melgoza, J. 2003. "Evolución reciente de la afiliación sindical y la regulación laboral," in E. de la Garza Toledo and C. Salas (eds.): *La situación del trabajo en México* (Mexico, DF, Plaza y Valdéz).

Ibarra, D. 2004. *La inversión extranjera,* Working paper, no. LC/Mex/L.599 (Mexico, DF, ECLAC).

Instituto Brasileiro de Geografia e Estatística (IBGE). 2002. *Síntese de indicadores sociais 2001: Sindicatos* (Rio de Janeiro).

———. 2003. *Presquisa Nacional por Amostra de Domicílios* (PNAD).

Instituto Nacional de Estadística Geografía e Informática (INEGI). 2002. *Encuesta nacional de empleo* (Aguascalientes).

Inter-American Development Bank (IADB). 2002a. "Closing the telecommunications gap," in *Latin American Economic Policies,* vol. 18 (Washington, DC).

———. 2002b. *Latin American Economic Policies,* vol. 18 (Washington, DC).

———. 2002c. "Más allá de las fronteras: El nuevo regionalismo en América Latina, Informe 2002," in *Progreso económico en América Latina,* annual report (Washington, DC).

———. 2002d. "The privatization paradox," in *Latin American Economic Policies,* vol. 18 (Washington, DC).

———. 2004. *Good jobs wanted* (Washington, DC).

———. 2005. "China ascendant: A snapshot of economic performance," in *Journal Ideas for Development in the Americas (IDEA),* Research Department (Washington, DC).

International Conference of Labour Statisticians (ICLS). 2003. *Guidelines concerning a statistical definition of informal employment, endorsed by the seventeenth annual Conference of Labour Statisticians* (Geneva), November–December.

International Labour Organization (ILO). 1999. *MERCOSUR socio-laboral, selección de documentos fundacionales, 1991–1999* (Buenos Aires).

———. 2002a. *Effect to be given to resolutions adopted by the International Labour Conference at its 90th session,* Governing Body (doc. GB.285/7/2), 285th session, seventh item on the agenda (Geneva).

———. 2002b. *Panorama laboral 2000: América Latina y el Caribe* (Lima).

———. 2003a. *Integración regional y libre comercio en las Américas: El desafío laboral en el MERCOSUR* (Lima).

———. 2003b. *Key indicators of the labour market (KILM),* 3rd ed. (Geneva), database.

———. 2003c. *Panorama laboral* (Lima).

———. 2004a. *Macroeconomic policies for growth and employment,* Governing Body (doc. GB.291/ESP/1).

———. 2004b. *Panorama laboral* (Lima).

———. 2005. *Generando trabajo decente en el Mercosur: Empleo y estrategia de crecimiento,* vols. 1–2 (Buenos Aires).

———. *Latin America and Caribbean labour information system,* database.

———. *Minimum wage* (Geneva, Conditions of Work and Employment Programme), database.

International Monetary Fund (IMF). 2004. *World economic outlook 2003* (Washington, DC).

————. *International financial statistics* (Washington, DC), database, http://ifs.apdi
.net/imf.

Islam, I. 2003. *Avoiding the stabilization trap: Towards a macroeconomic policy framework for growth, employment, and poverty reduction,* Employment paper, no. 53 (Geneva, ILO).

Islam, R. 2006. *Fighting poverty: The development-employment link* (Boulder, Lynne Rienner).

Jachimowicz, M. 2003. "Argentina's economic woes spur emigration," in *Migration Information Source,* http://www.migrationinformation.org.

Katz, J. 1998. "Aprendizaje tecnológico ayer y hoy," in *ECLAC Review,* Special issue (Santiago).

————. 2000a. *Cambios en la estructura y comportamiento del aparato productivo latinoamericano en los años 1990: Después del "Consenso de Washington," qué?* Serie desarrollo productivo, no. 65 (Santiago, ECLAC).

————. 2000b. *Reformas estructurales, productividad y conducta tecnológica en América Latina* (Santiago, ECLAC).

Kosacoff, B. 2000a. "Business strategies under stabilization and trade openness in the 1990s," in B. Kosacoff (ed.): *Corporate strategies under structural adjustment in Argentina: Responses by industrial firms to a new set of uncertainties* (Basingstoke, Hampshire, Macmillan).

————. 2000b. "The development of Argentine industry," in B. Kosacoff (ed.): *Corporate strategies under structural adjustment in Argentina: Responses by industrial firms to a new set of uncertainties* (Basingstoke, Hampshire, Macmillan).

————. 2000c. "The responses of transnational corporations," in B. Kosacoff (ed.): *Corporate Strategies under structural adjustment in Argentina: Responses by industrial firms to a new set of uncertainties* (Basingstoke, Hampshire, Macmillan).

Kostzer, D.; Mazorra, X. 2004. *Estrategias de crecimiento y de generación de empleo en Argentina,* Working paper, no. 14. (Buenos Aires, ILO).

Krugman, P.; Taylor. L. 1978. "Contractionary effects of devaluation," in *Journal of International Economics,* vol. 8.

Kulfas, M.; Porta, F.; Ramos, A. 2002. *Inversión extranjera y empresas transnacionales en la economía argentina,* Serie estudios y perspectivas, no. 10 (Buenos Aires, ECLAC).

Laos, E. H. 1999. "Apertura comercial, productividad, empleo y contratos de trabajo en México," in V. E. Tokman and D. Martinez (eds.): *Productividad y empleo en la apertura económica* (Lima, ILO).

Lapper, R. 2004. "Garment companies fight back for share of market," in *Financial Times,* July 27.

Lederman, D.; Maloney W. F.; Serven, L. 2003. *Lessons from NAFTA for Latin America and the Caribbean countries* (Washington, DC, World Bank).

León González Pacheco, A.; Dussel Peters, E. 2001. "El comercio industrial en México, 1990–1999," in *Comercio Exterior,* vol. 51, no. 7 (Mexico, DF).

Llamas Huitrón, I.; Garro Bordonaro, N. 2003. "Trabajo, formalidad, escolaridad y capacitación," in E. de la Garza and C. Salas (eds.): *La situación del trabajo en México* (Mexico, DF, Insituto de Estudios del Trabajo).

López, J. G. 1999. *Evolución reciente del empleo en México,* Serie reformas económicas, no. 29 (Santiago, ECLAC).

López-Córdova, E.; Mesquita Moreira, M. 2003. *Regional integration and productivity: The experiences of Brazil and Mexico,* Working paper, no. 14 (Washington, DC, IDB, Instituto por la Integración de América Latina y el Caribe, INTAL), July.

López de Silanes, F. 2002. *NAFTA and Mexico's reforms on investor protection* (New Haven, Yale University Press), mimeo.

López Zadicoff, P. D.; Paz, J. A. 2003. "El desempleo inteligente: Elegibilidad y participación en el PJH en condiciones record de pobreza y desempleo," 6th Congreso Nacional de Estudios del Trabajo, ASET (Buenos Aires), CD-ROM.

Lora, E.; Panizza, U. 2002. *Structural reforms in Latin America under scrutiny,* Working paper, no. 470 (Washington, DC, IADB), March.

Lustig, N. 1998. *Mexico: The remaking of an economy* (Washington, DC, Brookings Institution).

———. 2001. "Life is not easy: Mexico's quest for stability and growth," in *Journal of Economic Perspectives,* vol. 15, no. 1.

Lustig, N.; Ros, J. 2000. "Mexico: Trade and financial liberalization with volatile capital inflows," in L. Taylor (ed.): *External liberalization, economic performance, and social policy* (New York, Oxford University Press).

Maloney, W. F. 1999. "Does informality imply segmentation in urban labor markets? Evidence from sectoral transitions in Mexico," in *World Bank Economic Review,* vol. 13, no. 2 (Washington, DC, World Bank).

Maloney, W. F.; Mendez, J. N. 2004. "Measuring the impact of minimum wages: Evidence from Latin America," in J. J. Heckman and C. Pagés (eds.): *Law and employment: Lessons from Latin America and the Caribbean,* National Bureau of Economic Research conference report (Chicago, University of Chicago Press).

Margheritis, A. 1999. *Ajuste y reforma en Argentina (1989–1995)* (Buenos Aires, Nuevohacer).

Márquez, G. 1999. *Unemployment insurance and emergency: Employment programs in Latin America and the Caribbean—An overview,* paper presented at the Conference on Social Protection and Poverty (Washington, DC, IADB), February 5.

Marshall, A. 1992. *Circumventing labour protection: Non-standard employment in Argentina and Peru,* Research series, no. 88 (Geneva, International Institute for Labour Studies/ILO).

———. 1994. "Economic consequences of labour protection regimes in Latin America," in *International Labour Review,* vol. 133, no. 1.

———. 1996a. *Mercado de trabajo y seguro de desempleo,* report prepared for ILO/ETM (Santiago, Buenos Aires), mimeo.

———. 1996b. "Weakening employment protection in Latin America: Incentive to employment creation or to expand instability?" in *International Contributions to Labour Studies,* vol. 6 (Oxford, Oxford University Press).

———. 1997. *State labour market intervention in Argentina, Chile, and Uruguay: Common model, different versions,* Employment and training paper, no. 10 (Geneva, ILO).

———. 1998. *Empleo en la Argentina, 1991–1997: ¿Nuevas pautas de comportamiento después de la liberalización económica?* Working paper, no. 79 (Santiago, ILO/ETM).

———. 2001. "Política económica e instituciones laborales en la regulación del mercado de trabajo: Análisis comparativo de Argentina, México y Perú," in *CICLOS,* no. 21.

———. 2002. "El comportamiento del mercado de trabajo en los años 90: ¿Nuevas pautas?" in B. García Guzmán (ed.): *Población y sociedad al inicio del siglo XXI* (Mexico, DF, El Colegio de México).

———. 2003. "Empleo 'no registrado' en la Argentina: Estudio de sus salarios relativos," paper prepared for the ILO, Brasilia, project "Enfrentando los Retos al Trabajo Decente en la Crisis Argentina."

————. 2004. *Labour market policies and regulations in Argentina, Brazil, and Mexico: Programmes and impact,* Employment strategy paper, no. 2004/13 (Geneva, ILO), http://www.ilo.org/public/english/employment/strat/download/esp13.pdf.

Martin, G. 2000. "Employment and unemployment in Mexico in the 1990s," in *Monthly Labor Review* (Washington, DC, Bureau of Labor Statistics), November.

Martinez, D. 2004a. *El mundo del trabajo en la integración económica y la liberalización comercial: Una mirada desde los países americanos* (Lima, ILO).

————. 2004b. *The world of work in the context of economic integration and trade liberalization,* Working paper, no. 45 (Geneva, ILO, Policy Integration Department).

Mato Díaz, F. J. 2003. *Estudios sobre las experiencas europeas con los instrumentos de evaluación de las políticas del mercado de trabajo,* Serie macroeconomía del desarrollo, no. 21 (Santiago, ECLAC).

Máttar, J.; Moreno-Brid, J. C.; Peres, W. 2002. *Foreign investment in Mexico after economic reform,* Serie estudios y perspectivas, no. 10 (Mexico, DF, ECLAC), July.

McGuire, J. 1997. *Peronism without Perón* (Stanford, Stanford University Press).

Micco, A.; Pagés, C. 2004. *Employment protection and gross job flows: A differences-in-differences approach,* Working paper, no. 158 (Washington, DC, IADB).

Minella, A.; et al. 2004. *Inflation targeting in Brazil: Lessons and challenges,* Working paper, no. 19 (Basel, Bank of International Settlements).

Ministerio de Trabajo, Empleo y Seguridad Social (MTSS). 1996. *Políticas de empleo: Informe especial* (Buenos Aires).

————. 2004. *Salario mínimo vital y móvil* (Buenos Aires).

Montoya, S. 1996. "Capacitación y reentrenamiento laboral: Argentina durante la transición," in *Estudios,* vol. 19, no. 76.

Moreno, P.; Tamez, S.; Ortiz, C. 2003. "La seguridad social en México," in E. de la Garza and C. Salas (eds.): *La situación del trabajo en México, 2003* (Mexico, DF, Plaza y Valdéz).

Moreno-Fontes, G. 2004. *The impact of the 1985–2000 trade and investment liberalization on labour conditions, employment, and wages in Mexico,* PhD thesis (Geneva, Graduate School of International Studies).

Mortimore, M.; Buitelaar, R.; Bonifaz, J. L. 2000. *México: Un CANálisis de su competitividad internacional,* Serie desarrollo productivo, no. 62 (Santiago, ECLAC), March.

Mostajo, R. 2000. *Gasto social y distribución del ingreso: Caracterización e impacto redistributivo en países seleccionados de América Latina y el Caribe,* Serie reformas económicas, no. 69 (Santiago, ECLAC).

Munck, R. 1997. "Introduction: A thin democracy," in *Latin American Perspectives,* vol. 24, issue 97, no. 6.

Murillo, M. V. 2001. *Labor unions, partisan coalitions, and market reforms in Latin America* (Cambridge, Cambridge University Press).

Nelson, J. 1992. "Poverty, equity, and the politics of adjustment," in S. Haggard and R. Kaufman (eds.): *The politics of economic adjustment* (Princeton, Princeton University Press).

Novick, M. 2001. "Nuevas reglas de juego en Argentina: Competitividad y actores sindicales," in *Los sindicatos frente a los procesos de transición política* (Buenos Aires, CLACSO).

Ocampo, J. A. 2001a. "A new look at the development agenda," in *ECLAC Review,* no. 74 (Santiago, ECLAC), August.

————. 2001b. "Raúl Prebisch y la agenda del desarrollo en los albores del siglo XXI," in *ECLAC Review,* no. 75 (Santiago, ECLAC), December.

Oliveira, M. 2003. "Tendências recentes das negociações coletivas no Brasil," in M. A. Santana and J. R. Ramalho: *Além da Fábrica: Sindicatos, trabalhadores e a nova questão social* (São Paulo, Boitempo).

Organisation for Economic Co-operation and Development (OECD). 2001. *Employment outlook* (Paris).

——. 2002. *Economic survey: Mexico* (Paris).

——. 2004. *Economic survey: Mexico* (Paris).

Orsatti, A.; Calle, R. 2004. *La situación de los trabajadores de la economía informal en el Cono Sur y el Área Andina,* Working paper, no. 179 (Lima, ILO).

Orszag, P. 2001. *Unemployment insurance as economic stimulus,* policy brief (Washington, DC, Center on Budget and Policy Priorities).

Paes de Barros, R.; Corseuil, C. H.; Bahia, M. 1999. *Labor market regulations and the duration of employment in Brazil,* Texto para discussão, no. 676 (Rio de Janeiro, Instituto de Pesquisa Econômica Aplicada).

Paes de Barros, R.; Corseuil, C. H.; Foguel, M. 2000. "Os incentivos adversos e a focalização dos programas de proteção ao trabalhador no Brasil," in *Planejamento e Políticas Públicas,* no. 22.

Palley, T. I. 2004. "Escaping the debt constraint on growth: A suggested monetary policy for Brazil," in *Brazilian Journal of Political Economy,* vol. 24, no. 1.

Palma, G. 2003. *Trade liberalization in Mexico: Its impact on growth, employment, and wages,* Employment paper, no. 55 (Geneva, ILO).

Papademetriou, D. G. 2003. "The shifting expectations of free trade and migration," in J. J. Audley et al. (eds.): *NAFTA's promise and reality: Lessons from Mexico for the hemisphere* (Washington, DC, Carnegie Endowment for International Peace).

Pautassi, L.; Rossi, J.; Campos, L. 2003. *Plan Jefes y Jefas: Derecho social o beneficio sin derechos?* Documento de trabajo, no. 5 (Buenos Aires, CELS).

Perelman, L. 2001. "El empleo no permanente en la Argentina," in *Desarrollo Económico* (Santiago, ECLAC), vol. 41, no. 161.

Petrocella, D.; Lousteau, M. 2001. "FDI in Argentina during the 1990s," in W. Baer and W. R. Miles (eds.): *Foreign direct investment in Latin America: Its changing nature at the turn of the century* (New York, Harworth Press).

Pieper, U.; Taylor, L. 1998. *The revival of the liberal creed: The IMF, the World Bank, and inequality in a globalized economy,* CEPA working paper series 1, no. 4 (New York, Center for Economic Policy Analysis).

Pietrobelli, C.; Rabellotti, R. 2004. *Upgrading in clusters and value chains in Latin America: The role of policies,* Best practices series (Washington, DC, IADB, Sustainable Development Department).

Piore, M. 2004. *Rethinking Mexico's labor standards in a global economy,* (Cambridge, MA, MIT, Department of Economics), mimeo.

Pochmann, M. 1999. "Los costos laborales en Brasil," in V. E. Tokman and D. Martínez (eds.): *Inseguridad laboral y competitividad: Modalidades de contratación* (Lima, ILO).

Polaski, S. 2003. "Jobs, wages, and household income," in J. J. Audley et al. (eds.): *NAFTA's promise and reality: Lessons from Mexico for the hemisphere* (Washington, DC, Carnegie Endowment for International Peace).

Posthuma, A. 2004. *Industrial renewal and inter-firm relations in the supply chain of the Brazilian automotive industry,* Working paper, no. 46 (Geneva, ILO, InFocus Programme on Boosting Employment through Small Enterprise Development).

Pozzi, P. 2000. "Popular upheaval and capitalist transformation in Argentina," in *Latin American Perspectives,* vol. 27, issue 114, no. 5.

Prat-Gay, A. 2003. "Texto del discurso antes las comisiones de economía y hacienda del senado de la República Argentina," December 18.

Ramos, C. A. 2002. *Las políticas del mercado de trabajo y su evaluación en Brasil,* Serie macroeconomía del desarrollo, no. 16 (Santiago, ECLAC).

Ramos Francia, M.; Chiquiar Cikurel, D. 2004. "La transformación del patrón del comercio exterior mexicano en la segunda mitad del siglo XX," in *Comercio Exterior,* vol. 54, no. 6, June.

Ranis, P. 1997. *Clases, democracia y trabajo en la Argentina contemporánea* (Buenos Aires, Corregidor).

Rauber, I. 2000. *Tiempo de herejías* (Buenos Aires, Instituto de Estudios y Formación de CTA).

Rocha, S. 2001. *Workfare programmes in Brazil: An evaluation of their performance,* Working paper (Geneva, ILO, InFocus Programme on Socio-Economic Security).

Rodrik, D. 2001a. *Development strategies for the next century,* paper prepared for the seminar "Development theory at the threshold of the twenty-first century: Commemorative event to mark the centenary of the birth of Rául Prebisch" (Santiago, ECLAC).

———. 2001b. *Globalisation, social conflict, and economic growth,* Prebisch Lecture delivered at UNCTAD (Geneva, UNCTAD).

Rohter, L. 2002. "South American trading bloc frees the movement of its people," in *New York Times,* late edition (East Coast), November 24.

Ros, J.; Bouillon, C. 2000. "Mexico: Trade liberalization, growth, inequality, and poverty," in E. Ganuza et al. (eds.): *Liberalización, desigualdad y pobreza: América Latina y el Caribe en los 90* (New York, UNDP).

Ross, J. 1998. *The Annexation of Mexico: From the Aztecs to the IMF* (Monroe, ME, Common Courage Press).

Ruiz Durán, C. 2004. "Los desbancarizados: El problema de los mercados financieros segmentados," in *Comercio Exterior* (Mexico, DF), vol. 54, no. 7.

Saboia, J.; Saboia, A.L. 2004. *Caracterização do setor informal a partir dos dados do censo demográfico do Brasil de 2000* (Brasilia, ILO).

Salas, C.; Zepeda, E. 2003. "Empleo y salarios en el México contemporáneo," in E. de la Garza Toledo and C. Salas (eds.): *La Situación del trabajo en México, 2003* (Mexico, DF, Plaza y Valdéz).

Samaniego, N. 1998. "Programas de empleo e ingresos en México," in *Programas de empleo e ingresos en América Latina y el Caribe* (Lima, IADB/ILO).

———. 2002. *Las políticas del mercado de trabajo y su evaluación en México,* Serie macroeconomía del desarrollo, no. 18 (Santiago, ECLAC).

Shome, P. 1999. *Taxation in Latin America: Structural trends and impact of administration,* Working paper, no. 19 (Washington, DC, IMF, Fiscal Affairs Department).

Stallings, B.; Peres, W. 2000. *Growth, employment, and equity: The impact of the economic reforms in Latin America and the Caribbean* (Washington, DC, Brookings Institution Press/ECLAC).

Stallings, B.; Weller, J. 2001. "Employment in Latin America: Cornerstone of social policy," in *ECLAC Review* (Santiago), no. 75.

Stiglitz, J. E. 2003. "El rumbo de las reformas: Hacia una nueva agenda para América Latina," in *ECLAC Review* (Santiago), no. 80, August.

Suarez Dillon Soares, S. 2002. *O impacto distributivo do salário mínimo: A distribuição individual dos rendimentos do trabalho,* Discussion paper, no. 873 (Rio de Janeiro, Instituto de Pesquisa Econômica Aplicada).

Szretter, H. 1999. "Los costos laborales en Argentina," in V. E. Tokman and D. Martínez (eds.): *Inseguridad laboral y competitividad: Modalidades de contratación* (Lima, ILO).

Tokman, V. 2003. *Desempleo juvenil en el Cono Sur: Causas, consecuencias y políticas,* Prosur opciones (Santiago, Friedrich Ebert Stiftung).

Tokman, V.; Martínez, D. 1995. *The impact of labour costs on competitiveness and worker protection in the manufacturing sector of Latin America,* presentation at the Conference on Labour Market Policy in Canada and Latin America (Toronto, University of Toronto), mimeo.

Torre, J. C.; de Riz, L. 1991. "Argentina since 1946," in L. Bethel (ed.): *The Cambridge history of Latin America,* vol. 8 (Cambridge, Cambridge University Press).

United Nations Conference on Trade and Development (UNCTAD). 2000. *World investment report: Cross-border mergers and acquisitions and development* (Geneva).

———. 2001. *World investment report* (Geneva).

———. 2002. *World investment report: Transactional corporations and export competitiveness* (Geneva).

———. 2003a. *Trade and development report* (Geneva).

———. 2003b. *World investment report: FDI policies for development—National and international perspective* (Geneva).

———. 2004. *World investment report: The shift towards services* (Geneva).

United Nations Educational, Scientific, and Cultural Organization (UNESCO). 2004. *Education for all in Latin America: A goal within our reach.* Regional EFA monitoring report (Santiago).

Vadi, J. M. 2001. "Economic globalization, class struggle, and the Mexican State," in *Latin American Perspectives,* vol. 28, issue 119, no. 4.

Valdovinos, O. 1998. "Las relaciones del trabajo al final del siglo XX," in *Derecho Colectivo de Trabajo* (Buenos Aires).

Vega Ruíz, M. L. (ed.). 2001. *La reforma laboral en América Latina* (Lima, ILO).

Verdera, F. V. 1998. "Análisis comparativo de los programas de empleo e ingresos en América Latina y el Caribe," in *Programas de Empleo e Ingresos en América Latina y el Caribe* (Lima, IADB/ILO).

Waisgrais, S. 2003. *Wage inequality and the labour market in Argentina: Labour institutions, supply and demand in the period 1980–1999,* Discussion paper, no. DP/146/2002 (Geneva, International Institute for Labour Studies/ILO).

Weeks, J. 2000. *Exports, foreign investment, and growth in Latin America,* Working paper (London, School of Oriental and African Studies, Centre for Development Policy and Research).

Weller, J. 2001. *Procesos de exclusión e inclusión laboral: La expansión del empleo en el sector terciario,* Serie macroeconomía del desarrollo, no. 6 (Santiago, ECLAC).

World Bank. 2000. *World business environment survey,* database, http://info.worldbank .org/governance/wbes/front.htm.

———. 2003. *Land policies for growth and poverty reduction,* Policy research report (Oxford, Oxford University Press).

———. 2005. *Economic growth in the 1990s: Learning from a decade of reforms* (Washington, DC, World Bank).

World Commission on the Social Dimension of Globalization. 2004. *A fair globalization: Creating opportunities for all* (Geneva, ILO).

World Trade Organization (WTO). 1996. *Trade policy review: Brazil* (Geneva).

———. 2002. *Trade policy review: Mexico* (Geneva).

Yoguel, G. 2000. "Responses of small and medium-sized enterprises," in B. Kosacoff (ed.): *Corporate strategies under structural adjustment in Argentina: Responses by industrial firms to a new set of uncertainties* (Basingstoke, Hampshire, Macmillan).

Zapata, F. 1998. *El sindicalismo y la política laboral en México,* presentation at the twenty-first meeting of the Latin American Studies Association (Chicago), mimeo.

Zarsky, L.; Gallagher, K. P. 2004. *NAFTA, foreign direct investment, and sustainable industrial development in Mexico,* program policy brief (San Francisco, Inter-hemispheric Resource Center), January 28, http://www.americaspolicy.org/briefs/2004/0401mexind.html.

Zazueta, C.; de la Peña, R. 1984. *La estructura del Congreso del Trabajo* (Mexico, FCE).

Index

Agriculture sector: cheap imports'
impacts on, 91–92; employment
decline in, 19

Alfonsín, Raúl, 171, 186–188

Argentine economy: and crash of 2003,
59; credit boom in, 52; crisis of
2001–2002 in, 47; debt service and,
66–67; debt-to-GDP ratio in, 60*fig*,
61; and employment-output
elasticities, 47; export performance
and, 52–56; fiscal policy and, 206;
and foreign direct investment (FDI),
106, 107, 108*fig*, 119; and foreign
investment laws, 49–50; government
spending and, 68; growth in, 5, 46,
47*fig*; inflation targeting in, 62–63,
66; liberalizing reforms in, 49–51;
privatization and, 50; real
manufacturing wages in, 54; and
recovery from economic restructuring,
201–202; Tequila crisis and, 58;
transnationality index (TNI) and,
108–111, 111*tab*; value-added tax
(VAT) and, 69

Argentine Industrial Union (UIA), 176

Argentine labor force: education and
skill levels of, 12–13; female, 13,
14*tab*, 17; gender wage gap in, 31;
migration and, 11–12; and population
growth rates, 10; public employment
services for, 151; self-employment
and microenterprise creation
assistance for, 149; training programs

for, 150; urban, 14*fig*, 16; working
hours of, 36–38

Argentine labor market: demand in,
13–19; economic opening and, 41;
employment rates in, 16;
informal/nonprotected wage
employment in, 29, 141–142;
inspectors employed in, 142; sectoral
gains and losses in, 19–22;
unemployment rate in, 156, 158

Argentine labor market policies:
convertibility-liberalization program,
30, 31, 49, 51, 52, 56, 158; coverage
and impact of, 154, 155; for displaced
workers, 29; emergence and evolution
of, 157–158; for employment
creation, 145–147; for employment
protection, 133–136, 138;
expenditures on, 152, 153–154;
privatization, 171; "promoted"
temporary contracts, 139–140, 142,
147–148; reforms, public support for,
171; unemployment insurance,
144–145, 154, 158; widening of, 158;
worker training, 150

Argentine labor relations system:
collective bargaining systems in,
178–179, 197–198; control and
recognition of unions in, 169–170;
and economic restructuring, 170–173;
industrial, 169, 170; labor court
established in, 170; labor law trends
in, 194; labor movement in, 169, 192

237

About the Book

A rguing that economic policies in Argentina, Brazil, and Mexico favor markets over institutions and the international economy over the domestic—to the detriment of the work force in those countries—*Meeting the Employment Challenge* presents extensive evidence in support of placing employment concerns at the center of economic and social policies.

The authors discuss the challenges the three countries face in creating employment, as well as the evolution of the labor market since 1990 in terms of the quantity and quality of jobs. They then explore the impact of five policy areas on employment creation: macroeconomic policy, trade liberalization, foreign direct investment, labor market regulation, and labor relations. Their concluding recommendations offer concrete steps for balancing market forces and policy intervention in the interest of employment growth in a sound economy.

Janine Berg and **Christoph Ernst** are economists in the Employment Analysis and Research Unit of the Employment Strategy Department, and **Peter Auer** is chief of the unit, at the International Labour Office, Geneva.